THE CONTOURS OF JUSTICE

Communities and Their Courts

THE CONTOURS OF JUSTICE

Communities and Their Courts

James Eisenstein
Roy B. Flemming
Peter F. Nardulli

University Press of America,® Inc.
Lanham • New York • Oxford

Copyright © 1999 by
University Press of America,® Inc.
4720 Boston Way
Lanham, Maryland 20706

12 Hid's Copse Rd.
Cumnor Hill, Oxford OX2 9JJ

Library of Congress Cataloging-in-Publication Data

Eisenstein, James.
The contours of justice : communities and their courts / James
Eisenstein, Roy B. Flemming, Peter F. Nardulli
p.   cm.
Originally published: Boston : Little, Brown & Co., ©1988.
Includes index.
1. Criminal courts—Pennsylvania—Erie County. 2. Criminal
courts——Michigan—Kalamazoo. 3. Criminal courts—Illinois—
Du Page County. 4. Criminal courts—United States—States. I.
Flemming, Roy B. II. Nardulli, Peter F. III. Title.
KF9223.Z95E37 1999 345.73'01—dc21   99—22101 CIP

ISBN 0-7618-1406-X (pbk: alk. ppr.)

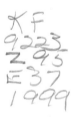
^{TM} The paper used in this publication meets the minimum
requirements of American National Standard for Information
Sciences—Permanence of Paper for Printed Library Materials,
ANSI Z39.48—1984

TO JOHN, MARGUERITE, AND CHARLES

*who grew up while this book
was conceived, researched, and written*

Preface

This book presents an approach to understanding criminal courts. Our argument is quickly summarized. First, criminal courts are worth trying to understand because they make decisions that people find significant and fascinating. Second, understanding these courts is difficult: the widespread belief that courts merely apply something called "Law" inhibits understanding; courts differ in ways that matter, and these differences produce the contours of justice; each criminal court is a formidably complex organization that defies simple explanation. Third, it is useful to approach the challenging task of making sense of the courts' complex puzzles by thinking of them as communities.

Students who read earlier versions of this book gave us useful evaluations, many of which are incorporated here. One realization merits explicit discussion. The belief that courts can be understood simply by applying something called "Law" has a powerful grip on the public mind. Most readers therefore begin with a strong presumption that courts are relatively simple institutions. The question, "How do courts work?" calls forth the response, "By applying Law." But courts are as complex and difficult to understand as any other highly developed social or political institution, and the notion of Law helps little to unravel their complexity. Throughout this book, we return to this complexity because we recognize that most readers believe that Law provides a useful and simple key to understanding, and that they will resist the idea that it is in fact incomplete and misleading.

In place of the notion of Law, we offer the metaphor of courts as communities. The metaphor builds on a rich body of empirical research on courts and the criminal justice system. The metaphor weaves together the many poorly-integrated elements produced by prior work. This book, however, did not result from merely reviewing previous research. Rather, the metaphor was devised during intensive field research in nine middle-sized criminal courts. We introduce and demonstrate its usefulness by applying it to these nine courts.

The research reported in this book could not have been undertaken without generous support by the National Institute of Justice and the National Science Foundation. Grant 79-NI-AX-0062 and Grant 81-IJ-CX-0027 came from the National Institute of Justice. The National Science Foundation Grants were SES-8308989, SES-8309609, and SES-83-08705. The views expressed and conclusions reached herein are those of the authors and do not necessarily represent the official views or policies of the Department of Justice or the National Science Foundation.

A project of this magnitude required assistance by many individuals. The following worked on the Illinois portion of the study: David Chambers, Keith Emmons, John Carroll, and Michael Bass performed important tasks as graduate assistants. Arthur Jameson and Robert Illyes were invaluable as computer consultants. Karen Wilson, Kathy Wilson, Carol Freund, Karla Kraus, Tammy Turner, and Darlene Riccuito were assistants whose performance belied their undergraduate status. Ann Nardulli contributed untold hours to sorting and organizing the Q-sort data. Students who very ably collected the case file data were Jan Powell, Frank Saibert, Ann Fohne, Laurie Edgar, Rick Morris, Scott Rubemeyer, Rich Hampton, Lisa Lindsay, David Bowers, and David West. Florence Edmison and Laurie Mitchell devoted many hours to typing interview transcripts. Jean Baker, Shirley Burnette, Lorena McClain, and Velma Sykes all contributed much to typing tasks. Anna Merritt did her normal outstanding job of editing. Special thanks is due the Director of the Institute of Government and Public Affairs at the University of Illinois, Samuel K. Gove, for his support of this project and his tolerance for the disruptions it caused.

These people provided invaluable assistance in collecting the case data in Michigan: Jan Johnson, Janet Van Tiem, Peter Kalawert, Donna Larson, Elizabeth Lenihan, Michael Draving, Laura Skiragis, Rolf Heubel, Steven Rosenberg, Sharon Hansen, Stephen Roach, Scott Mahoney, and Robert Sydlow. Meg Falk, a graduate student at Wayne State, ably performed various tasks relating to all phases in the field research. Evelyn Cloutier Lappen devoted many hours to preparing and sorting the Michigan Q-sort data, clipping newspaper articles, and a number of other important chores. Carol Wesson, Nancy Michaels, and Linda Laird provided typing assistance.

Outstanding assistance was provided by many people supporting the research effort in Pennsylvania. Thanks go to: Mark Kessler, for his outstanding participation in all phases of the project as the principal research assistant; Rick Feiock, Jeff Webster, Paula Carta, Tony Filippello, Terry Kline, and Mindy Morrison for a fine job collecting case file data in the field; Diane Colonna, Colleen Young, Chuck Kimmel, and Leslie Castaldi, for performing varied chores during the early and middle phases of the research; Louise Foresman, for her heroic labors in preparing, organizing, and sorting more than 17,000 cards for the Q-sort; Martha Waldman, for assistance during the later stages of the project; Chris Hopwood, for doing just about everything; Bob Rutchick, for computer assistance; Bonnie Grove, Mary Jane Johnson, Audrey Smith, Elena DeLuca, Joanne Ostergaard, Melanie Romig, Georgene Searfoss and especially Jan Walther, for a fine job in editing and typing data forms, reports, drafts, letters, and so on, often on short notice; Lynne Kaltreider, Lee Carpenter, and Traci Fabian for high-quality editorial assistance on many of the chapters; Marva Hillard for an outstanding job in the difficult transcribing of interviews; Greta O'Toole for competently handling all budget preparation and financial administration; and Irwin Feller, Director of the Institute for Policy Research and Evaluation, for crucial support throughout.

We also wish to acknowledge contributions by the individuals who assisted the project generally. A number of past and present employees in the National Institute of Justice provided wise and useful guidance and encouragement, particularly Carolyn Burstein, Debbie Viets, Linda McKay, and Cheryl Martorana. Thanks are also extended to Felice Levine of the National Science Foundation. Our advisory panel participated actively and productively in the early stages of implementing the research, and made a number of excellent suggestions. The panel consisted of James Gibson, Tom Church, Milt Heuman, George Gish, Magnus Seng, and Clifford Kirsch. Especially perceptive, helpful, detailed comments on an earlier draft from Tom Church, Herb Jacob, and Karen O'Connor led to a number of substantive revisions. Of course, without cooperation and participation by the judges, attorneys, court personnel, and others who gave generously of their time and insights, the study could not have been undertaken.

The entire project truly was a joint enterprise. Research of this magnitude cannot be undertaken by an individual. The fortuitous blend of skills each of us brought to the project enriched the final products substantially.

Contents

THE CONTOURS OF JUSTICE:
COMMUNITIES AND THEIR COURTS

Metaphors for Understanding Courts: Law vs. Community

Part One provides the foundation upon which the rest of the book rests. In Chapter One we explore several vital preliminary questions. What is there about criminal courts that so compellingly draws the interest and attention of Americans? What functions do courts perform? What images of courts do people bring to the task of trying to understand them?

In Chapter One we argue that criminal courts perform significant symbolic functions along with helping to determine what happens to defendants. We treat them as political institutions charged with a job: disposing of defendants who face criminal charges. In trying to understand courts, most Americans apply a metaphor that draws upon traditional views of what "Law" is and how it operates. We believe this metaphor fails to provide a useful guide, and argue that the alternative metaphor of courts as "communities" presented in Chapter Two is superior.

In Chapter One we also present the view that courts everywhere in the United States are similar enough to permit applying one approach to the task of understanding them, but at the same time different enough to make the job both interesting and challenging. Finally, we describe the nine courts we studied, why we chose them, and how we went about gathering the information presented in Part Two.

We describe in Chapter Two how we came to adopt the metaphor of courts as communities. The very fact that we think a metaphor is useful carries assumptions about the nature of courts that we address explicitly at the outset.

Scholars who study courts believe they are one of the most complex political institutions around. The diversity they display complicates the already challenging task of learning about them. During the field research, these characteristics of courts became even clearer to us. Going into a new jurisdiction with the intent of learning how its criminal courts operated resembled putting together a jigsaw puzzle. Unlike the thousand-piece puzzles sold in stores, however, court puzzles provided no pictures of what the solution looked like. In fact, the content of the solution depended on the questions asked. Furthermore, no pieces were provided. We had to fashion the pieces from the information received in interviews and during the analysis of data on defendants' cases and on the characteristics of the principal decision makers. At times, equally credible sources provided information that produced differently shaped pieces depicting the same phenomena. When it came to assembling the pieces, some necessary ones turned up missing; others that should have fit did not. The pictures that resulted consequently provided only an approximation of reality.

The problems we encountered differed little from those faced by most efforts to understand human institutions. The challenge is to devise techniques that most effectively overcome the obstacles to understanding. In Chapter Two we argue that employing the metaphor of courts as communities provides just such a technique. We describe what we mean by "community" and the related concept of "county legal culture." We then demonstrate how the components of the notion of community can be applied to examine courts. We conclude by discussing the proximate factors that contribute to the outcomes of individual defendants' cases.

CHAPTER ONE

Approaches to Crime and Criminal Courts

INTRODUCTION

Anyone who looks at the local news, reads the newspapers, listens to talk shows, or gossips with the neighbors knows that crime, criminal justice, and criminal courts attract nearly everyone's enduring interest and morbid fascination. Criminal violence grabs people's attention because it taps deep insecurities about physical well-being and safety. Headaches, illnesses, barked shins, and awful hangovers remind human beings that their bodies are fragile, their skins easily punctured. Of course, crimes against property, far more prevalent than those against persons, also produce unease. But violent crimes add a special flavor to physical vulnerability, for they show that pain, injury, and death itself come unexpectedly from attacks by other human beings. The mass media tap and awaken these fears with their heavy emphasis upon violent crime as "news."

Concern about violent crime impels strong desire for assurance that we are safe from it. We seek and find comfort in reassurance that "something is being done." News about the arrest of violent criminals, stories of trials, pronouncements of guilty verdicts, and imposition of harsh punishment provide such psychological comforting by symbolic demonstration that something *is* being done.

Weighty as they are, these considerations do not fully explain the symbolic or psychological functions performed by courts. Western democracies instill attitudes in citizens that imbue courts with significance that goes beyond reassurance about physical safety. Images of "law," the formal architecture of courtrooms and their black-robed judges, and the frequent use of symbols like "justice" and "due process" express values basic to social and political life.

To convey the special status of this traditional notion of law, we will refer to it by the symbol "Law." The traditional view, often compatible with religious belief in a higher being and higher law, regards Law as sanctified, akin to God's Law. Courts provide forums in which the basic values of a democratic society find expression. Government's power, and the power of its agents such as the police, is to be limited, subject to outside and independent control. When the lowliest or most despised criminal is afforded an attorney, a full jury trial with cross-examination of witnesses, and an opportunity to challenge the validity of the government's actions, it provides a dramatic, indeed theatrical reaffirmation of such fundamental values as equality and limited government that underlie our democracy. Americans expect their government to meet high standards of conduct. They want "due process" and "justice" to prevail and limits to be placed on police conduct. Courts in general, and criminal trials in particular, offer the most prominent and recurring forums for convincing citizens that these values actually limit the awesome coercive power of the government.[1]

The dual symbolic functions courts perform, reassuring people that violent criminals are being punished and that basic values of limited government restricted by Law are guiding officials' actions, profoundly shape Americans' thinking about them. Reading and learning about courts is different from trying to understand how school boards, sewer authorities, the Post Office, or even legislatures work. We need to acknowledge and understand just how our approach to learning about courts will be shaped by the fact that the symbols they produce are potent. Otherwise, the powerful symbolic functions courts provide, without anyone's realizing it, can seize control of our approach to the subject and crowd out our ability to understand what courts do in their routine, day-to-day activities.

---

[1]For a cogent discussion of how courts and Law serve to embody the most fundamental values in democratic societies, and how criminal trials in particular serve to express and renew them, see Thurmond Arnold, *The Symbols of Government* (New Haven: Yale University Press, 1935), and Stuart Scheingold, *The Politics of Rights* (New Haven: Yale University Press, 1974).

THE TRADITIONAL "LEGAL" METAPHOR

Human society generally, and that of the United States in particular, is too complicated for people to apply to it sophisticated models of how things work as they go about living each day. By necessity, they employ vastly simplified models, capable of being applied quickly, to explain and understand. This oversimplifying is resorted to especially when the phenomena people want to understand are distant and experienced indirectly. We will refer to these models as "metaphors," loose analogies which convey understanding, but which are oversimplified and rough.

The highly symbolic views of criminal courts and Law held by most American citizens produce a persistent, relatively unchangeable, and powerful set of beliefs employed to understand courts. We call this set of beliefs the "legal metaphor." Nearly every student, many professors of law, and most judges, lawyers, and politicians rely on it.

It would take many pages to describe fully the content of the legal metaphor, its origins, and its use in understanding courts. We will describe only the barest outlines of its principal components. At its heart rests the notion of Law as a set of rules transcending time, geography, and the circumstances surrounding specific cases. These rules embody the values expressed by the words carved in stone on the Supreme Court's temple-like façade, "Equal Justice Under Law." In the traditional view, law is "a complete body of rules existing from time immemorial and unchangeable except to the limited extent that legislatures have changed the rules enacted by statutes.... "[2] It exhibits the characteristics of being uniform, general, continuous, equal, certain, and pure.[3] Courts, judges, and attorneys provide the setting and the personnel who simply apply the law to specific circumstances (cases) that arise. The outcome is determined by the content of the Law. Judges and lawyers merely employ the techniques and skills their special knowledge and training have given them to

---

[2]This phrase comes from Jerome Frank, a well-known "legal realist" who sharply challenges the traditional view. See his *Law and the Modern Mind* (Garden City, N.Y.: Anchor Books, 1963), p. 35.

[3]See Frank, ibid., p. 53.

produce the inevitable "right" result. These are the classic words of the noted English jurist, Sir William Blackstone:

> The judgment, though pronounced or awarded by judges, is not their determination or sentence, but the determination and sentence of the law. It is the conclusion that regularly follows from the premises of law and fact. . . . [4]

The unsophisticated version of the legal metaphor that most people apply to criminal cases raises only a few questions. Did the evidence show that the defendant "did it"? Were the rules followed? Was the convicted defendant punished appropriately? More elaborate versions are focused on the content of criminal statutes, the elements that must be proven by the prosecution, the strength of the evidence, the procedures for presenting evidence and questioning witnesses, the rules on instructing the jury, and guidelines for imposing the sentence. The standard of proof of guilt in a criminal case, "beyond a reasonable doubt," and other elements encompassed by the notion of "due process" also form part of more sophisticated versions.[5]

Both versions, however, focus on formal rules and procedures, relegating attorneys and judges to the nominal role of carrying out the functions assigned to them. Both ignore the many features in the context and setting in which the case is resolved. To the extent that the metaphor explicitly assigns a societal function beyond "doing justice," it is to "control crime," ensure "due process," or do both.[6] Finally, the metaphor deals primarily with full-fledged jury trials,

[4]Quoted by Wilfred E. Rumble, Jr., *American Legal Realism* (Ithaca, N.Y.: Cornell University Press, 1968), pp. 49–50.

[5]For a treatment of the due process notion, see the discussion of national legal culture below, pp. 12–14 and Table 1–2. Few systematic studies have been done on public opinion toward the rights of defendants or commitment to due process. It appears that attitudes toward due process are mixed, and knowledge of its content spotty. A public opinion survey found that 93 percent knew that everyone accused of a serious crime had the right to be represented in court by an attorney, but 56 percent said it was up to the accused to prove his or her innocence. See National Center for State Courts, *The Public Image of Courts* (Williamsburg, Va.: National Center for State Courts, 1978), Table 1–5, p. 9.

[6]The distinction between the "Crime Control" and "Due Process" models of the criminal process was first and best described by Herbert Packer. See *The Limits of the Criminal Sanction* (Palo Alto, Calif.: Stanford University Press, 1968), especially Chapter 8, "Two Models of the Criminal Process."

treating bench trials and guilty pleas as exceptions to the "real" and central mechanism.

The legal metaphor's appeal comes from two sources — its reliance on the concept of Law, which ties it to revered and deep values, and its role in providing symbolic reassurance that threats to well-being posed by violent criminals are being dealt with. These sources are powerful, and the reassurance that criminal courts' operations provide is real. Our quarrel with the legal metaphor is simply that it provides a poor tool to employ in trying to understand courts.

CRIMINAL COURTS IN THE UNITED STATES

This book reflects our belief that the legal metaphor provides a fundamentally misleading understanding of how criminal courts work. We recognize, however, that no matter how convincing our argument, the powerful hold of the legal metaphor for many readers will be little loosened. In fact, the continuing parade of highly publicized trials and Supreme Court decisions employing the rhetoric of the legal metaphor and conveying the image of adherence to its principles guarantees its frequent reinforcement, offering apparent proof of its validity. Thus, we approach our task with a good deal of humility. Society will not and cannot abandon the legal metaphor. It is too deeply embedded in belief structures. Most of our readers will not completely reject it, for it is a familiar tool for crafting explanations of aspects of the world. We can, however, offer an alternative metaphor that can uneasily coexist with the legal metaphor in our intellectual tool box, to be taken out and employed on occasions when innate curiosity and desire to really "understand" take control. And it can guide thinking about policy decisions when proposals to reform courts' manner of operating surface by suggesting what will work and what won't.

In Chapter Two, we introduce this alternative metaphor — the notion that criminal courts can be thought of as "communities." But before describing the community metaphor, we need to address two questions. First, how does our approach draw upon and extend prior empirical research on criminal courts? Second, what do we assume about what courts do and how they should be studied?

The view of criminal courts as communities is consistent with much previous research. It is part of a developing tradition arguing that the traditional view, which relies on the legal metaphor, is un-satisfactory.

Previous empirical research that went beyond using the "legal metaphor" falls into three categories. One group of studies relied upon characteristics of the individuals who dispose of cases. This "individual approach" focused primarily upon the backgrounds, attitudes, and role perceptions of key decision makers.[7] A second looked to the institutional and organizational context in which cases were disposed. The "organizational approach" examined how the "triads" of judge, prosecutor, and defense attorney who handled a case came together and interacted with one another. It also looked at the policies and practices of the organizations, such as the district attorney's office, which employed members of the triad.[8] The third (the "environmental") approach spread its net more widely, studying the characteristics of the communities that the courts served. It sought to consider the economic and social composition of the communities and the content of their political and legal culture.[9]

All three approaches contributed to our understanding of courts, but each had limitations. Studies adopting the individual approach often used incomplete and indirect measures of attitudes, and typically looked at the link between attitudes and behavior for one aspect (usually sentencing) of one participant's behavior (the judge). Studies using the organizational approach typically did not empirically measure many crucial variables, relying instead on impressionistic observations, unsystematic interviews, and untested assumptions. The

[7]See especially John Hogarth, *Sentencing as a Human Process* (Toronto: University of Toronto Press, 1971); James Gibson, "Judges' Role Orientations, Attitudes, and Decisions: An Interactive Model," 72 *American Political Science Review* (1978), p. 911; Austin Sarat, "Judging in Trial Courts: An Exploratory Study," 39 *Journal of Politics* (1977), p. 368; Greg Caldeira, "The Incentives of Trial Judges in the Administration of Justice," 3 *Justice System Journal* (1977); and Larry R. Baas, "Judicial Role Perceptions: Problems of Representativeness, The Identification of Types, and the Study of Role Behavior," Paper delivered at the Midwest Political Science Association Meetings, Chicago, Ill., 1972.

[8]For a thorough review of this literature, see Peter F. Nardulli, "Organizational Analyses of Criminal Courts: An Overview and Some Speculation," in Nardulli, ed., *The Study of Criminal Courts: Political Perspectives* (Cambridge, Mass.: Ballinger, 1979).

[9]See especially Martin Levin, "Urban Politics and Judicial Behavior," 1 *Journal of Legal Studies* (1975); Thomas Church, *Justice Delayed: The Pace of Litigation in Urban Trial Courts* (Williamsburg, Va.: National Center for State Courts, 1978); Roy B. Flemming, *Punishment Without Trial* (Boston: Longman, 1983); and Herbert Kritzer, "Political Culture, Trial Courts, and Criminal Cases," in Nardulli, ed., op. cit.

environmental approach drew heavily on the notion of legal culture, but rarely defined it or assessed its content empirically. It looked unsystematically and impressionistically at the links between factors like public opinion, parties, and the media on the one hand and major participants in case disposition on the other. Thus, all three lacked internal rigor and completeness. More seriously, studies adopting one approach hardly ever examined factors regarded as significant by the others, producing a fragmented and unintegrated body of findings. Finally, nearly all the major studies focused upon criminal courts in major metropolitan centers.

A major objective of our research, then, was to address some of these weaknesses. We sought to develop an integrated approach by researching individual, organizational, and environmental factors in each of nine middle-sized jurisdictions and by comparing our findings across all nine.

What basic assumptions about what courts do and how they should be studied guided our research? In the discussion that follows we do not seek to describe criminal courts comprehensively. Most readers already have a pretty good idea of what they are and what they do. Rather, we present our position on some questions upon which there is disagreement.

One of the most controversial of these questions involves the courts' function. The typical answers are quite familiar, including "to deter crime," "to punish criminals," "to protect society," and to treat or meet the needs of the criminal in order to prevent future wrongdoing. These approaches focus on what courts *should* do, not on *what* in fact they do. But because many institutions and individuals seek to deter crime, protect society, and treat criminals, such approaches do not identify that which is unique about courts.

It is not difficult to isolate the special task of courts. They process defendants who are apprehended by the police and formally charged with criminal offenses. They determine who will be convicted by a plea of guilty or a guilty verdict following trial and who will obtain a not guilty verdict or dismissal. Of course, the police play a pivotal role by determining most often who is brought to court and what charges they initially face. They sometimes administer physical punishment of their own. But the *official* labeling of someone as a convicted criminal, and the determination of legitimate punishment can be done only by a court. Prison officials, probation and parole officers, and parole boards rely upon courts to decide who falls under their control.

Table 1–1

Examples of Political Outcomes Allocated
by Criminal Courts for Several Classes of Recipients

Type of recipient	Tangible outcomes	Intangible outcomes
General local community	personal safety, expenditure of tax dollars	symbolic reassurance, peace of mind, satisfaction or discontent about "justice"
Defendants	physical freedom, personal safety, employment prospects, money spent on bail, attorney's fees, fines, court costs	psychological discomfort, shame, anger, family turmoil
Court	public employment, income from fees, appointment to cases, enhanced career prospects	work satisfaction or dissatisfaction, self-esteem, sense of purpose

The function of courts—to process defendants—is clearly political.[10] Like other political institutions, criminal courts allocate both tangible and intangible values such as money and freedom in an authoritative manner. Their decisions are authoritative because they are "legitimate," that is, they are actions of government backed by the ultimate right to employ force. Thus courts affect who gets what. Several categories of people make up the "who," including the local community, defendants and their families, and the people employed by the courts and related agencies. The scope of things encompassed by the "what" is equally broad, and includes personal freedom, safety, and money. Table 1-1 summarizes how courts affect who gets what.

It is not just the functions criminal courts perform in society that make them political, however. The way in which courts operate exhibits characteristics that are typically associated with politics. For instance, the principal decision makers such as judges and prose-

---

[10]We adopt the classic definitions of politics provided by David Easton (the process by which values are authoritatively allocated for a society) in *The Political System* (New York: Knopf, 1960) and by Harold Lasswell (the process that determines who gets what, when, and how in society) in *Politics: Who Gets What, When, How* (New York: McGraw-Hill, 1936).

cutors exercise substantial discretion; that is, they freely choose between significantly different courses of action. Thus, the judge's discretion to sentence a defendant to prison or grant probation or the prosecutor's decision to drop all charges resembles discretionary decisions made by legislators and mayors. Furthermore, the recruitment of judges, prosecutors, and public defenders involves them in a political process. Prosecutors and some judges, in fact, win office in partisan elections. They seek the support of party officials, raise campaign contributions, and woo voters. Those who come to office by appointment also participate in a political process, seek support, try to outfox competitors, and shape their behavior to ensure reappointment. Finally, participants in criminal courts interact with one another to produce decisions in ways not unlike those legislators or agency heads engage in. Charles Lindblom's apt description of the "play of power" in politics also fits what happens in courts: decisions result from human interaction shaped by rules, personalities, and tactics.[11] Understanding courts involves some of the ways of thinking that many use to describe the play in a game.

Weighty consequences flow from recognizing that courts are political institutions that share many characteristics with legislatures, administrative agencies, and executives. This realization suggests above all that concepts and metaphors useful for understanding these other political bodies may also apply to courts. The misconception that courts are different because they deal with Law, and the mistaken belief that law and politics represent opposing ways of making decisions, lose their surface appeal when we understand that courts are political. The mystery and aura that surround courts and black-robed judges, characteristics that impede looking at them as they are, also fade as we see that they make political decisions. Of course, courts are not just like school boards and legislatures. The language used and the formal procedures adopted, which are part of what we call "national legal culture," distinguish courts from other political institutions. But because they are fundamentally political, we should look at such things as career ambitions, the influence of constituencies, personal values and political beliefs, personalities, and pressures exerted by organizational superiors to understand how courts process defendants.

[11]See Charles E. Lindblom, *The Policy-Making Process*, 2nd ed. (Englewood Cliffs, N.J.: Prentice-Hall, 1980), especially Chapters 5 and 6.

Two sources of confusion about criminal courts need to be confronted to complete our discussion of them. First, most trial courts in the United States handle both criminal and civil cases. This book is focused upon how the criminal portion of their work is conducted. Of course, many of the same judges and lawyers deal with both types, and so the manner in which each is handled depends in part on the other. Second, though we concentrated earlier on perceptions of *violent* crime and punishment of violent criminals, most cases and defendants involve nonviolent offenses against property or public order.[12] Media coverage and citizens' perceptions of crime and criminal courts focus on violence. But to understand criminal courts, it is necessary to recognize that defendants accused of violent crimes are but a few among the many processed.

SIMILARITIES AND DIFFERENCES
IN AMERICAN CRIMINAL COURTS

In order to devise a metaphor useful in understanding how criminal courts everywhere operate, these courts must resemble one another enough to make such a general approach possible. They must also differ enough to make the effort interesting and worth the trouble. Luckily, American criminal courts display just such an elegant combination of similarities and differences. Only the participants' accents in a jury trial suggest where in the United States it is being held. The events a defendant facing a serious charge experiences, from initial appearance before a judge to imposition of sentence, differ only in relatively minor ways.

What accounts for such striking similarities in procedure in a nation as diverse as ours? The answer rests in the notion of "national legal culture"—shared values and attitudes about how persons

---

[12]Data from the FBI on arrests made in 1980, the year in which we conducted our field research, show that only about 20 percent of the more than 2,300,000 arrests made for its "index" crimes (murder, rape, robbery, aggravated assault, burglary, larceny-theft, motor vehicle theft, and arson) were violent. Inclusion of less serious crimes like petty theft and drunkenness reduces this proportion dramatically. See Table 4–1, "Estimated number of arrests, by offense charged, United States, 1980," in Timothy J. Flanagan and Maureen McLeod, eds., *Sourcebook of Criminal Justice Statistics*—1982 (U.S. Department of Justice, Bureau of Justice Statistics. Washington, D.C.: U.S. Government Printing Office, 1983), p. 390.

charged with crimes should be treated. Many of these values, and the procedures that implement them in practice, find expression in the U.S. Constitution. "No person shall be held to answer for a capital or otherwise infamous crime, unless on a presentment or indictment of a Grand Jury," states the Fifth Amendment. It continues:

> nor shall any person be subject for the same offense to be twice put in jeopardy of life or limb; nor shall be compelled in any criminal case to be a witness against himself, nor be deprived of life, liberty, or property without due process of law. . . .

Other amendments prohibit unreasonable searches and seizures and excessive bail, and guarantee a speedy public trial, assistance by counsel, and the right to subpoena and cross-examine witnesses. The Supreme Court has extended application of virtually all these procedural guarantees to the states. Most of them appear anyway in the constitutions of the individual states. They are taught to students in civics classes and, more significantly, to every law student.

These provisions and the many appellate court decisions specifying how they are to be implemented explain both why the sequence of stages in criminal cases and many of the procedures used along the way are alike everywhere. Table 1–2 presents the formal steps every defendant convicted of a serious crime experiences. Common procedures include the opportunity to file and argue motions challenging the admissibility of a confession or physical evidence alleged to have been improperly obtained, the conduct of a standard ritual before a plea of guilty is entered, and the voicing of objections during questioning of witnesses.

The national legal culture also dictates a common cast of participants and organizational structure. Everywhere defendants appear before a judge who presides over the interactions of a prosecutor representing the government and a defense attorney representing the defendant. Because every defendant charged requires such treatment, established procedures arise for scheduling court appearances and assigning a judge, prosecutor, and defense attorney. Judges, prosecutors, and many defense attorneys provided to poor defendants (public defenders) belong to organizations that coordinate their activities and establish common policies.

Along with the broad similarities found in the stages of criminal cases, in the procedures employed, and in the personnel and supporting organizations, American criminal courts also exhibit differ-

Table 1–2

Common Stages in All "Serious" (Felony)
Criminal Cases

1. *Initial arraignment* before a judicial official (magistrate), usually within twenty-four hours of arrest. Defendant is informed of the charges lodged. Eligibility for bail is determined, and if eligible, a bail type and amount are set.

2. *Determination of "probable cause,"* that is, whether there is probable cause that the crime charged did occur and that the defendant committed it. Probable cause can be determined by a grand jury or by a preliminary hearing (sometimes both), depending on the jurisdiction.

3. *Determination of guilt or innocence* in a trial-level court. Hearings on motions challenging the evidence or raising other defenses must be permitted at some time between the finding of probable cause and the final disposition. Determination of legal guilt or innocence can take the form of a dismissal, a guilty plea, or a verdict in a trial conducted before a jury or before a judge.

4. *Imposition of sentence* on convicted defendants following their conviction.

---

ences. Some are relatively minor, such as procedural variations in how potential jurors are chosen or whether a prosecutor's filing of an "information" can substitute for a grand jury indictment. Differences in selection and organization of judges, prosecutors, and defense attorneys have more extensive consequences. The same is true of the techniques used to schedule cases (calendaring) and to assign people to handle them (case assignment). The informal structure of relations among the people who work in courts, the values and informal norms that guide their behavior, and shared understandings about how they treat one another and dispose of cases also vary widely. But by far the most significant differences rest in how defendants fare. What proportion spend how much time in jail, unable to post bail, before their cases are concluded? How many are convicted and how many not? What proportion of convictions come from guilty pleas? Finally, how severely are convicted defendants punished? Criminal courts in the United States produce very different answers to these questions. Part of the challenge in understanding them requires describing and explaining this variety, a task we undertake in subsequent chapters.

THE APPROACH GUIDING
THE EMPIRICAL RESEARCH

How should one go about designing research that will generate better understanding of how criminal courts operate? Just how should what be studied? A natural way to start answering these questions is to draw upon our own previous research and the work of others faced with these questions. But this experience is not sufficient. We need a guiding principle to help decide what to study and how to study it.

One way to convey the problem is to imagine trying to learn how large universities in the United States operate. Who should be studied? If students were interviewed, they would begin talking about midterm and final examinations. Faculty would complain about grading exams and overwork. Administrators would grumble that neither students nor faculty understood the realities of running the institution and raising money. The research could not be conducted solely by talking with any one of these groups. Furthermore, the array of other possible topics is bewildering. What about the funding policies of the state legislature and governor, the work of the board of trustees, or the athletic department's influence? Clearly, a focus, a criterion of relevance, must be adopted to guide research on such complex social institutions as universities and courts.

Conceiving of courts as political institutions provided our research with a powerful initial guide. It not only helped us sort through published research to identify factors to study, but provided a map that helped arrange and suggest the relationships among these factors. It revealed how important what happens to defendants is, a principal though by no means complete answer to the question, "Who gets what as the result of courts' activities?" And it called our attention to categories of explanations commonly used in understanding politics that could be applied to research on courts.

DESIGN OF THE RESEARCH:
WHAT WAS STUDIED, AND HOW?

Two theoretical considerations guided us in selecting courts to study. First, the advantages of comparing criminal courts dictated examining a number of jurisdictions. At the same time, our intention to measure systematically many factors and integrate the three approaches meant that each court selected had to be studied in depth, limiting the number of courts three people could research. Second, we did not want to study large metropolitan jurisdictions. Not only had they been covered in most previous research, leaving us with little knowledge of other courts, but their size and complexity would have prevented studying more than two or three of them. The very smallest courts, those with one or two judges, had too few cases and decision makers to permit quantitative analysis. Practical considerations involving the cost of travel and ease of access led us to stay in our home states, Illinois, Michigan, and Pennsylvania.

We finally selected nine courts in counties with populations of between 200,000 and 1,000,000. Almost fifty counties in the three states fell into this range. Because we could not study intensively enough counties to provide a representative cross-section of the set of fifty, we decided to select the research sites in a way that would facilitate assessing the influence of environmental characteristics. Consequently, our research design called for studying three matched sets of triplets among middle-sized courts. We wanted large differences in the social, political, economic, and geographical features in the counties in the *same* state so that we could consider the effects of these differences. We also wanted counties with the same characteristics but in different states. We therefore selected three wealthy, Republican, suburban "ring" counties (Du Page, Oakland, Montgomery); three "autonomous," conservative counties (Peoria, Kalamazoo, Dauphin); and three "declining," more industrial, Democratic, and poorer counties (St. Clair, Saginaw, Erie). The geographical location of the counties and data on their population, income, and voting patterns appear in Figure 1–1. Table 1–3 identifies and summarizes the principal characteristics we sought to match in each set of triplets.

How well did we succeed in choosing the three sets of triplets? We were not able to obtain perfect matches, "identical triplets." Consequently, our counties displayed a few noticeable differences within each set. Oakland, with just over a million people, was significantly larger than Montgomery and Du Page, each of which had about 650,000. Because blacks are more often defendants, assessments of the fairness of courts usually ask if black defendants receive equal treatment. Therefore, ideally the proportion of blacks in each set of triplets should be similar. The black population in the declining

Figure 1–1

Location and Characteristics of Research Sites

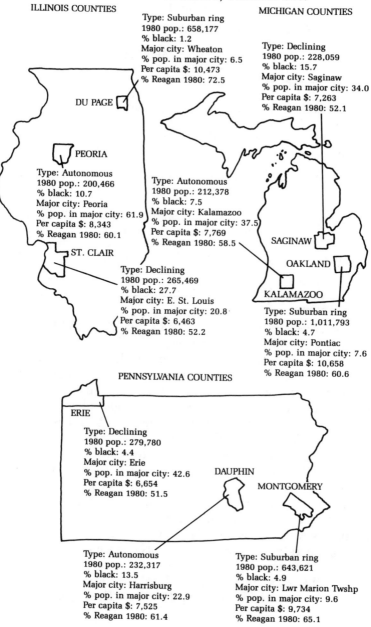

ILLINOIS COUNTIES

Type: Suburban ring
1980 pop.: 658,177
% black: 1.2
Major city: Wheaton
% pop. in major city: 6.5
Per capita $: 10,473
% Reagan 1980: 72.5

DU PAGE

PEORIA

Type: Autonomous
1980 pop.: 200,466
% black: 10.7
Major city: Peoria
% pop. in major city: 61.9
Per capita $: 8,343
% Reagan 1980: 60.1

ST. CLAIR

Type: Autonomous
1980 pop.: 212,378
% black: 7.5
Major city: Kalamazoo
% pop. in major city: 37.5
Per capita $: 7,769
% Reagan 1980: 58.5

Type: Declining
1980 pop.: 265,469
% black: 27.7
Major city: E. St. Louis
% pop. in major city: 20.8
Per capita $: 6,463
% Reagan 1980: 52.2

MICHIGAN COUNTIES

Type: Declining
1980 pop.: 228,059
% black: 15.7
Major city: Saginaw
% pop. in major city: 34.0
Per capita $: 7,263
% Reagan 1980: 52.1

SAGINAW

OAKLAND

KALAMAZOO

Type: Suburban ring
1980 pop.: 1,011,793
% black: 4.7
Major city: Pontiac
% pop. in major city: 7.6
Per capita $: 10,658
% Reagan 1980: 60.6

PENNSYLVANIA COUNTIES

ERIE

Type: Declining
1980 pop.: 279,780
% black: 4.4
Major city: Erie
% pop. in major city: 42.6
Per capita $: 6,654
% Reagan 1980: 51.5

DAUPHIN

MONTGOMERY

Type: Autonomous
1980 pop.: 232,317
% black: 13.5
Major city: Harrisburg
% pop. in major city: 22.9
Per capita $: 7,525
% Reagan 1980: 61.4

Type: Suburban ring
1980 pop.: 643,621
% black: 4.9
Major city: Lwr Marion Twshp
% pop. in major city: 9.6
Per capita $: 9,734
% Reagan 1980: 65.1

17

Table 1–3

Classification and Characteristics of Counties

	"Ring" triplets	"Autonomous" triplets	"Declining" triplets
Location			
Michigan	Oakland	Kalamazoo	Saginaw
Illinois	Du Page	Peoria	St. Clair
Pennsylvania	Montgomery	Dauphin	Erie
Principal characteristics			
Geography	suburbs "ringing" a major city	free-standing	free-standing
Economy	wealthy, low unemployment	moderate income and unemployment	low income, high unemployment
Politics	very Republican, very conservative	Republican, conservative	weakly Democratic, moderate

counties, however, ranged from Erie's scant 4.4 percent to St. Clair's 27.7 percent, with Saginaw between at 15.7 percent.

The relative size of a county's major city determines, among other things, the geographical dispersion of attorneys and lower courts, and the number of defendants arrested by the largest police department. We found differences within two sets of triplets here. Among the declining counties, St. Clair's largest city, East St. Louis, accounted for only about one-fifth of the county's population, and Saginaw and Erie contained one-third and two-fifths respectively. St. Clair's proximity to St. Louis placed it in the metropolitan media market, though too few residents commuted to St. Louis to qualify it as a suburb. In the autonomous set, the city of Peoria dominated its county with 62 percent of its population, but Kalamazoo with 34 percent and Harrisburg with 23 percent did not. Harrisburg, being Pennsylvania's capital, experienced more turnover in its population and had a number of state employees living in the area.

Nevertheless, as Figure 1–1 and Table 1–3 suggest, though we did not get identical triplets, we did get siblings. The declining counties of Saginaw and St. Clair had about the same number of people as Erie. All ranked below the other two counties in their state in per capita income, had higher rates of unemployment, and had more people receiving public assistance. The declining counties also voted Democratic more often than either the autonomous or ring counties. In contrast, the ring county in each state gave strong support to Republican candidates, had the highest per capita income, and had the lowest rate of people on public assistance. Their residents read newspapers and watched the television channels based in the nearby metropolitan centers of Chicago, Detroit, and Philadelphia. In sharp contrast to the adjoining big city, no ring county had a large black population. Thus, despite some differences within each set of triplets, the family resemblance was clear enough in such features as economic well-being, relation to other population centers, size of population, and partisan political composition to warrant comparison of the court communities within each type of county.

We gathered three kinds of information on the nine courts during 1980. First, we went to the court records to obtain information on the defendants handled. In addition to recording the charges lodged and the outcomes, we gathered data on the evidence, the defendant's characteristics, the dates and outcomes of each stage in the disposition of the case, and the identity of the judge, prosecutor, and defense attorney. Information on more than 7,400 defendants resulted. Second, we conducted interviews with approximately 300 judges, prosecutors, defense attorneys, and other major participants such as court administrators, county council members, and newspaper reporters. The interviews were open-ended, taking the form of guided discussions covering a standard outline of topics. Nearly all were tape recorded and transcribed. Finally, we asked the individuals interviewed to fill out several questionnaires. One gathered information on their background, prior career, and political and community activities. Another assessed their attitudes toward several basic issues in criminal justice: commitment to due process, belief in punishment for criminals, and the need for "efficiency" in handling cases. A third measured an aspect of personality, Machiavellianism, to ascertain the extent to which respondents sought to manipulate other people. Finally, we asked each interviewee to rank other participants in the county on such factors as legal ability, trustworthiness, and the quality of his relationship with them. We refer to these evaluations as the "Q-sort" data because the technique used to gather them is called a Q-sort.[13]

Detailed descriptions of the research methodology, including the content of the measures just described and the statistical techniques used to analyze it, have appeared in other places.[14] In this book, we will discuss the results of the analysis conducted on the quantitative data, but we will not present the rather involved statistical analyses themselves.[15]

Obviously, these nine counties do not constitute a representative random sample of middle-sized jurisdictions in our three states. Even if we could have expanded our research to study enough counties to obtain a valid random sample, it could be asked if these three states are representative of all states or if the focus on middle-sized jurisdictions does not limit the conclusions that can be drawn. Though in a narrow sense such criticisms are valid, they miss the mark. The research is designed to increase our understanding of how courts work; nobody can study everything. Furthermore, one needs to know the factors that shape how courts work and the content of the patterns found in their operation before the broadly focused surveys with random samples needed to determine the frequency with which such patterns appear can be conducted. For the purposes we sought to achieve, the group of counties selected and the techniques applied in studying them are appropriate.

---

[13]The Q-sort involved asking each respondent in the study to answer questions about other respondents. For instance, we gave judges the names of every assistant prosecutor and public defender and asked them to rank each on a five-point scale of trustworthiness. Similarly, prosecutors ranked each judge and the defense attorneys. When these results were combined, we had a measure of how judges as a group ranked each attorney on such characteristics as trustworthiness and trial ability. For further discussion of the Q-sort, see Chapter 4, note 7.

[14]For a discussion of this research, see James Eisenstein, Peter F. Nardulli, and Roy B. Flemming, *Final Report: Explaining and Assessing Criminal Case Disposition: A Comparative Study of Nine Courts*, submitted to the National Institute of Justice, April 29, 1982, especially Chapters 1 and 2.

[15]We have published a detailed presentation of the results of our statistical analysis elsewhere. See Nardulli et al., *The Tenor of Justice* (Urbana, Ill.: University of Illinois Press, forthcoming, 1987).

SUMMARY

Criminal courts attract interest because they deal with criminal violence, a topic that fascinates and threatens. They provide symbolic reassurance that criminals can be controlled and punished. Also, however, they express other fundamental values, and demonstrate that government faces limits in dealing with individual citizens. We view courts as political not only because of the dual symbolic functions they perform, but also because they help determine who gets punished and who does not as the result of government action.

In trying to understand criminal courts, most Americans draw upon the notion of Law, the metaphor based on the traditional view of the nature of law. Too powerful to be dislodged, it nevertheless provides a poor tool to use for understanding the complexities of criminal courts in action. We propose an alternative metaphor, viewing courts as communities.

Though courts display enough variation to make studying them difficult and interesting, national legal culture imposes common values and procedural stages that make them similar enough to permit comparison. In undertaking empirical research to examine and understand their variation, we adopted an eclectic approach drawing from three existing approaches — the individual, organizational, and environmental. We gathered information from court records and interviewed more than three hundred participants in the courts of nine middle-sized jurisdictions in Michigan, Illinois, and Pennsylvania.

Before embarking on a description of these courts in Part Two, we need to explain fully how the metaphor of courts as communities can be used to enhance our understanding. This is our task in Chapter Two.

CHAPTER TWO

The Criminal Court Community

ORIGINS OF THE METAPHOR: COURTS AS COMMUNITIES

Criminal courts command interest principally because of what happens to defendants there. Hence, focusing on the outcomes of defendants' cases was a natural starting point for our efforts to understand criminal courts. As we began conducting interviews and strolling through courthouse corridors, simple curiosity expanded the list of the phenomena that called for understanding. How (and why) did techniques for scheduling cases, arriving at plea bargains, and engaging in other chores associated with disposing of cases differ among our counties? What significance did the variations have? Why did we find ourselves discussing the personalities and policy goals of chief judges and head prosecutors?

This broader focus to the challenge of understanding criminal courts has served us well. We cannot abandon examining case outcomes as a major theme. Looking just at outcomes, however, fails to provide general insights into the dynamics of the disposition process, factors that determine how all defendants who come to court fare. And it helps little in the vital task of assessing the effects of reform proposals undertaken in Chapter Eleven.

In this chapter we describe the metaphor that evolved to achieve this broader understanding of criminal courts. We had emphatically rejected the legal metaphor described in Chapter One when we began our field research. In its place we relied upon a variety of concepts drawn from each of the three approaches employed in previous research on courts.[1] But we lacked a unifying metaphor that could help us assemble the individual pieces of the puzzle these concepts provided.

The metaphor of courts as communities evolved as we informally discussed our experiences at the end of a day of interviewing. We would share tidbits of information, offer pieces of the puzzle, and try to fit them together. Perhaps knowing that the jurisdictions had fewer active participants than those we had previously studied and read about nudged us toward applying unarticulated conceptions of community to the task. Some of the people we interviewed either used the word "community" or described things that brought it to mind. Regardless of its origins, the end result was the metaphor that guides our descriptions of criminal courts. In the following pages we present the principal components of the metaphor of courts as communities.

THE NOTION OF COMMUNITY

Our initial understanding of the concept of community lacked specificity and rigor. In refining it, we turned for help to discussions of it by sociologists. We quickly found that its use in sociology was, as two authors described it, amorphous and malleable,[2] and that it carried strong emotional overtones. Our task was to forge from its components a conception that would prove useful in understanding courts.[3] The concept of culture is so intertwined with community

[1]These concepts (some of the principal ones) included "courtroom workgroups," "sponsoring organizations," "decision-maker attributes and attitudes," "local legal culture," and the "environmental context."

[2]See the Introduction by Colin Bell and Howard Newby in Bell and Newby, eds., *The Sociology of Community: A Selection of Readings* (Portland, Ore.: Frank Cass, 1974), p. xiv.

[3]Like all efforts to aid understanding by means of analogies, there is danger of overdoing this application of notions drawn from the concept of community to criminal courts. Even if we succeed in carefully qualifying and circumscribing our presentation, inevitably some among both critics and admirers will exaggerate our position. Clearly, we believe that the operation of criminal courts exhibits enough characteristics found in discussions of the concept of community to allow us to apply the analogy profitably. Obviously, though, courts are not just like residential communities. There is considerable disagreement on just what the essence of communities is. Fur-

that it warrants separate discussion. In the section following this we consider the relationship between court communities and "county legal culture."

The emotional overtones that the term community introduces can hopelessly compromise its usefulness. For many people, the word symbolizes an idealized view of the "traditional community" that existed in a past and happier era, a "better" place characterized by "warmer" and tightly knit interpersonal relations, with cooperation crowding out conflict. As such, it contrasts with the cold, impersonal, and conflict-dominated character of modern life.[4] Our use of the word implies no judgment about the merits of traditional or modern communities. Merely to say "community" leaves open the question of interpersonal dynamics within it, including the level of conflict.[5] Therefore, the existence of a court community does not require strong agreement, low conflict, or similarity in its members' attributes. As we explain below, the crucial elements are common workplace and interdependence. These are likely to be found in all criminal courts. People locked in conflict are no less interdependent. The actions of each influence the other. If attitudes differ sharply and conflict is rampant, these features do not mean there is no court

---

ther, though consensus on some characteristics can be identified, courts differ from it in several ways. Most significant is departure from the focus on residence and geographical boundedness. We substitute "occupation" for "residence," defining the community as composed of individuals whose occupation leads to interdependence. There is a geographical component, to be sure. The jurisdiction of the court provides some boundaries, and interactions among community members tend to occur within the physical confines of the courthouse. But this approach differs markedly from many definitions of community that depend upon domicile. See, for example, Norbert Elias, who offers this definition: "A community, one can say, is a group of households situated in the same locality and linked to each other by functional interdependencies which are closer than interdependencies of the same kind with other groups of people within the wider social field to which a community belongs." "Towards a Theory of Communities," the Foreword in Bell and Newby, op. cit., p. xix. Our definition is built on functional interdependencies that arise from *occupation* alone, not proximity of households.

[4]See Norbert Elias, ibid., p. xi, for a discussion of the emotional overtones associated with the notion of community.

[5]Norbert Elias, ibid., p. xix, comments that "interdependencies between people are completely neutral features of communities or societies—neutral in terms of cooperation and conflict; they can give rise to either." He goes on to observe that when problems arise among interdependent people, they can be handled through either cooperation *or* conflict.

community. Rather, they tell us something about its significant *characteristics*. Adjectives like "fractured" or "conflictual" rather than "close-knit" and "cooperative" will be appropriate. In fact, intense conflict between individuals and organizations in court communities probably is quite common.

Among the various usages of "community" in social science, two appear most transferable to courts: the notion of community as a neighborhood, and "undercover communities" within formal organizations. Norbert Elias, who has written on the theory of communities, provides a description of "undercover" communities in organizations that seems especially applicable to courts:

> [T]hey are beehives of personal groupings and interdependencies full of bonds of sympathy and antipathy, affection and emotional loathing, with a gossip flow and gossip struggles structured in accordance with the power differentials and many other characteristics of residential communities.[6]

Many of the principal features of courts that correspond to elements embodied in the concept of community are contained in Elias's description of undercover communities within formal organizations. *Interdependencies* is perhaps the foremost. Members of a community depend upon one another because of their residence in the community.[7] Most conceptions of community trace interdependence to the shared interests that emanate from *common residence* in a geographical locality. Our application to courts transforms this notion to *common workplace*, with the interdependencies stemming from occupation. Strong emotional undercurrents and grapevines carrying gossip and information in communities are another important feature found in courthouses. Elias attaches special significance to grapevines:

> One of the most ubiquitous manifestations of these emotive aspects of community bonds is the community grapevine. . . . it is structured in accordance with the structure of the community itself and particularly with its distribution of power chances — usually uneven.[8]

[6]Elias, ibid., p. xxx.

[7]Elias states: "The concept of interdependence, in other words, conveys as the others do not the peculiarly compelling nature of human bonds." Op. cit., p. xviii.

[8]Ibid., p. xxviii.

These and other attributes of communities mentioned in the literature suggest a number of specific aspects of criminal court communities worth exploring. In fact, we draw upon the metaphor to guide efforts to understand how a specific criminal court works. Thus, many of the questions one would ask when trying to learn about a residential community can be usefully applied to criminal courts. Who are the inhabitants of the community? How do they depend upon one another? What is the structure of status and power among them? What are the principal organizations and groups to which inhabitants belong, and how do these organizations function? What technologies are employed in the community to do its work? How does the geography of the community shape its dynamics? In the following pages, we will examine how the asking and answering of each of these questions can assist in studying criminal court communities.

Applying the concept of court community to comparative research such as ours suggests the potential of looking at how communities differ. This theme is a recurring and controlling one in this book. Court communities vary on each of the attributes we will discuss. Here is just one example: some will be heavily influenced by a strong local political party organization in selecting judges and prosecutors; recruitment in places with weak parties will be shaped by other forces. We also will seek to identify factors that help explain *why* court communities differ from one another. In Chapter Ten we consider this question in detail. The size of the jurisdiction, and therefore the number of individuals in the community, appear especially important. But structural and cultural factors stemming from differences among the states, and variation in the political and economic characteristics of the counties and the practices and policies of the principal sponsoring organizations also deserve consideration. Part of this discussion will be focused on the role played by "county legal culture." Before discussing the attributes of "community" that apply to courts, we need to consider the special part that county legal culture plays in the metaphor.

COUNTY LEGAL CULTURE
AND COURT COMMUNITIES

The concept of culture has a leading part in discussions of the nature and dynamics of communities. Recent use of the idea of local legal culture in studies comparing aspects of court operation makes it especially pertinent to our approach.[9] This research argues that the notion of local legal culture finds concrete expression in the perceptions of those who participate in the courts' activities, that its content varies, and that this variation helps explain differences in the way in which courts work.[10] In this book, we will use the expression county legal culture instead of local legal culture to emphasize that, at least in most places in the United States, state trial courts' jurisdictions extend to county boundaries. Though minor differences in legal culture might be found in different localities within the same county, the geographic concentration of judges and activities in one county courthouse (and often the physical concentration of attorneys' offices in the immediate neighborhood) ensures that the most appropriate unit of analysis for examining legal culture is at the county level.

Definition of County Legal Culture

Examining in detail the various academic treatments of the notion of culture, the alternative definitions and the problems that different definitions create could occupy us for many pages.[11] For our purposes in this chapter, however, we can dispense with such an inquiry and merely present the definition we will use.

We assert without elaboration the commonly accepted view that culture shapes both the behavior of individuals and the character of communities. We also accept the view that political culture is a central aspect of culture, and that legal culture in turn is part of political culture. We will focus primarily on county legal culture. We recognize that a national legal culture is widely shared throughout the

[9]See, for example, Thomas Church, *Examining Local Legal Culture: Practitioner Attitudes in Four Criminal Courts* (Washington, D.C.: National Institute of Justice, 1982). For an excellent summary of earlier research and a bibliography, see Herbert Kritzer, "Political Culture, Trial Courts, and Criminal Cases," in Peter Nardulli, ed., *The Study of Criminal Courts: Political Perspectives* (Cambridge, Mass.: Ballinger, 1979).

[10]See especially Thomas Church, *Justice Delayed* (Williamsburg, Va.: National Center for State Court, 1978). For an early treatment of the subject, see Martin Levin, "Urban Politics and Judicial Behavior," 1 *The Journal of Legal Studies* (January 1972), pp. 193–221.

[11]For earlier discussions of these topics, see Lawrence Friedman, "Legal Culture and Social Development," 4 *Law and Society Review* (1969), pp. 29–44; Austin Sarat, "Studying American Legal Culture: An Assessment of the Survey Evidence," 11 *Law and Society Review* (1976), pp. 427–488; Church, *Examining Local Legal Culture*, op. cit., and Thomas Church, "The 'Old and the New' Conventional Wisdom of Court Delay," 7 *Justice System Journal* (1982), pp. 395–412.

United States, but because we want to examine differences in courts, we need not consider it. We must, however, recall a point made in Chapter One—that national legal culture sculpts county legal cultures throughout the United States, producing a common set of beliefs and accepted procedures. Finally, some differences stem from variation in state legal culture, and so we must briefly discuss it.

Our view of county legal culture is that it consists of the values and perceptions of the principal members of the court community about how they ought to behave and their beliefs about how they actually do behave in performing their duties. This is a narrow definition. We exclude the beliefs of the general public and elected legislative and executive officials, and we do not include the patterns of actual *behavior* as part of culture. Some degree of consensus must exist before one can say that a distinctive county legal culture exists. Though precise measures of how much agreement is needed to say that sufficient consensus is present are difficult to specify, the level of shared attitudes and beliefs has to be fairly high. Finally, there must be some stability of perceptions and beliefs for them to qualify as part of county legal culture.

Our research uncovered five recurring themes as we assessed the content of the county legal culture in the nine jurisdictions we studied. In the discussion that follows we present each of them.

Self-Awareness as an Attribute of County Legal Culture

First, the degree to which members consciously recognize the existence of a court community varies. In some counties, such self-images are weak; in others, respondents refer frequently to the existence of a community. Du Page and Montgomery counties provided a nice contrast. Similar in their wealth, their conservative Republicanism, and their location next to major metropolitan centers, they differed in the specificity and content of their self-images. In Du Page, the sense of community was not as strong. Sharp conflict between the prosecutor's office and the defense bar, a sense of loss stemming from what many believed to be the formerly high level of cooperation, and disintegrating cohesion in the Republican party all worked against a strong sense of community. Instead, several distinct subcommunities resembling cliques developed. In Montgomery, the Republican party's centralization and ideology led to shared beliefs that the people throughout the offices in the county courthouse were part of "one family."

One way in which both the existence of a sense of community and its deterioration became evident was by expressions of nostalgia and discontent at perceived violations of previous patterns of inter-action. In Du Page, defense attorneys described the new set of pros-ecutors as "heavy handed" and lacking a sense of justice. In Erie, a public defender, unhappy with recent tension and mutual criticism flowing between his office and the district attorney's, described what he desired:

> I want to see a good strong DA's office with quality, competent people. And I want a good strong defense office with quality, competent people. Because working together with good profes-sional tension, I think, is gonna increase the quality of criminal justice.

Several other components of self-image illustrate this aspect of culture. In all the suburban ring counties respondents contrasted themselves favorably with the big, bad metropolitan center and its courts. Du Page saw itself as "not like Chicago" and Montgomery as "not like Philadelphia." But more than negative comparisons came out. People in all three ring counties regarded themselves as leaders in unspecified "quality," in innovation, and in administration. Oak-land respondents felt their court was the "premier circuit" in Mich-igan. In several counties, the court community (including defense attorneys) saw itself as "holding the line" against a siege of crime. Both Peoria and Montgomery defense attorneys, for example, ex-pressed antidefendant attitudes, and saw themselves as participating in a cooperative enterprise to see that dangerous criminals did not stalk the streets of Peoria or that Philadelphia blacks did not prey on Montgomery's wealthy white bedroom communities.

Common Beliefs About Interpersonal Relations

Shared beliefs on how community members treat one another and generally conduct themselves are a second major theme in court cul-tures. In a number of counties, we learned the commandment "don't rock the boat." A Montgomery attorney explained why he did not seek to overturn Republican area leaders' decision not to nominate him for a county office by telling us: "I decided that I maybe should not do that because around here when you put up a stink, they gen-erally hold it against you when it's over." Another explained that class-action civil suits or suits challenging the operation of the criminal system "upset" the bar, and that "upsetting the bar would be rocking the boat." A Dauphin county private attorney commented "Dauphin county has a very conservative bar. Nobody rocks the boat."

Trustworthiness, keeping one's word, was another common rule of interpersonal behavior. A person familiar with Erie's courts expressed these themes well: "Everybody tries to work together. Everybody sort of trusts each other around here that nobody is going to pull anything funny on anyone else."

Attorneys who cooperated, who sat quietly in the boat, could expect to build "credit" that could be drawn on in times of need. As a part-time public defender in Montgomery county explained:

> You go along. I've never raised a point that the DA's petition has been filed late because I know I do it all the time. . . . You wind up doing favors for people, for a judge. You might do this or that. So you call in your dues. And everybody's got dues.

An Erie public defender described a similar accounting system:

> Everybody, by virtue of being a good guy, has so many chips a year that he can cash in. You go in to a judge and you say, "Look, judge. I'm busting my buns every day in this dang court, and I need a break on this case." It has nothing to do with justice, nothing to do with law. I need a break. Okay! You get so many chips a year that you can cash in.

Finally, a spirit of cooperation in some counties supported practices that rewarded conformists and provided benefits to many. In Montgomery County, attorneys with new babies passed out cigars to the judges, a signal that they were eligible for appointment to a guardianship worth about $1,000. In St. Clair County, the police and prosecutor traditionally conducted what the community called the "fall roundup." One defense attorney described it: "On drug cases, they would go out and issue a couple of hundred drug cases at one time, and all the private bar would get rich for a couple of months. They'd wind up dismissing half of them."

Shared Attitudes About How Cases Are Processed

A third component of court culture deals with handling of cases. By far most significant is the notion of the "going rate"; that is, the appropriate sentence given the offense and the defendant's prior criminal record. We report just a few of the many statements made about appropriate sentences. An experienced Peoria defense attorney told us:

> Talking about the state's attorney's office, I think that there's no fooling around when you want to sit down and plea bargain there. They know that you're there to bargain, and you try to give them the benefit of your wisdom in the practice, not only for defendants. Hell, we have to live in the community, and we're not interested in taking some guy who's guilty of multiple murders and heinous felonies, for Christ's sake, and putting him on the goddamned street. We try to get the proper sentence. I myself feel after thirty years' experience that I know as much about sentencing and what should be the sentence as the judges know, if not more so, in a lot of situations.

A Montgomery judge referred to an "informal consensus" that developed among his colleagues. "We have a policy around here that there's gonna be some jail time after the second or third offense for retail theft, definitely after the third one." Finally, an experienced private defense attorney in Montgomery observed that:

> There have been many cases where a DA has made a deal with me and I look at him and I say, "Hey, that's not enough. You're too low on the case." The guy says he wants a $250 fine. I say, "No, make him pay $500." Because it's fair.

Another aspect of county legal culture pertaining to how cases should be handled deals with the appropriateness of judicial acceptance of plea bargains, including a specific sentence. In Montgomery County, a former prosecutor known as a harsh sentencer explained why he hesitated to reject many pleas as too lenient.

> Because the system doesn't permit it. . . . The system is set up so that the prosecutor plea bargains. And he plea bargains because the system demands him to plea bargain. Otherwise the system fails. So I've got to live with that, even though I don't approve of it.

But at the opposite end of the same state, plea bargaining occurs without specification of sentence. Told that this was the practice in Montgomery, a crusty veteran Erie judge retorted:

> I've told them, "If you're going to tell me the sentence, get a computer. You don't need a judge." I'll make up my own mind with the presentence report and everything. I don't need the advice of an attorney.

An equally sharp contrast differentiated the two counties in attitudes on whether part-time public defenders should be allowed to represent private criminal clients. In Montgomery County, it was established practice and unquestioned. In Erie, it was felt that part-time defenders absolutely should not handle any private criminal cases. A final example on the handling of cases came from Peoria. When several charges arising from the same incident could be brought, the prosecutor's office began to file separate indictments with a single charge, increasing its conviction rate. To be practical, defendants who went to trial had to face all indictments in one proceeding. Other members of the court community, however, disapproved of the practice. Before long, judges began granting defense motions to separate the charges, forcing the prosecutor to go to trial on each. The prosecutor's office had to stop the practice.

Not all counties exhibited as much agreement over the handling of cases as those just described. The Oakland prosecutor came to office vowing to eliminate plea bargaining and increase sentences. He went so far as to criticize some of the judges publicly for their lenient sentences. When the judges tried to take some of his office space to provide additional judicial chambers, he refused to accommodate them. Though things had settled down by the time our field research began, memories of these sharp disagreements lingered. In Kalamazoo, the prosecutor lost the support of the police union and faced public criticism from it because of changes in screening of cases for prosecution. Thus, though consensus on such matters often appears, it is neither inevitable nor permanent.

Special Language as an Aspect of Culture

The presence of shared special language and commonly understood nonverbal communication is another significant component of county legal culture, arising regardless of the general level of conflict or cooperation. In Oakland County, everyone referred to the former practice of scheduling a day for the appearance of attorneys in every case scheduled for the upcoming trial term as the "cattle call." Poor cases that prosecutors stalled in bringing to trial were known as "dogs." Almost everyone in Dauphin referred to the Wednesday court sessions regularly scheduled to handle pleas and minor offenses as "Junk Court." Experienced attorneys who knew well a hard-line, tough-sentencing judge in Montgomery would sometimes grab their neckties and hold them up in a hanging gesture when they walked into his courtroom. In St. Clair County, a combination of code words and silence came to signify a recommendation of probation. An assistant explained:

> [The prosecutor] has told us that he doesn't want us always in
> the posture of recommending probation. It looks bad. So when
> we take a plea [where probation is appropriate] we usually say,
> "The defendant will plead to the charge and we will stand silent
> at sentencing." . . . Well, to the judge, that is his cue that this is
> a probationary offense. We are not going to object to probation.
> We are not going to do anything. We are just going to stand
> there while the judge makes up his mind. There is really no
> difference between us recommending it or the judge giving it
> except in terms of who is doing the asking for it.

Culture and a Sense of Tradition

Finally, members of the court community in each of the counties
had in varying degrees a sense of history that they call upon to explain and to evaluate current patterns. A common theme of such
remarks dealt with the "loss of cooperation." Defense attorneys in
Du Page and St. Clair compared present levels of cooperation and
performance in the prosecutor's office unfavorably with those of the
past. Nearly everyone in Kalamazoo regretted the loss of harmony
that had characterized relations among the judges. In Erie, many
discussions of the prosecutor's office in 1980 began with what happened when an incumbent prosecutor died in office more than six
years earlier. Stories about eccentric members of the community, past
and present, were a primary source of entertainment in informal bull
sessions in nearly every county. Some of the "lore" or "conventional
wisdom" that is conveyed socializes new members and guides incumbents' behavior. In Saginaw, many people believed a former
prosecutor's defeat for reelection could be attributed to opposition
by the police officers' organization. This credit enhanced the ability
of the police to receive careful consideration for their interests from
incumbents who planned to seek reelection. In counties with an ideology of "don't rock the boat" and "cooperate with the other side,"
stories of what happened to nonconformists were more than entertainment. They served as object lessons.

INHABITANTS OF COURT COMMUNITIES

Residential communities, by definition, consist of people who live in
a common geographical locale. It is the sharing of a common workplace and interaction in the performance of their jobs that define

the membership of criminal court communities. These communities have a readily identifiable "core" at any given time, consisting of the judges, prosecutors, and defense attorneys who spend almost all their time dealing with criminal cases. Others may be just outside this core, such as a judge or part-time assistant prosecutor or public defender who spends a significant percentage of time on noncriminal matters. Beyond that, the criteria for inclusion in the community become less clear-cut. As defense attorneys move from "regular" to "occasional" status, their membership becomes increasingly questionable. "Outsider" defense attorneys present special problems. They enjoy all the formal authority regulars possess when it comes to disposing of a case. But they are subject to very few of the sanctions applied to regulars, and frequently have little idea of the routines that regulars have established among themselves. In some places, other individuals may approach full membership in the community — a prominent bail bondsman, an experienced court administrator, or a veteran newspaper reporter assigned to cover the courthouse.

The higher-status members of the criminal court community share more than a common workplace and linked occupations. All are lawyers, sharing the relatively high status that this profession accords its members and the common experience of attending law school and practicing law. Though women attorneys are beginning to appear in the ranks of assistant prosecutors and public defenders, few serve as judges, office heads, or established private defense counsel.

Though our research did not focus extensively on nonlawyer members of the community, such as courtroom staff, clerks, office secretaries, and court administrators, they are part of the community and participate actively in many of its activities, including the grapevine. Here, the proportion of women is much higher.

The size of the core community depends to some extent on the combinations of technologies employed to assign cases to judges, prosecutors, and defense counsel. The procedures used can result in a handful of specialists who spend full time on criminal cases, or a diffuse group most of whom participate sporadically. The stability of membership can also vary. Where turnover among assistant prosecutors and public defenders is high, and where those who leave drift into civil practice, stability will be lower. Smaller courts in stagnant counties with zero or negative population growth exhibit greater stability.

What is the status of defendants in the court community? An apt analogy can be drawn between their status and that of tourists in resort communities. Tourists come to the community for a brief stay, but they are not part of it. They are outsiders, temporary "summer people" who are fed, housed, and processed by the yearlong residents. The permanent residents may be cohesive or riven by conflict. But they share a perspective, a grapevine, the memory of important past events, a special vocabulary, and patterns of nonverbal communication that visitors do not. Though tourists come to the community voluntarily and defendants do not, both may complain about the food, the accommodations, and the treatment they receive from the natives. Thus, both tourists and defendants are physically present, but temporarily. They affect the community's operation significantly. In fact, they are a principal reason for its existence in both instances; however, they are not a *part* of the community.

INTERDEPENDENCIES IN COURT COMMUNITIES

Empirical research on criminal courts demonstrates convincingly that the principal participants in the work of criminal courts depend heavily upon each other.[12] This interdependence, perhaps more than anything else, makes applying the notion of community to courts productive. The question is not so much whether such intense interdependence exists, but why it is not immediately evident to everyone. The answer perhaps rests in lingering adherence to symbolically potent visions of a "combat" image of courts, as places where Law is applied by independent and trained judges who assess the arguments of autonomous professional advocates.

The extent of familiarity among members of a court community shapes significantly the quality of interdependence. There are degrees of familiarity, of course. Merely recognizing the face and name of the opposing attorney is a form of familiarity, but one unlikely to affect interaction. Knowledge of the opponent's reputation for skill, honesty, and the like provides more significant information. But in-

[12]This point is so well established that it is hard to decide which works to cite and which to leave out. For an early and good statement, see Abraham Blumburg, *Criminal Justice* (Chicago: Quandrangle Books, 1967). Only narrowly focused research designs do not reach this conclusion, but they do so by omission.

timate understanding of others' past behavior patterns, strengths and weaknesses, and the like, especially if derived from first-hand experience, leads to a type of familiarity that deeply colors interactions.

Several factors affect the quality and degree of familiarity among members of a court community. The size of the community; that is, the number of members, is both the most obvious and most telling. But the size and nature of the towns and cities in the jurisdiction also have a role. Where the population is small, the chances increase that court community members know one another from grammar school, volleyball league, or church. Communities with stable populations and low levels of migration show greater familiarity.

The scope of interdependence; that is, the number of ways and places in which interactions take place among members of the court community also warrants attention. Clearly, size has a big part here too. In small jurisdictions, attorneys and judges are unable to specialize in one area of law. The likelihood that a defense attorney will also appear before a judge on a civil matter is higher; the probability that a part-time prosecutor will have dealings with defense attorneys on noncriminal matters likewise is greater. The expectation that young assistant prosecutors and public defenders currently specializing in criminal law will have to deal with one another on a variety of matters in their subsequent careers also rises as the jurisdiction is smaller. But the degree of specialization among the bar may depend on other local factors besides sheer size. In assessing the scope of interdependence, nonoccupational ties are also relevant. In counties with stable populations such as Erie and St. Clair, family, financial, and political ties among court community members appeared to be more frequent than in more mobile counties like Kalamazoo, Peoria, and Dauphin. Finally, established career paths within counties contribute to dependence when success in obtaining subsequent jobs requires approval or support by members of the court community.

STRUCTURE OF STATUS AND POWER

A significant attribute of a community is the structure of status and power among its members. Judges clearly rank at the top of the hierarchy of status in court communities. Their salaries exceed the incomes of all but the most prominent and experienced private defense attorneys. The trappings of power—their own chambers and courtrooms, the black robes and elevated daises—and the deference shown when they are addressed as "Your Honor" attest to their high prestige. Status differences among the judges show little variation, but the rest of the community displays a considerable range. A few members of the community elite may approach the judges' status (the head prosecutor and established private defense attorneys). At the other extreme are assistant public defenders and some high-volume regular defense attorneys. Just as in other types of communities, courts sometimes encounter both "deviants" and "outsiders." The deviants are physically present, but not regarded as full members because they fail to conform to standards of behavior or dress regarded as important. Their deviance sometimes brings on some sort of punishment, making them object lessons to others who might contemplate similar behavior. They remind others that norms specifying what is proper will be enforced. Outsiders, visitors from other communities, pose special problems because they are unfamiliar with local practices and are not subject to the sanctions and pressures that residents are.

The distribution of influence is less clear-cut than that of status. Judges' high status gives them an initial but not overwhelming advantage. Dominance in formal status does not invariably translate into actual influence. Most of the crucial decisions producing an outcome in a case result from joint interaction among the three members of the triad: the judge, prosecutor, and defense attorney handling a case. Thus, influence among the major actors in criminal cases flows in all directions. Though influence in triads is reciprocal, patterns of interdependence are neither uniform nor in perfect balance. Reciprocity is both uneven and variable from triad to triad. Even the rare instances in which unilateral decisions determine outcomes, as when a prosecutor drops all charges spontaneously or a recalcitrant defendant stubbornly insists on a jury trial, the other participants must adjust accordingly. When we move from individual cases to look at general disposition patterns and the work lives of participants, the extent of interdependence broadens. It is here that differences in the content and quality of interdependence found can help characterize court communities.

What determines the balance of influence? Certainly role is one major component. But, as we have seen, the higher status of judges does not guarantee they will control interactions and outcomes. The specific circumstances of cases can interact with personal characteristics to alter the balance. The ages of the triad members, particularly if they differ substantially, can also significantly shape the balance of influence. Differences will be found in the content and quality of interaction between a new twenty-nine-year-old assistant prosecutor and an established privately retained defense counsel twice his age, or between that same defense attorney and a judge with whom he has dealt for two decades. Some young attorneys recognize this difference well, as the comments of a perceptive Dauphin County prosecutor on courtroom behavior indicate:

> I: But you don't shout and walk away, and turn your back [to the judge]?
> R: No. And believe me, in our Dauphin County courts, there's no judge that would let a young attorney get away with that.
> I: What about an old attorney?
> R: Yeah. They probably would, maybe because many of the judges were contemporaries. Twenty years from now, when my contemporaries are sitting on the bench, people that I've socialized with, that I have dinner with, they're gonna give me much more leeway than they're going to give to a younger person.

An experienced defense attorney in another county conveyed the flavor of his interactions with a judge who formerly served as his boss when he was an assistant prosecutor. The judge had agreed to extra effort to help reduce the backlog:

> You know what I told [him]? I said, "You're a goddamn fool."
> . . . Now, I can talk to him like that because we're friends and I'm greatly concerned.

These observations suggest a general feature of communities that can be used to understand courts—the structure and influence of "age cohorts" or "generations." The distribution of age and experience among the most active members of the court community, which varies from position to position and from jurisdiction to jurisdiction, affects the extent to which generational effects appear. At the time of our research, the five Erie judges had served together for a number of years, knew each other well, and (at least for the three who handled most criminal cases) enjoyed a close personal and working relationship. The public defender's office, previously staffed by experienced and respected attorneys, had undergone huge turnover. The newly elected DA brought in a mixture of inexperienced assistants and veteran prosecutors from a previous era. The judges' cohesiveness, under strong leadership by the chief judge, combined with their declining energy and interest, thwarted the prosecutor's efforts to bring about changes in the calendar and created numerous problems in trying to deal with the workload. The inexperience of the public defenders' staff compounded these problems. This "age and generation" factor affects court communities in indirect but telling ways.

A related feature of communities is the forming of cliques. Our research suggests that the extent to which cliques coalesce within both the court community at large and specific sponsoring organizations varies from jurisdiction to jurisdiction. Though many of the reasons for the development of these cliques remain elusive, two did appear. One relates directly to the political structure in the county, particularly the political party structure. Where parties are strong, and especially where conflict arises within party structures, cliques form. Even in counties where the dominant party was fairly cohesive (as in Montgomery), cliques gathered based on whether individuals participated in the political life of the dominant party. The second is based on similarities in age and in prior experiences (law school classmates, family friendships, and the like).

No one is surprised when the existence of cliques sometimes leads to significant conflict and animosity. In one county, our question to a judge at the core of one group about the management style of the chief judge, who headed the rival clique, elicited a response that proves judges are not always one big happy family:

> We've got a bastard in our county who's a dictator and he does what he wants. You could quote me. He's a first-class bastard. I tell you, he's a bastard. He does what he wants to do. He wants to be the leader.

Research on communities has devoted substantial attention to "community power structure." These researchers ask, "Who is influential in the community?" or "Who makes what decisions?"[13] In

[13]An extensive literature on community power, spanning both political science and sociology, blossomed in the late 1950s and early 1960s. For a general review of some of the major perspectives and research findings, see David Ricci, *Community Power and Democratic Theory: The Logic of Political Analysis* (New York: Random House, 1971), and Nelson Polsby, *Community Power and Political Theory* (New Haven: Yale University Press, 1963).

court communities, the questions become, "Are some individuals especially influential, or is influence more widely shared?" and, "Who are the most influential in shaping what happens?" The answer seems to be that the degree to which chief judges or head prosecutors or public defenders dominate the setting of general policies that affect their organizations does differ from one court to another. We found, for example, that the chief judge in Erie and St. Clair and the prosecuting attorney in Kalamazoo and Peoria each wielded greater influence than their counterparts in the other jurisdictions.[14] Sometimes, this influence results from force of personality and solid credentials as a community insider. But on occasion, a strong-willed outsider such as Du Page's prosecuting attorney can significantly shape the thrust and content of a court system's policies by unilaterally exercising his available authority. The factors that determine interdependence recombine continually as cases come to court and judges, prosecutors, and defense attorneys assigned to each engage one another in disposing of them. Further, major changes result from the passing of generations and the entry of new personalities into crucial positions. The result is a gradually changing mosaic of interactions within jurisdictions and distinctive patterns in these mosaics between them.

EMOTIONAL UNDERCURRENTS AND GRAPEVINES

The social "underlife" of a courthouse readily becomes apparent to anyone who works there or conducts research requiring physical presence for any length of time in courtrooms, hallways, and offices. After all, attorneys, their secretaries, court clerks, and others who work in courthouses are people, too. But the nature of their informal social networks is not often featured either in popular or scholarly accounts of courts.[15] The rivalries, grudges, friendship groups, petty

[14] See James Eisenstein, Peter Nardulli, and Roy Flemming, *Explaining and Assessing Criminal Case Disposition: A Comparative Study of Nine Counties*, Final Report to the National Institute of Justice, Washington, D.C., April 29, 1982, Chapters 12 and 17.

[15] Scholars who study formal organizations, however, have been sensitive to the importance of communication, including informal communication. For an early discussion, see Herbert A. Simon, Donald W. Smithburg, and Victor A. Thompson, *Public Administration* (New York: Knopf, 1956), Chapter 10, especially the discussion of

jealousies, and noble acts of humanitarian goodwill found in courts are probably no more frequent or intense than elsewhere in society; but neither are they less frequent. And just as these considerations shape the functioning of administrative bureaucracies and legislatures, so too do they shape the operation of courts.

The vigorous health of courthouse grapevines is particularly noteworthy. A number of respondents attested to the presence of a grapevine. A public defender in Erie commented:

> I don't know how it is in other counties, but in this county the courthouse is just the fastest grapevine I've ever seen. If I fire a secretary at 9 o'clock, the whole courthouse knows about it by 9:30.

Our research discovered grapevines in each county, usually equaling Erie's in scope and vigor. Because the courts sat in the courthouse with other elected county officials everywhere but in Oakland, the grapevine extended well beyond the justice system.

The intricate and varied structure of these grapevines defies comprehensive description, but we can provide illustrative examples. An individual in the Montgomery PD's office provided a glimpse of its grapevine's tentacles:

> You know, you have to be here for a few years to realize how the grapevine works. All right. One of our secretaries is now a secretary to a judge and somebody else in this office is now a crier to a judge, and he's friendly to the secretary. The secretary comes up here to drink coffee with these secretaries and they

---

informal communication, pp. 226–228. They state (at p. 227), "The informal communication system is at the same time indispensable, inevitable, and somewhat annoying." The author of a recent public administration textbook devotes the first section, of a chapter titled "The Dynamics of Organization," to communication, remarking that "Every major theory of organizations has included, explicitly or implicitly, assumptions about the nature, roles, and processes of communication in a given organizational setting." George J. Gordon, *Public Administration in America*, 3rd ed. (New York: St. Martin's Press, 1986), p. 216. Students of organizations have conducted some empirical research on informal communication and grapevines in organizations. A study by H. Mintzberg, "The Manager's Job: Forklore and Fact," 4 *Harvard Business Review* (1975), pp. 49–61, found that managers spent most of their time at work in oral communication; they utilized gossip, opinion, and facts garnered from it. For a discussion of research in informal communication and a bibliography, see Keith Davis, "Methods for Studying Informal Communication," 28 *Journal of Communication* (1978), pp. 112–116.

have lunch together every day. So it spreads back. It just goes back and forth.

The reach of the grapevine inspired wonder among court community members. A prosecutor in Erie reported that among the judges disagreements arising at their meetings seemed to always leak out:

> It's part of the grapevine. When the judges have a meeting, usually someone is there—either the court administrator, tipstaff, or somebody. And word comes out. It's that way. It's that type of place.

The number of people on the receiving end usually seemed to be large. In Saginaw, a shifting group of judges and established attorneys ate lunch at a special table in a hotel restaurant close to the courthouse. One judge observed that news went "from the courthouse to there to everywhere" so that more than half the Saginaw bar knew important court goings-on within a week.

The grapevine served the straightforward function of providing court community members with information useful in the performance of their jobs. When a new judge or assistant prosecutor took office, it became essential to learn about their characteristics. An experienced prosecutor commented that it took a new assistant about a year to "get the book" on defense attorneys.

> But the book is made on a new assistant, for instance, within months after that person's arrival. Soft, tough, easy to get along with, hard to get along with, hang-in-there, realistic approach to cases, sloppy in court, effective. Anywhere where two or more lawyers meet, it's a topic of conversation.

Supervisors relied upon the grapevine to acquire feedback on the performance of their staff. Peoria's head public defender bore responsibility for an office staffed by experienced private attorneys paid a lump sum to represent all indigents assigned to them. Because the courthouse lacked a central office where the staff gathered, the boss relied on the grapevine to monitor performance and make sure public defender clients were not slighted so that assistants could devote more time to private practice. Montgomery's public defender needed to utilize the same technique to assess the performance of the large group of attorneys hired (for the magnificent sum of $40) to represent clients at preliminary hearings held in one of the twenty-nine district courts scattered around the county. One supervisor in this office explained:

> I get feedback at cocktail parties, at social occasions . . . two
> weeks ago I was over having a few drinks after work and some-
> body decided to corner me and say, "You know so and so? Well,
> don't send him to another hearing." . . . It may not be a letter
> in writing complaining about somebody's representation or lack
> thereof, but the feedback does come in.

The Erie public defender actively sought information from people
plugged in to the grapevine.

> The court reporters know who's doing a good job and who isn't,
> and you talk with them. You know, we only have five judges.
> And lawyers talk. I'm not one to sit around and listen to bull-
> shit. . . . But I do zero in on professional criticism by a lawyer.

The grapevine's function of passing on information inevitably
expands in some circumstances to perform the social-control tasks
the literature on community assigns to gossip networks. Private attorneys appointed by Oakland judges to represent indigents assigned to
their courtrooms did not receive additional appointments if they acquired a reputation for going to trial unnecessarily. In Erie, the ex-
prosecutor's allegedly poor performance became a matter of public
knowledge throughout the community, resulting in his amazingly
poor third-place finish with 10 percent of the vote in his quest for
renomination. Though these results flow from the unconscious and
natural operation of the grapevine, some participants deliberately
plant messages to say indirectly what they cannot say face to face.
In Saginaw, the judges felt they could not publicly or directly criticize
the prosecutor for overcharging even though they felt the practice
overloaded the court's docket. But they could and did use the grapevine. "I know [the prosecutor] has got a lot of messages back," a judge
observed, "because I intend it that way."

Though our knowledge of grapevines falls short of comprehen-
siveness, we know that differences in their scope, structure, and
significance abound. Most of those we encountered can be characterized by adjectives like "effective" and "extensive," but not everywhere. In Du Page, personal rivalries and interoffice conflict produced a fragmented grapevine that infrequently bridged the chasms
found in the community. Oakland resembled a vineyard, with distinct grapevines rooted in individual courtrooms that were loosely
connected to other courtrooms and generally separated from grapevines established in other county offices in different buildings.

These differences suggest some of the factors that shape the grapevine's structure and role in each county. These include the geography of the courthouse, how concentrated private attorneys' offices are in the vicinity of the courthouse, availability of convenient informal meeting places, richness of kinship and friendship ties among community members, degree of conflict versus cooperation present, and content of county legal and political culture.

SPONSORING ORGANIZATIONS IN COURT COMMUNITIES

The study of residential communities accords a big role to a variety of organizations — churches, the Elks, the volunteer fire department, the PTA, labor unions, and so on. Residents' attitudes and behavior depend in part on the groups to which they belong. Furthermore, participation by group leaders in community affairs is an important mechanism through which the interests shared by the members of the organization are represented.

In court communities, most members belong to organizations that serve analogous functions. Assistant public defenders and prosecutors in particular find the office in which they work significant. It recruits, trains, pays, and assigns them responsibilities. It can also fire them. In a sense, assistant prosecutors and public defenders are "sponsored" by these organizations. For convenience, we refer to these offices as "sponsoring organizations."[16] The structure, composition, policies, and activities of these sponsoring organizations affect the behavior, interactions, and dynamics of daily life in court communities.

Judges also belong to a sponsoring organization, though it exhibits fewer characteristics of traditional hierarchical bureaucratic organizations than does the public defender's or especially the prosecutor's office. Judges do not depend on their organization for their hiring, their salary, or their promotion. It cannot fire them. Nonetheless, some aspects of organization operate. The judges usually hold reg-

[16]For an earlier discussion of sponsoring organizations, see James Eisenstein and Herbert Jacob, *Felony Justice: An Organizational Approach to Criminal Courts* (Boston: Little, Brown, 1977), Chapter 3.

ular meetings, presided over by a chief judge who bears responsibility for assigning tasks, appointing committees, and overseeing administration of the court. Occasionally, a chief judge will acquire enough influence to be an effective leader of a judges' organization.

The private defense bar displays even less organization in most counties. Occasionally, however, defense attorneys will form their own organization or form and run a committee of the local bar association. With or without a formal organization, defense attorneys almost always communicate with one another. Other organizations sometimes relevant to the life of a court community include police agencies, probation departments, and administrative units, such as elected clerks of court, who are not under the judges' control.

TECHNOLOGY IN COURT COMMUNITIES

The concept of technology intertwines with that of culture. Technology refers to the tools and machines of a community, the procedures for using them, and the social relations arising from their use.[17] Our use of the word goes beyond the overly narrow conception of technology as nothing more than tools and machines. The methods used to find, divide, and clear land, plant and harvest crops, and make fire are part of the technological component of a primitive community's culture. University communities employ a technology to decide what classes will be offered, who will teach them, at what times and in what rooms they will be taught, and who will enroll in them. Student and faculty preferences must be matched, and information on solving the scheduling problem effectively conveyed. Tools and procedures include registration forms, course schedule books, long lines, hand and computer filing systems, and other paraphernalia all too familiar to anyone who has gone to college.

Court communities face extremely difficult challenges in solving analogous scheduling problems. Among the choices to be made are:

Determining when various civil and criminal cases will be scheduled for action;

[17]Larry D. Spence, "An Introduction to a Theory of the Politics of Technology," unpublished revision of a paper given at the Instituto de Estudios Superiores de Administración, Caracas, Venezuela, March 29, 1976.

Deciding which judges will hear what kinds of cases and during which
days, weeks, and months of the year;

Deciding which prosecutor and defense attorney (if the defendant is
too poor to afford a lawyer) will be present at each scheduled stage
in a case.

Several difficulties arise in devising procedures for making such
decisions. Judges, the District Attorney, and (in most counties) the
Public Defender make independent choices about how to assign personnel to cases. All three participants are extremely busy, producing
many conflicts in schedules. Predictions on how long a case will take
are very difficult to make, creating much uncertainty and numerous
last-minute disruptions.

Courts use a bewildering array of techniques to solve these problems. To begin to describe even a small portion of them would soon
become incredibly boring. But the implications of the procedures are
crucial in shaping the way in which criminal court communities go
about their work, so some general discussion of these techniques is
needed.

The decisions made by the judges establish the rhythm to which
prosecutors and defense attorneys dance. Judges can be assigned for
a set period exclusively to hear either civil or criminal cases; that is,
given a "specialized" docket. Alternatively, judges can deal with a
mixture of civil and criminal cases during the same period. If judges
handle a specialized docket, their assignments can be switched as
frequently as every few months, or never. Regardless of the type of
docket, a choice must be made between scheduling trials continuously and fitting pleas, hearings, and other short matters between
them, or concentrating all jury trials during the specified periods.
Table 2–1 depicts the resulting combinations. The picture is further
complicated by the option in "mixed dockets" with "periodic trial
terms" to have a judge hear both civil and criminal trials during the
same term or to alternate hearing just one type from term to term.

The techniques outlined in Table 2–1 determine how judges will
be deployed. But they specify nothing about which judges get particular cases. Individual calendar systems assign cases early in the process to a specific judge who sees them through to final disposition.
Participants consequently know long in advance which judge will
preside over final disposition. Master calendars assign cases to individual judges from one large pool. Often, no one knows with cer-

Table 2–1

Alternative Techniques for Organizing Dockets and Trial Terms

Type of trial term	Type of docket assignment		
	Mixed (Judges hear civil and criminal cases.)		Specialized (Some judges hear only criminal cases.)
Continuous (Trials scheduled with no breaks)	Judges hear both civil and criminal cases. Civil and criminal trials are scheduled continuously, with other proceedings squeezed between trials.		A designated group of judges hear only criminal cases. Trials are scheduled continuously, with pleas & other matters squeezed between trials.
Periodic (Trials scheduled for specific periods)	"Rotating" systems: Civil and criminal cases heard in different periods by all judges	"Pure" mixed systems: Civil and criminal cases heard during the same trial term by all judges.	A designated group of judges hear only criminal cases. Trials are conducted only during specified trial terms.

tainty which judge will hear the case until minutes before walking into the courtroom. Regardless of which system is employed, when it comes time to say which judge gets which case, the decision can be made randomly, sequentially by sending a case to the "next available courtroom," or by an official such as the chief judge, court administrator, or someone in the prosecutor's office. Because trials take much longer than guilty pleas, some courts use different procedures to schedule each.

Though we have focused on the case scheduling and assignment technologies employed by judges, we could just as easily have described the procedures, forms, and tools prosecutors' offices use to perform such tasks as assigning personnel to cases, reviewing their performance, approving cases for prosecution, and determining the content of plea bargains. Public defenders must devise techniques for performing many of these tasks. The variety found in technologies that these offices employ rivals that described in detail for judges.

The full significance of what might at first blush seem to be technical and mostly unimportant administrative detail becomes evident only when we examine closely the dynamics of interaction in a court community. The effects both on the working lives of members of the community and the outcomes of cases, though not readily apparent, are profound. The role that court communities' technologies play will become clearer as we describe in detail several courts in the following chapters.

SPATIAL RELATIONS AND GEOGRAPHY

The significant part that topography and geography play in shaping communities generally has some counterpart in court communities, though it is less influential. Judges whose chambers adjoin develop closer personal ties. Public defender and prosecutor offices with centrally located coffeepots or conference rooms often find that these spots turn into informal meeting places where internal cohesion and esprit are built. Where courtrooms sit in buildings separate from other county offices, as in Oakland, the grapevine's reach is shorter. At the opposite extreme, some courthouses concentrate much activity in one place. The case assignment room in Montgomery County served as a nerve center, gathering place, and communication node in the courthouse grapevine. In Erie, the coffee room and snack bar on the third floor served a similar function, as a young public defender explained:

> The coffee room is a great center for news distribution. That's the main place. You can talk in a more relaxed way there, where you're not competing at the moment. . . . I don't know how to explain it, but you can sit there and socialize with the District Attorney as though he were on the same level. . . . Those things are removed for that moment.

Though in prior research on criminal courts relatively little heed is given to such factors, many of the sponsoring organization leaders we interviewed displayed keen sensitivity to questions of space and location. Several head public defenders felt that they benefited substantially from being housed outside the courthouse, thereby avoiding links in their clients' minds with the prosecutor and judges' courtrooms.

LINKS TO OTHER COMMUNITIES

Just as a residential community cannot be understood without taking into account how it is affected by neighboring communities and the broader social, political, and economic environment, so too we must consider criminal court communities' links to the outside. Obviously, many basic and relatively stable features of court communities result from decisions made outside the community. The state constitution or statutes determine the size of the court's jurisdiction, the sources of funds for paying salaries and meeting expenses, and similarly vital features. Such provisions structure the dynamics of a court community's work life in countless ways that become so much a part of the continuing nature of things that they are barely recognized. Comparing court communities in different states, however, reveals their significance. Pennsylvania law gives elected county officials the responsibility for choosing public defenders; in Illinois, the trial judges choose them. Public defenders in Pennsylvania, especially if they enjoy county officials' support, deal with judges on matters of court policy from a stronger position than that of their counterparts in Illinois.

Characteristics of the procedural rules that guide the processing of cases also emanate from outside the local court community. The state legislature or state Supreme Court can establish speedy trial rules, require grand jury indictment or abolish grand juries, and determine the timing and form of pretrial motions. More significantly, the legislature determines the capacity of the state prison system by authorizing and funding construction of new facilities. It can even alter the basic framework of sentencing laws. In recent years, a number of states have sought to reduce judges' discretion in sentencing and to increase the severity of sentences. When implemented, these laws usually do not have the full effect their authors intended, but certainly they profoundly affect how individual court communities process cases.[18] Less significant but more frequent are small changes

---

[18]An extensive literature on the reform of sentencing and its influence has been produced in the past decade. For a comprehensive bibliography of this work up to 1982, see A. Blumstein, J. Cohen, S. E. Martin, and M. H. Tonry, eds., *Research on*

made by the state legislature in the criminal code, changes that require some adjustments by criminal court communities throughout the state.

The legal metaphor assigns great importance to another external source of influence that is said to restrict the discretion of local court community decision makers. The traditional view assumes that the decisions of federal and state appellate courts establish precedents and procedures that trial courts are obliged to and actually do follow. In practice, actions and decisions by state appellate courts draw scorn and ire from many trial judges, and their influence on day-to-day activities is limited. Some behavior may be modified by anticipating possible reversal or reprimand by a higher court. Many of the accommodations take the form of symbolic rituals that complicate and prolong public ceremonies without changing the substance of outcomes. The elaborate ritual followed in guilty-plea ceremonies, devised in response to appellate court reversals, does not appear to reduce significantly the frequency or alter the content of plea bargains. Defense attorneys file numerous motions to forestall potential appeals based on incompetency of counsel allegations. But few participants interviewed cited these motions as significant shapers of outcomes.

Higher courts do exert some indirect, subtle, lasting effects on case disposition. Decisions prohibiting judges from indicating to the attorneys what the sentence will be before the guilty plea is entered drives the practice underground, reduces its frequency, and generates intricate rituals for achieving the same result by devising special code words and procedures.

Supervision of public defenders and prosecutors by officials such as the state Attorney General is virtually nonexistent. Only in the realm of judicial administration and budgeting does there appear to be significant limitation on local autonomy, and even here, its extent varies widely from one state to another.

Indirect effects emanating from the general context of the state in which a jurisdiction is located also appear to affect court communities. These contextual factors shape revisions in the criminal code or sentencing practices. Both state political culture and inter-

---

Sentencing: The Search for Reform (Washington, D.C.: National Academy Press, 1983). For a recent study, see L. Goodstein and J. Hepburn, *Determinate Sentencing and Imprisonment: A Failure to Reform* (Cincinnati: Anderson Publishing, 1985).

action among judges, prosecutors, and others in state meetings produce some "norming effects" on things like severity of sentences and technologies used. Michigan courts tended to use individual calendars; in Pennsylvania, master calendars dominated. Thus, states exhibit a state legal culture that produces differences on matters not encompassed by the national legal culture.

If effective limits on court communities exist, they emanate mostly from the local community. Decisions that affect the capacity of the jail and the size, policies, and performance of police departments (which determine the number and characteristics of the cases and defendants with which the court must work) exert an especially strong and direct influence. Other factors operate more slowly and indirectly. This is not the place to review the spotty literature examining such things as the effects that judicial and prosecutorial elections, local political parties, local budgetary authorities, the mass media, and public opinion have on the operation of courts.[19] Treating courts as communities suggests the relevance of such outside ties to understanding behavior and places them in a broader context.

A final point about the relationship between court communities and the general environment in which they exist. Though court communities certainly reflect the characteristics of the broader context, they clearly are not microcosms. Every study of political decision-making elites finds that they come from the better-educated, higher-status, higher-income segments of society. Though in a sense it came as no surprise, the contrast between composition of the permanent residents of the criminal court community on the one hand and the visiting defendants on the other is striking. Blacks were a significant minority in many jurisdictions, and provided a higher proportion of defendants than the size of their population. In Saginaw, Dauphin, Erie, Oakland, and St. Clair, a defendant population with a high proportion of blacks confronted a nearly all-white court community. The effects of this situation cannot be ascertained, but certainly it did nothing to alter black images of white domination.

---

[19]Among the sources whose authors look at such factors are Levin, op. cit.; Jack W. Peltason, *Fifty-Eight Lonely Men* (New York: Harcourt, Brace, 1961); James Eisenstein, *Counsel for the United States* (Baltimore: Johns Hopkins University Press, 1978); Richard Richardson and Kenneth Vines, *The Politics of the Federal Courts* (Boston: Little, Brown, 1970); and Herbert Jacob, *The Frustration of Policy: Responses to Crime by American Cities* (Boston: Little, Brown, 1984).

PROXIMATE CAUSES OF CASE OUTCOMES

The metaphor of criminal courts as communities provides a useful way to summarize much of what we have to say about how to understand courts. The general context in which decisions about each of the defendants who come to court can be described and understood by drawing upon the elements of the metaphor presented in this chapter. Our inquiry into the workings of criminal courts, however, is meant to go beyond such a broad description. We also want to know what happens to defendants, how their case outcomes differ among the counties, and why. To find this information, we need to examine the factors that influence the outcome of specific cases. These "proximate" or case-specific characteristics help explain why a prosecutor dismisses a case, a defendant accepts a plea of guilty negotiated by his attorney, or a judge imposes a two-year sentence in a burglary case. The brief discussion that follows justifies our examination of some of these proximate causes of case outcomes in the descriptions of the nine courts found in Part Two.

Prior research on criminal courts identifies three sets of factors that determine why specific cases turn out as they do: the characteristics of the case and the defendant; the attitudes and values of the courtroom triad; and the mixture of personalities and characteristics among the members of the triad.

Relevant defendant characteristics include age, race, sex, wealth, and prior criminal record. The seriousness of the offense charged and the strength of the evidence available define the parameters of possible outcomes. The attitudes of the judge, prosecutor, and defense attorney on the importance of due process for defendants, the value of punishment, and the importance of "efficiency" color their actions. So too do other characteristics such as their experience in their position, the extent to which they partake of the county legal culture, their career aspirations, and their personalities and style of interpersonal interaction. Finally, the distinctive personal characteristics of the particular mixture of triad members interact with case and defendant characteristics. It makes a difference if judge, prosecutor, and defense attorney all believe strongly in punishment, if two of the three are easygoing and the third is abrasive.

The number of combinations of characteristics of decision makers, cases, and defendants is astonishing, even in courts that handle less than a thousand cases a year. Furthermore, the way in which these factors interact displays bewildering complexity. In later chapters we will describe this complexity in some detail and identify factors (such as seriousness of the offense charged) that exert the most significant influence in shaping outcomes.

The kaleidoscopic combinations of proximate factors that combine to determine how individual cases are handled suggest a final characteristic of court communities. The task they perform, disposing of criminal cases, is extremely complex. The problems associated with getting the participants together are substantial; cases pose different problems from those such administrative agencies as the postal service and welfare departments face; and the decisions made arouse strong emotions and evoke beliefs about the nature of society and personal security. As we hope to show in the following chapters, the ways in which criminal court communities grapple with the important and complex tasks given them are varied and fascinating.

SUMMARY

The concept of community brings to mind a number of attributes commonly associated with towns and small cities. Our metaphor of courts as communities rests on the assumption that the interdependencies arising from a common workplace produce a similar collection of attributes.

We begin elaborating these attributes by discussing five elements of county legal culture, the beliefs of core members of the court community about how things ought to work and how they do work. We then discuss the inhabitants of the community, their interdependencies, the structure of status and power among them, the nature of grapevines and emotional undercurrents, and the sponsoring organizations that send prosecutors and public defenders to courtrooms, hire, train, and fire them, set and enforce office policies, and perform other tasks that shape behavior. Sponsoring organizations for judges and defense attorneys display fewer of these features, but still exert some influence over behavior.

The technology used by courts, though little studied, has a large part in shaping the rhythm and dynamics of court communities' operations. The details of the ways in which the judges' dockets are organized, how trials are scheduled, and how individuals are assigned to specific cases constitute the core of a court's technology. The physical arrangement of the courthouse and the offices within it, and the geography of the county along with the distribution of attorneys within it are also examined. Finally, we discuss relationships between individuals and organizations and the larger environment. We conclude the chapter by discussing briefly the factors that shape how cases are decided, which is background necessary to understanding the descriptions in Part Two.

Criminal Court Communities in Nine Middle-Sized Courts

Describing complex social phenomena is difficult. Try explaining the game of baseball to someone totally unfamiliar with it. Where do you begin? The rules? The statistics? A portrait of a team? A description of a game, batter by batter?

We argue in Chapter One that criminal courts rank among the most complex political institutions. Solving the puzzle that each criminal court presents poses a daunting challenge: devising and describing clearly a framework that helps us understand all criminal courts makes solving one court puzzle seem easy.

We believe the most effective way to communicate how our community metaphor helps us to understand criminal courts is to apply it, which requires detailed dissection of the structure and operation of one court community. As this description proceeds, we will need to explain and illustrate in more detail many of the concepts and processes mentioned briefly in Chapter Two. What does a case-scheduling technology look like? How does a court organize to dispose of the cases brought to it? In the first three chapters in Part Two we examine these and other questions by focusing on Pennsylvania's "declining" county, Erie.

Our snapshot of Erie and the other eight counties was taken in 1980, and our description pertains to their condition at that time. Data on such items as population, arrest rates, defendants' attributes, and case outcomes thus reflect conditions in 1980, not the current state of affairs. To demonstrate the value of the metaphor of courts as communities, the date of the snapshot is pretty much irrelevant. Like the larger communities they serve, court communities change constantly, sometimes slowly, sometimes with amazing rapidity. To construct a complete picture of a criminal court takes so much effort that by the time any study is completed and published, the court has already undergone significant change. Unavoidably, then, all in-depth analyses of courts are in a sense out of date; but this datedness is much less significant than it seems at first.

It would take another twenty-four chapters to describe the other eight counties in as much detail as we have Erie. Mercifully, we can shorten substantially the task of meeting our objective to impart understanding of how courts differ, the *contours* of justice. In Chapters Six and Seven we describe one court (Michigan's "autonomous" county, Kalamazoo; and the suburban "ring" county in Illinois, Du Page) by sketching briefly what is described in detail for Erie. By referring back to the appropriate sections of the description of Erie, we can convey the essential features of these two courts much more quickly.

In the same way, a summary view of how all nine courts operate, emphasizing their similarities and differences, can be presented in two chapters resting on the foundations of the earlier descriptions. In Chapter Eight we summarize the principal features of all nine court communities. Chapter Nine completes the progress of Part Two from a detailed narrow focus on one court to a broad treatment of the principal features of all nine courts by looking at the patterns of case outcomes they produce.

CHAPTER THREE

Introduction to Erie County: People, Crime, and Defendants

A SKETCH OF ERIE COUNTY

For residents of Erie County, Pennsylvania, it takes as long to get to Chicago as to Philadelphia. Erie feels isolated from the rest of Pennsylvania. Bordering both Ohio and New York, and equidistant from Pittsburgh and Cleveland, it is close to neither. The long, cold, hard winters, with many large snowfalls because of its proximity to Lake Erie, increase its physical isolation for much of the year.

In earlier times, Erie was an important commercial center. Founded in 1795, it serviced pre-Civil War trade in salt and lumber by virtue of its good harbor on Lake Erie.[1] After 1865, manufacturing flourished, especially in iron and other metalworking industries. By 1900, an industral economy was well established. Much of Erie's industry had departed, however, by the time we began our field research in 1980. Though large manufacturers such as General Electric, Hammerhill Paper, and Zern Industries still operated, economic decline was under way.

The city of Erie mirrored economic decline in its population figures. These peaked in 1960 at 138,440, but dropped to 129,265 in 1970 and 119,123 in 1980. A substantial number, 43 percent, of the county's people resided in the city of Erie proper. In fact, outside of Erie city and suburban Millcreek, only eight of the county's forty-two political subdivisions had a population of at least 5,000.

---

[1]For a history of the city, see Edward Wellejus, *Erie: Chronicle of a Great Lakes City* (Woodland Hills, Calif.: Windsor Publications, 1980). Wellejus, a local newspaperman, wrote the book with the support of the Erie Chamber of Commerce.

The entire county's population grew a scant 0.6 percent between 1970 and 1980, to just under 280,000. Relatively few new residents migrated into the area. Data on the economic well-being of its people—median per capita income and median household income— confirmed these impressions. Erie ranked below all but St. Clair, another declining county, on both measures among the nine counties in our study.[2]

Descendants of succeeding waves of immigrants, first English and Scots, followed by Irish, then Poles and Germans, and finally Italians, made up the county's population. Though the ethnic identity of many loosened, Poles and Italians retained much of theirs. Roman Catholics were more than half the city of Erie's population. The 1980 census found only 9.7 percent of the city's people to be black; countywide, blacks made up but 4.4 percent, slightly higher than the 1970 figure of 3.2 percent.

Its industrial base and diverse ethnic population made Erie county's long tradition of voting Democratic, which began in 1876, no surprise. The Republican candidate for president in 1964, Barry Goldwater, received only 30 percent of the vote. Though Ronald Reagan won 51.5 percent of the county's votes in 1980, this was a lower margin than in any of the other eight counties. The concentration of Democrats in the city of Erie compensated for the predominance of Republicans in the suburbs and rural areas, giving the Democrats a healthy registration edge in 1980 of about 26,000, or 58 percent of the registered voters. The GOP accounted for 37 percent, with 5 percent registered independent.

In the years preceding our research, however, the Democrats' traditional domination of elections had eroded. By 1980, they could no longer translate their registration advantage into solid control of the county. Their party organization was weak. The labor unions' influence had eroded along with the area's industrial base. Candidates'

[2]Household median income in Erie County in 1979 was $16,766; thus, half its households received less. Though about $650 higher than St. Clair county's household median of $16,119, it fell far below the middle county among our group of nine, Peoria (at $19,399). Du Page ranked first at $27,509, a substantial 64 percent higher than Erie. Per capita income figures show a similar pattern: $6,654 for Erie, $6,463 for St. Clair, but $8,343 for Peoria and $10,473 for Du Page. U.S. Bureau of the Census, *1980 Census,* Table 180, "Income Characteristics in 1979 for Counties: 1980." Other measures of wealth and economic well-being (unemployment rate, public assistance rate) also attest to Erie's economic difficulties.

ethnicity and religion competed with party affiliation and economic status in voters' calculations. Our examination of recent voting patterns in federal, state, and county elections concluded that Erie was only a "weak democratic" county.[3] Thus, in 1980 the political landscape included:

a Democratic mayor in Erie;

a Democratic district attorney who won a hotly contested primary, but was unopposed in the general election;

a Republican County Executive elected in 1977;

a Republican judge who carried the city of Erie but lost in the rest of the county.

An individual well versed in the county's politics summed up these mixed results for us: "This county makes no sense if you talk about voting patterns."

In some respects, the city of Erie was a fine illustration of the survival of the "old politics," in which ethnicity, political party organizations, and patronage were dominant. Erie's mayor came from the ranks of the old-style ethnic politicians in the Northeast. First elected in 1965, he built a strong political organization, using jobs and favors to establish a base solid enough to win him a fifth consecutive term in 1985. The old politics, however, took a shattering blow in 1977. Over the opposition of the newspaper, the courthouse, and much of the political establishment, the voters approved adoption of a "home-rule" charter. It abolished some county-wide offices along with the three-person Board of Commissioners, the principal organ of government. A Republican County Executive and seven County Council members, most of them relative newcomers to politics and a majority Democrats, assumed the duties of the three old-style commissioners. Thus, Erie's political environment held an uneasy mixture of tradition and reform, a Democratic predisposition without dominance, and shifting voting patterns for some offices but not others.

The political landscape outside the government had few prominent features. Few groups or organizations actively participated in

[3]These data are drawn from Peter Nardulli, James Eisenstein, and Roy B. Flemming, *Sentencing as a Sociopolitical Process: Environmental, Contextual, and Individual Level Dimensions.* Unpublished Final Report submitted to the National Institute of Justice, Washington, D.C., June 30, 1983, Table 3–4.

politics. Though labor unions had once been powerful and the county's votes for president were Democratic, the ideological climate was not strongly "liberal." A politically active lawyer summarized the views of most people we spoke with about the ideological cast of the county:

> Typical liberal groups are not very well organized or vocal here. . . . They have them but they're not really able to get a lot of input or a lot of coverage or move anybody around much the way they do in a bigger city. . . . They have a tendency to vote Democratic, but it's still an extremely conservative community. I have a lot of Polish clients, and those guys are conservative. . . . The National Organization of Women in Erie County doesn't get to first base. . . . This is a tough community to crack.

On the other hand, the political ideology of elected officials was not rigidly right-wing or even conservative.

In order to compare the ideological cast of the electorate in our nine counties, we examined the voting records of each county's U.S. congressman and the electoral margins given candidates in presidential elections who presented an ideological image (Goldwater in 1964, Nixon and Wallace in 1968, Nixon in 1972, Reagan in 1980). The combined measure placed Erie behind only St. Clair on the "liberal" side.[4]

By this measure, most of the other counties displayed distinctly more conservative tendencies. As the discussion above suggests, however, Erie's liberalism was relative. We classified it as only "moderately liberal."

CRIME IN ERIE COUNTY

Criminal courts process defendants apprehended by the police and charged with a criminal offense. Their activities inevitably reflect the outcome of the processes that determine how many people come to court charged with which crimes. But courts exercise very little influence over the quantity or content of their workload. For the most part, courts wait passively for whatever comes their way. Of course, the nature and extent of crime determines the general outlines of the caseload. But the activities and policies of law enforcement agen-

[4]Ibid., Table 3–5.

cies, particularly local police departments, and the decisions of lower courts also shape the workload of trial courts. Our description of the criminal court community in Erie appropriately begins with a brief sketch of its patterns of crime, the raw material from which cases are derived. Before looking at crime in Erie, however, we review briefly how the common measures of crime are obtained and what they mean.

Everyone forms opinions about how much crime there is. But typical comments like "The crime situation is bad," or "People just aren't safe any more" convey little information. Furthermore, people differ on the crimes they regard as serious, indeed on the actions they regard as criminal, just as the legislatures that write criminal statutes differ. Getting a precise measure of crime is impossible. Public opinion surveys that ask people to relate the crimes committed against them or their families are now conducted regularly, but they are expensive and do not provide a completely reliable measure of crime.[5] The most widely disseminated measure, compiled by the FBI from data supplied by local police departments, conceals much. Victims of many crimes fail to report them to the police out of fear, shame, apathy, or cynicism.[6] Even when victims contact the police, a "crime" may not be recorded and forwarded to the FBI. Police departments must exercise discretion in judging which incidents reported actually constitute a crime, and which citizens' claims are to be believed.[7] Furthermore, internal police department policies and procedures affect what gets reported and how.[8] Even policies on how police are

[5]For a discussion of the victimization studies and their problems, see Wesley Skogan, "Crime and Crime Rates" in Wesley G. Skogan, ed., *Sample Surveys of Crime Victims* (Cambridge, Mass.: Ballinger, 1976).

[6]A number of scholars have written upon this "dark figure" of crime, the difference between reported crime and "real" crime. See, for example, Donald Black, "The Production of Crime Rates," 35 *American Sociological Review* (1970), pp. 733–748.

[7]The term "unfounded" is applied when citizen reports of crimes are deemed false or the facts do not meet the requirements for a criminal violation. For an early discussion of the process of unfounding, see "Police Discretion and the Judgment That a Crime Has Been Committed: Rape in Philadelphia," 117 *University of Pennsylvania Law Review* (1968), p. 281.

[8]The Washington, D.C., police department reported a significant drop in the rate of serious crime in the early 1970s by reclassifying many thefts from "over $50" to "under $50." At that time, thefts of more than $50 met the definition of a "serious" crime. See David Seidman and Michael Couzens, "Getting the Crime Rate Down: Political Pressure and Crime Reporting," 8 *Law and Society Review* (1974), pp. 457–494.

deployed affect the number and type of crimes viewed directly by police on patrol, and which of them result in arrest. Changes in any of these practices can shift the figures reported to the FBI without altering the "real" level of crime occurring.

When referring to FBI crime rate data, we will call them "crimes reported *by* the police" rather than the FBI's "crimes reported *to* the police" to recall how vulnerable these figures are to error, manipulation, and change. One advantage they possess is that they are available for nearly all jurisdictions. Consequently, they provide the only readily available source of information about differences in crime rates among jurisdictions. One should remember, though, that these figures are not very reliable.

Our purpose is not to compare actual rates of crime, but to examine the contours of justice, the differences in criminal court communities' ways of going about their work. Consequently, the weaknesses in FBI data are less damaging because they define the set of crimes potentially available for processing in court. Of course, other crucial steps must occur to transform such crimes into court cases. An arrest must result, and the police must decide to bring the arrested defendant to court for prosecution. Thus, our use of these data can be thought of not as providing an indication of "crimes known to the police," but as "matters that could result in a court case."

Keeping in mind these qualifications, what do the FBI data reveal about Erie County in 1980? The rate of "serious" crimes, defined as the total of reports of murder, manslaughter, rape, arson, aggravated assault, burglary, theft, and auto theft, was 3,420 per 100,000 of population.[9] The breakdown by type of crime among these "Part I offenses" appears in Table 3-1. The seriousness of these offenses obviously varied tremendously. Getting raped ranks above having your purse stolen from the library stacks while you get a drink of water. Yet both count equally in the measure of serious crime. The overwhelming proportion of Erie's crimes involved property. Indeed, larceny-theft alone accounted for 58.6 percent of "serious" crimes

[9]These figures are from *Uniform Crime Report: Commonwealth of Pennsylvania Annual Report — 1980,* compiled by the Pennsylvania State Police, Bureau of Research and Development.

Table 3–1

*Number of "Serious" Crimes Reported
in Erie County, 1980[a]*

Offense	Number reported	Percentage of those reported
murder	14	.1
manslaughter	2	b
rape	67	.7
robbery	324	3.4
assault	425	4.4
burglary	2,333	24.4
larceny	5,599	58.6
car theft	708	7.4
arson	79	.8
Total	9,551	99.8

[a]Pennsylvania State Police, *Uniform Crime Report: Commonwealth of Pennsylvania, 1980* (Harrisburg, Pa., 1981), page B-21.

[b]Less than 0.1 percent.

reported, and burglary for another 24.4 percent.[10] Thus, the "serious crime rate per 100,000," which is found by dividing the 9,551 reported crimes by the county's population and multiplying by 100,000, consisted primarily of larcenies and burglaries. Four of every five crimes reported involved one or the other.

The specific percentages of Part I crimes accounted for by burglary and larceny-theft vary somewhat from place to place. But the pattern in Erie held true almost everywhere. The initial source of serious cases that *could* have come to court — serious crimes reported

---

[10]The FBI defines larceny as "the unlawful taking, carrying, leading, or riding away of property from the possession or constructive possession of another." Shoplifting, pocket-picking, purse-snatching, thefts from autos, and other crimes not involving force or violence are common examples. Burglary involves "the unlawful entry of a structure to commit a felony or theft." Robbery requires confrontation between victim and criminal involving use of force or threats to use it to take something of value. Federal Bureau of Investigation, *Uniform Crime Reports for the United States: 1979* Washington, D.C.: U.S. Government Printing Office.

by the police—involved mostly crimes against property, especially larceny and burglary.[11]

What about "less serious" crimes, those classified by the FBI as "Part II" crimes? They consist of such acts as drunk driving, underage drinking, disorderly conduct, vandalism, forgery, and minor assaults. Of course, more of these occur. In Erie county, police reported 11,455 such crimes to the FBI in 1980.[12]

How much of a crime problem did Erie face? The question invites *comparison*. Meaningful comparisons that communicate useful information must be devised and interpreted carefully, however. The murder rate can quadruple without affecting the FBI's serious crime rate much. In Erie the rate per 100,000 would go from 3,420 to 3,435. By the same token, a rash of thefts can produce a misleading impression of a huge jump in "serious" crime. If we compare rates between jurisdictions for each of the categories separately, such problems diminish. Nothing can remedy the unreliability of these data, however, and therefore they should be viewed skeptically.

So many categories of crime could be examined that our eyes would begin to roll and our brains ask, "So what?" Consequently, we will provide only a few statistics comparing Erie's rates of reported crime with those of other geographical areas. Figure 3–1 contrasts Erie's "crimes to population rate" to those in the city of Philadelphia, in all of Pennsylvania, and in the United States in four categories: all Part I crimes, and the more serious crimes of violence, larceny, and burglary. The chart shows that Erie's overall crime rate and violent crime rate (the first two sets of bars) were significantly lower than the rate in Philadelphia and the United States as a whole, but about the same as for the state of Pennsylvania. Larceny and burglary rates also nearly matched the statewide figures; and though they fell below the nationwide and Philadelphia rates, the differences were not as great. Not shown are comparisons with the other two Pennsylvania counties. Here too, Erie's rates were lower. Compared to many other places, except for smaller rural counties, Erie's crime problems appear not to be too serious.

An alternative measure of crime compares trends over time within the same jurisdiction. Reported property crimes increased rapidly in

---

[11]For Pennsylvania as a whole, larcenies accounted for 50.7 percent of Part I offenses, burglaries 27.5 percent. Ibid.

[12]*Uniform Crime Report: Commonwealth of Pennsylvania*, op. cit., p. C-29.

Figure 3–1
Erie's Reported Crime Rate in Perspective

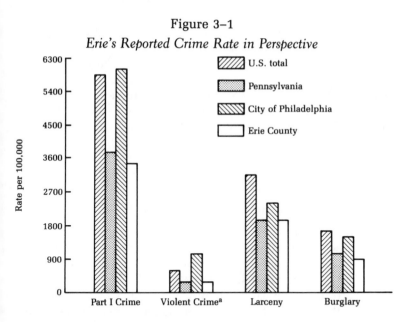

aMurder, manslaughter, rape, aggravated assault.

Erie's overall crime rate fell considerably below that for the entire United States and for Philadelphia, but nearly equaled the rate for the state of Pennsylvania. This pattern also held when just violent crimes were examined. As the shortness of the second set of bars shows, however, violent crimes constituted a small proportion of crimes generally. Two kinds of property crime, larceny and burglary, represented by the last two sets of bars, together account for a major share of reported crimes in each of the four jurisdictions compared.

Source: Federal Bureau of Investigation, U.S. Department of Justice. Crime in the United States: 1980 (Washington, D.C.: U.S. Government Printing Office, 1981), Tables 3, 6

Erie from 1971 to 1974, but remained relatively constant afterward and even showed a decline between 1979 and 1980.[13] The rate of violent crime between 1971 and 1980 showed a steady but very slow increase. A final comparison can be applied to *where* in the county

[13]For a more complete discussion of changes in crime rates in Erie and our other eight counties, see Peter F. Nardulli, Roy B. Flemming, and James Eisenstein, *The Tenor of Justice* (Champaign-Urbana, Ill.: University of Illinois Press, 1987), Chapter 4.

crimes occurred. More than 70 percent of reported crimes of violence came from the city of Erie, though as shown it had 43 percent of the county's population.[14] But property crime displayed a more even distribution, with 49 percent of those reported occurring in the city. Therefore the quality of the evidence produced by the city of Erie's police force, especially when dealing with violent crime, significantly affected the way in which the criminal caseload as a whole was handled.

ARRESTS IN ERIE COUNTY

Data on actual *arrests* reflect the patterns found in the composition of reported crime and more accurately measure crimes available for court processing. Police in Erie county made 2,021 arrests for the 9,551 Part I crimes reported.[15] More than half (53.5 percent) involved thefts; arrests for burglary accounted for another 24.2 percent. Adding auto thefts, four of every five arrests for serious crimes involved property. A total of 368 violent crime arrests were made, a majority of them (60 percent) for aggravated assault. Figure 3–2 illustrates the composition of arrests for Part I offenses.

A much higher proportion of less serious crimes, almost 70 percent, resulted in arrest, producing nearly 7,900 arrests for Part II crimes. But more than 55 percent came from just four offenses: disorderly conduct, liquor law violations, drunkenness, and drunk driving. Though some of those arrested for these offenses found their way to the trial court we studied, clearly Part II arrests involved violations far less serious than the notorious crimes that made the newspaper and television news.

Combining Figure 3–2 with data from Table 3–1 depicts visually the attrition in numbers between crimes reported by the police and actual arrests. Figure 3–3 compares reported crimes and arrests for four categories of crime side by side. The "real" incidence of crime, because it is unknown, is not shown.

---

[14]*Uniform Crime Report: Commonwealth of Pennsylvania,* op. cit., Table 9.

[15]Data on arrests are drawn from *Uniform Crime Report: Commonwealth of Pennsylvania,* op. cit., Table 9.

Figure 3–2

Composition of Arrests for Serious Crimes in Erie County, 1980

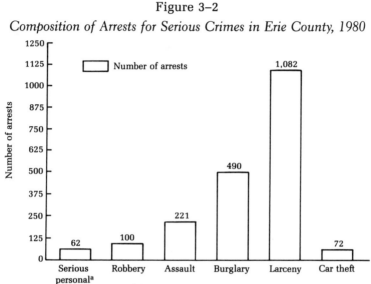

^aIncludes murder (14), manslaughter (6), arson (9), and rape (33).

Serious crimes against the person formed a small proportion of arrests for Part I crimes in Erie. The first three bars, encompassing all Part I crimes against the person, account for fewer arrests than burglary. Arrests for larceny clearly dominated.

Source: Pennsylvania State Police, Bureau of Research and Development. Uniform Crime Report, Commonwealth of Pennsylvania: Annual Report, 1980. Table 9, Part I Arrests Reported by County . . .

FROM ARREST TO COURT: SCREENING DEFENDANTS

The journey to trial court began for defendants with their arrest. But not everyone arrested finished the trip. The group of persons arrested formed the initial pool from which actual defendants were selected. The police did not always bring everyone arrested for arraignment to Pennsylvania's lower courts, the district justice courts. Some cases never left these courts, because of a finding of no probable cause, a dismissal, or a guilty plea to one of the minor charges that those who presided over the lower courts were authorized by

Figure 3–3

Comparison of Reported Crimes and Arrests for Serious Offenses in Erie County, 1980

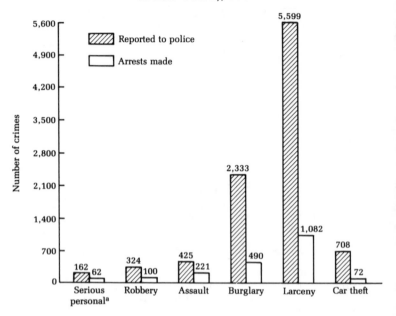

[a]Includes murder (14 reported, 14 arrested), manslaughter (2 reported, 6 arrested), arson (79 reported, 9 arrested), and rape (67 reported, 33 arrested).

For all offenses, the number of arrests covered only a small fraction of crimes reported to the police. The specific ratio of "reported crimes to arrests" varied. One arrest occurred for every five burglaries or larcenies reported; for serious personal offenses and robbery, it was one in three; for assault, about one in two. The prevalence of larceny and burglary illustrated in Figures 3–1 and 3–2 is demonstrated here also.

Source: See Table 3–1 and Figure 3–2

state law to accept.[16] Part of the task in solving the puzzle of how a criminal court works, then, must include understanding what happens between arrest and the first appearance in the trial court.

[16]Pennsylvania law authorizes district magistrates to accept pleas to third-degree misdemeanors and summary offenses. Summary offenses carry a maximum penalty of thirty days in jail; third-degree misdemeanors carry a sentence of ninety days to a year.

Our research design excluded direct examination of the behavior or policies of the police. Thus, we have no direct information about Erie County's sixteen law-enforcement agencies. We did, however, ask Erie's prosecutors to comment on their capabilities. They expressed high regard for the professionalism and skill of the State Police in investigating and obtaining evidence. The suburban Millcreek Township department also received high marks. Together, these two agencies patroled areas that accounted for about one third of the county's reported Part I offenses. When we asked one administrator in the prosecutor's office about the Erie city police, though, he replied:

> Oh! I'm glad you asked. Probably one of the worst police departments that I've ever had the pleasure to do business with. It's a complete political organization. . . . It's just an absolute mess that is controlled completely by the Mayor and is used by the Mayor as a political force.

Erie prosecutors described sloppy investigations, refusals to conduct additional investigations, and failure to notify defendants of their constitutional rights. More than half the Part I offenses reported in 1980 came from the city. The smaller departments, which ranged from seventeen officers to a force of one, also attracted criticism as "very understaffed, undereducated" organizations. Thus, Erie's prosecutors complained about the work of police agencies that served areas accounting for two-thirds of reported serious crimes.

Unlike their counterparts in Michigan and Illinois, prosecutors in the Pennsylvania counties exerted no effective control over police charging policies. In Erie, the number and content of charges defendants faced both upon initial arraignment and at the probable-cause hearing depended solely on decisions made by the sixteen police agencies. This freedom from prosecutorial control in filing charges was a significant factor shaping the court's workload. Furthermore, the seventeen district justice courts were scattered throughout the county, making it impossible for the DA's small staff to attend more than a handful of preliminary hearings. Thus, Erie's prosecutor could not alter charges or dismiss petty or weak cases before defendants came to the trial court.

Though formally charged with the duty of dismissing cases where probable cause could not be established by the arresting officer, the district justices who presided over them, like their brethren throughout the state, saw no point in assuming this responsibility. Chosen in partisan elections for a six-year term from the geographical areas they serviced, Erie County's district justices feared possible adverse consequences from throwing out cases unless the police or victim or both agreed. This combination sometimes occurred. Data collected by the Administrative Office of Pennsylvania Courts for 1980 found that 17 percent of the criminal complaints brought before District Justice Courts resulted in a dismissal; prosecution was withdrawn in another 11 percent, and almost as many were either settled or resolved by a guilty plea.[17]

We do not know how many of the cases disposed of in one of these ways involved serious crimes. Certainly some such cases did drop out. But the prosecutors' assertions that many "junk" cases came to the trial court probably reflected reality. The views of a public defender toward district justices provided support for this view. "They have such a close working relationship with the police they refuse to dismiss cases. They don't want to hurt the feelings of the cops. And it's an outrage." In fact, prosecutors told us that some district justices refused to dismiss charges, even when they attended the preliminary hearing and requested dismissal. This suggests that some cases brought to the trial court involved minor crimes or lacked strong evidence, making them candidates for dismissal or guilty pleas followed by very mild sentences.

ERIE'S CASES AND DEFENDANTS

What kinds of cases and defendants survived the journey to court? To answer questions like this, we hired college students to transfer information from the official court files and prosecutor's files to our standardized form for 594 defendants whose cases ended during the first eight months of 1980.[18] These data were then entered into a computer file and readied for analysis. Figure 3–4 presents the results of our breakdown of the most serious charge lodged against each defendant at arrest. Because the proportion of serious personal offenses such as murder, rape, attempted robbery, robbery, and sim-

[17]Administrative Office of Pennsylvania Courts, *1980 Annual Report*, Table 21.

[18]For a description of the methodology used to sample cases, obtain information about them, and prepare it for analysis, see Nardulli et al., *The Tenor of Justice*, op. cit.

Figure 3-4

Composition of Erie County's 1980 Caseload: Most Serious Charge at Arrest

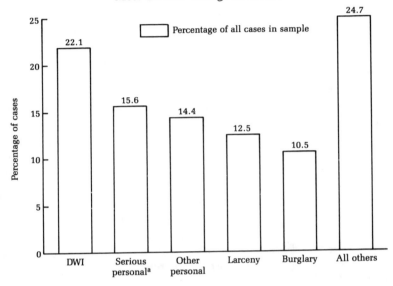

^aIncludes murder, manslaughter, rape, robbery, attempted robbery, aggravated assault.

DWI (driving while intoxicated) was the most frequent charge against Erie defendants. Crimes against the person, the second and third bars, made up 30 percent. Larceny and burglary accounted for nearly one case in four. Thus, cases brought to court contain a higher proportion of serious crimes than the mixture of crimes reported to the police (Figure 3-1) or making up arrests (Figure 3-2).

Source: Erie sample of disposed cases.

ilar violent crimes was low, we combined them in this figure into one category, "serious personal offenses."

Compared to arrests, the mixture of crimes that came to the trial court in Erie contained a much higher proportion of more serious matters. The result is expected: the work of a trial court should be focused on such cases. But the absolute number of defendants charged with less serious crimes remained high. Drunk driving, burglary, and theft were the most serious charge for 45 percent of the defendants. If minor assaults, crimes against property, nonserious drug cases, and other miscellaneous crimes are added, well over 60 percent of the cases involved something less than the crime of the century.

Who were the people who found themselves facing criminal charges? Nearly all (86 percent) were men. Only for property crimes like shoplifting and passing bad checks did women appear frequently. Defendants averaged in their late twenties. Only 24 percent were married. As a group, Erie's defendants did not qualify as hardened criminals. In fact, nearly half found themselves in court for the first time. Blacks appeared in court almost ten times as frequently as their proportion of the county's population, but they still were only about 30 percent of defendants.

Our research could not answer other important questions about these defendants. How much money did they have? What work, if any, did they do? Undoubtedly, the answers would resemble those for nearly every criminal court: defendants in state courts are poor, with relatively little education, few job skills, and sporadic employment history. The practice of hearing drunk driving cases in the trial court in Pennsylvania, however, raised the average age, the proportion married, and the number of first offenders in Erie's defendant population above those in most jurisdictions.

SUMMARY

Chapter Three begins our demonstration of how the community metaphor can be used to unravel the puzzles criminal courts present. It provides a general description of the larger community the Erie courts served and the nature of crime, arrests, and defendants in Erie County. The county was somewhat isolated, and faced problems such as economic decline and stagnant population growth. The political system was also changing, with a weakening predisposition to support Democratic candidates for office. The rate of "serious crime" as defined by the FBI's Part I offenses fell considerably below that of the United States and the state's major city, Philadelphia. It was slightly lower than the statewide average, and less than that of the other two counties in Pennsylvania we studied. Data on crimes, arrests, and charges against defendants reflected the predominance of property offenses. Though the proportion of serious crimes against the person rose at each successive stage of the disposition process, most cases that came to the trial court still involved a property offense or drunk driving. Defendants typically were unmarried white males with no prior arrest record.

In Chapter Three we described the context in which Erie's criminal court operated and introduced the cases and defendants it processed. What can we say about the characteristics of the criminal court community itself? Chapter Four presents our answers to this question.

The Criminal Court Community in Erie

SIZE, COMPOSITION, AND COMMUNICATION IN THE COURT COMMUNITY

Erie's criminal court community displayed several features that reflected the characteristics of the county it served. We begin our description of the court community by looking at these characteristics.

People tended to stay in Erie County. In 1980, 90 percent of its population had lived there at least since 1975, the highest proportion among our nine counties.[1] Among the five "Standard Metropolitan Statistical Areas" (SMSAs) in our nine counties, the Erie SMSA showed the lowest rate of migration into the area (10 percent) from 1975 to 1980.[2] The low influx of newcomers meant that people tended to know each other. Despite its population of 280,000, the county, and especially the city and its suburbs, exhibited the famil-

---

[1] The mean number of people among the nine counties who had lived in the county since 1975 was 81.8 percent, 8.2 percent below Erie's figure. These data were calculated from the U.S. Bureau of the Census, 1980, Table 174: "Geographical Mobility and Commuting for Counties: 1980."

[2] The excess of emigrants to immigrants in the Erie SMSA between 1975 and 1980 amounted to 4.2 percent of its population. For Saginaw and Peoria, this figure was 4.0 percent and 1.6 percent respectively. The Harrisburg SMSA (Dauphin County) and Kalamazoo SMSA gained .7 percent and 2.2 percent respectively. See U.S. Bureau of the Census, 1980, Table 8: "Mobility Status Between 1975 and 1980: Immigrants for SMSA by SMSA of Residence in 1980," and Table 9: Outmigrants from SMSAs Between 1975 and 1980 by SMSA of Residence in 1975: 1980."

iarity and extensive network of social ties usually associated with small towns. One person told us:

> Erie's an interesting community in that there are a lot of people in this community who are related to one another. I mean with strings, and cousins and distant cousins—that's the problem. A lot of the marriages—I can think of several older Republican families, and their families have married. There are a lot of small (100 to 200) industrial firms that have been run by older Erie families. It's in the school board; it's in the government; it's just everywhere.

These patterns facilitated the development of another feature of small towns, a highly effective and extensive community grapevine. An attorney who had lived in Pittsburgh commented that

> you could go over into another segment of Pittsburgh and nobody would know you. Here, someone once said, if you break a window at 10th and State, by the time you hit 6th and State, it's in the morning newpaper. There are grapevines all over the place.

Like many newspapers serving smaller towns, Erie's morning and evening papers combined a conservative editorial policy with "community boosterism." Published by the same company, both papers' editorials called for harsher sentences, and the morning paper's managing editor was described as a "hard-line criminal justice man." Nevertheless, because the papers wanted to project an image of Erie as a nice community with few serious problems, they did not sensationalize crime, single out individuals for criticism, or engage in in-depth investigative reporting on the courts. A content analysis of the papers' coverage of crime found fewer and shorter articles about crime and the courts than in the other two Pennsylvania counties.[3] Furthermore, the papers deliberately refrained from reporting an important feature of sentencing policy. One attorney told us that

> [E]verybody knows that prostitutes get six months or a year, and get out in ten days because the press doesn't follow it up. The press is there when the judge sentences them, but the press doesn't follow up, and the judge cuts them loose.

[3]Both Dauphin and Erie had morning and evening papers published by the same company. Combining both papers, faithful readers of Erie's papers would have found 2.0 articles per day, compared to Harrisburg's 2.75. About 40 percent of Erie's articles were at least ten paragraphs long; in Harrisburg, it was 63 percent.

In fact, a prosecutor claimed that a reporter had written a story describing this practice, only to have it killed by his editors.

The newspapers' treatment of the courts probably also reflected the effects of social and business ties common in small communities. The head Public Defender's law firm and several of the judges had served as legal counsel to editors or publishers. Another attorney told us of his friendship with the editor: "We do things in charitable organizations together. It's a small town . . . everybody knows everybody."

The criminal court community reflected many of the characteristics of the larger community just described. Lawyers referred to the Erie County bar as "small," even though more than three hundred lawyers practiced there. As one stated, "It's an easy place to get to know everybody." Furthermore, a relatively small group of people formed the core of the criminal court community. Three of the five judges heard most of the cases. Nine attorneys staffed the district attorney's office and fourteen the public defender's. Together, these twenty-eight people handled half the cases. A group of about fifty private attorneys joined the prosecutors and judges to handle the other half of the caseload. But just five of them represented about 40 percent of defendants with private counsel. Thus a core group of thirty-three people disposed of about 70 percent of the caseload.

Familiarity extended to other participants as well. One attorney summarized the results of his analysis of about 700 of his case files: "The same names appeared over and over again. . . . You see family names. . . . You'll get the father, the older brother, the younger brother, the sister, the mother." Another lawyer said that the judges, being political creatures, also knew many of the defendants. A third told us, "Basically, you see the same [police] officers. . . . There are a lot of detectives but there are only a few that do any work."

The Erie court community's small size and the familiarity of its members with one another undoubtedly contributed to the effectiveness of its grapevine. It was so well developed and visible to everyone that many of the quotations used in Chapter Two to introduce the notion of the grapevine came from people in Erie. A public defender confirmed our suspicion about its effectivenss when we asked if there were *any* secrets in the county: "I'll tell you. Probably not very many. Because if you get around and know the people, you'll find out."

The grapevine, the court community's small size, and the familiarity of its members together provided the conditions for developing strong social ties that went beyond the courthouse. The description of an experienced defense attorney's ties to people in the District Attorney's office illustrates these relationships:

> [One] is a personal friend of mine. He's over at my house; I'm over at his. A lot of those guys are personal friends. I have a corporation with another prosecutor. That's the thing that's unique about this county. Most of the lawyers — there's a couple of cliques — where everybody knows everybody else. After trial we go out and have dinner. . . . That's just the way we are.

Of course, criticism and conflict usually gave way to moderation and cooperation under such circumstances. One attorney explained, "Sometimes you have to be very careful whom you criticize in this town just because you never know who you're talking to." Mutual accommodation and working things out provided the principal formula for dealing with each other. A prosecutor explained,

> Detectives get along pretty well with defense attorneys, too. There's not a great deal of animosity. . . . The police get along with the DAs; the DAs get along with the defense attorneys.

A significant feature of Erie's court community was the ability to talk things over. This same prosecutor said that he shared a goal with public defenders, that if their client needed a break, they should "come see me." The ability to "talk about it" extended to judges: "I don't really have a problem walking in and seeing them at just about any time subject to their schedule," observed a prosecutor. A former public defender explained why Erie was a nice county in which to practice:

> It's a little bit looser than a lot of counties in Pennsylvania where the judges don't even want to talk to the lawyers. We have easy access to our judges.

And a full-time prosecutor, when asked what one needed to know to understand Erie's court, replied:

> My experience here has been that it's — I don't want to say that it's a family operation necessarily — but it's a fairly close inter-personal sort of operation, with some notable exceptions, like the Public Defender's office . . . in terms the relationships, most of them are based on individual relationships with each

> other. Like given lawyers in this office and given probation of-
> ficers on the third floor, or even given lawyers and judges.

He continued his description later:

> The judges' secretaries make a big difference too. . . . It's all part
> of the wheels, the wheels of the system. The court administrator
> is the same as you. You have to know how to handle him . . .
> he's our age, he worked on our campaign right along with us,
> he's a hell of a nice guy.

Thus, cooperating, "going along," and adhering to established ways
of treating others and doing things received powerful support in Erie.

If social relationships encouraged cooperation, they also provided
the means for punishing those who refused. A prosecutor explained
how he would get a postponement in a trial's starting date if key
witnesses were unavailable when the 180-day deadline was about to
expire:

> So I'm gonna have to lean on the defense counsel to get a waiver
> of the 180-day rule. The judge will do it for me if necessary. He'll
> just lean on the defense counsel. This is a small town.

And a nonlawyer familiar with the court's operations explained that
attorneys who violated widely accepted informal rules of behavior
"suffered in some way down the line" in their dealings with the
judges. Thus, the high degree of familiarity and interdepenency
characteristic of Erie's criminal court community heightened communication among its members and facilitated adherence to implicit
rules. Personal rivalries and conflicts were there too, especially among
the heads of the principal offices, but not extensively enough to
threaten the prevailing mood of cooperation and accommodation.

GEOGRAPHY OF ERIE'S
CRIMINAL COURT COMMUNITY

Where people worked subtly shaped the structure and dynamics of
Erie's criminal court community. Here we explore the effects of the
layout of the courthouse.

Public officials liked the façade of the old courthouse (built in 1852)
so much that they built a new wing duplicating it in 1929. Behind
these two buildings, traditional in appearance with marble columns

and staircases, sat the newest addition, built in the 1970s. Here were housed county officials on the first floor, four of the five judges and the District Attorney's office on the second, the Public Defender, probation department, and coffee room on the third, and the jail on the fourth.

These arrangements facilitated communication. A few steps led judges from their chambers to their courtroom or their brethren's quarters. The District Attorney's cramped quarters forced frequent encounters among its staff, a pattern reinforced by the practice of gathering to work, meet, and shoot the breeze in the centrally located conference room. Any judge's chambers could be reached in thirty seconds. In Chapter Two we described the courthouse coffee room as a center for socializing, gossiping, and nourishing the grapevine. The presence of other county offices on the first floor guaranteed that the grapevine would carry information about everybody's activities. It was also a convenient shorthand in discussing relations between the court (the "second floor") and its source of funds (the "first floor").

Erie experienced few of the problems in getting defendants in custody from jail to courtrooms that many other courts find maddening. A two-floor elevator ride provided all the transportation needed. The presence of shackled defendants in elevators, hallways, and entrances did, however, create a distinctive, incongruous, and somewhat unsettling atmosphere in the courthouse. Special passageways and elevators kept jailed defendants out of sight in most other courthouses. The size of the jail also presented a problem. Only six years old, it reached its capacity by 1980, and could accommodate only twenty defendants in its work-release program. These space limitations narrowed the sentencing options: If someone was sent to jail, frequently someone else had to be released.

THE JUDGES

Unlike other enforcers of rules such as baseball umpires, judges find that their prestige, formal authority, and active participation place them at center stage in criminal courts. What kind of people are they? What attitudes, personality quirks, and decision patterns describe them? How do they get along with one another and with other members of the court community? These questions are a never-ending source of fascination and worry to other members of the court community. Though we can provide only brief answers, they will contribute much to understanding the criminal court community.[4]

Five older, experienced "home-town boys" formed Erie's judiciary in 1980. One handled the juvenile docket; another devoted himself to probate. Only during trial terms did these two judges handle adult criminal cases, and then only by presiding over cases sent to them for trial. Our discussion consequently is focused on the three men who handled most of the criminal workload.

These three judges had served a total of thirty-five years. The youngest had already passed his sixtieth birthday and seventh year on the bench. The other two were sixty-four and sixty-seven, with thirteen and fifteen years' experience. Each indicated they were Republicans, though one of the other two was a Democrat, and the last an independent. Born and raised in Erie county, all three won election as District Attorney between 1964 and 1970. Their election campaigns for DA and judge familiarized them with the county and its people. Commenting on his experience in campaigning for judge, one concluded that

> I think it is an advantage because you tend to have a better feeling for people, and I think you've got a better feeling for problems, people's problems, practical problems. . . . I think it's easier to understand how people get into a situation that has led to some difficulty that ended up in court.

Their attitudes toward criminal law were distinctly conservative. In an article in *Pennsylvania Law Journal,* one publicly criticized the Warren Court's criminal law decisions, especially those such as *Miranda* dealing with confessions, as tipping the balance too far in favor of defendants; he went on to chastise the Pennsylvania Supreme Court for adhering too strictly to such decisions.[5] In an interview with us, an Erie judge expressed views that reflected the tone of the entire court on such issues:

> The criminal law has become so much more detailed and complex, and in my opinion a little nauseous, and I'm losing interest.

[4] An entire book could be devoted just to answering such questions about judges. For an example of in-depth description of judges, see Willard Gaylin, *Partial Justice: A Study of Bias in Sentencing* (New York: Knopf, 1974).

[5] Lindley R. McClelland, "Keep the Balance True," *Pennsylvania Law Journal,* Vol. II, no. 9 (March 5, 1979), p. 2.

> I really am opposed to a lot of criminal law decisions in Penn-
> sylvania. . . . Frankly, I think they're basically absurd. . . .

All three scored low on our measure of the extent to which they
believed in the due process guarantees for criminal defendants (the
"due process" scale). When the attitudes of all five judges as a group
were compared to those of judges in the other counties, only one
other county's judges (Dauphin) scored lower. Questions measuring
"belief in punishment" showed Erie judges ranked fourth.[6]

Long service together and ideological compatibility facilitated good
relations and a sense of comradery among the judges, one of them
saying,

> Three of us have been district attorneys . . . all of us have been
> defense attorneys for a longer period of time, so we're pretty
> familiar with criminal law. I mean, I think we think alike without
> even talking. . . . I could tell you what the President Judge thinks
> about criminal law without even talking to him.

Personal relations among four of the five judges appeared congenial,
even close. Referring to the President Judge, one commented that
"He's over here every day talking to me and we're very close friends."
The four normally gathered for morning coffee in the coffee room,
engaged in social banter, shared opinions, and discussed common
problems. The fifth judge, however, did not share in this fellowship.
Younger, stern and aloof in personality, and strong in his views, his
operating style differed sharply from that of his colleagues. We heard
stories of his conflicts with the President Judge, praise for his willingness to work hard, and descriptions of his distant manner. Prosecutors and defense attorneys ranked him as the least responsive to
them and least involved in trying to encourage guilty please in order
to avoid a trial.[7]

---

[6]For a complete comparison of the attitude scores for judges, prosecutors, and
public defenders, see Table 8–1.

[7]The Q-sort (see note 13, Chapter 1) asked respondents to evaluate community
members in other positions on a variety of measures, including several on their responsiveness and involvement. For judges, the "involvement" score was constructed
from these questions: "Is it easy or difficult to talk to this judge informally with opposing counsel about the disposition of cases?" "How active a role does this judge
play in seeking to affect whether a case will be tried, dismissed, or pled?" "Some
judges dislike and try to avoid trials; others seem to enjoy them. What about this
judge?" The responsiveness score was constructed from these questions. "Is it easy

The chief judge, called the President Judge in Pennsylvania, exercised strong leadership, though his influence varied from one area to another. One judge described these differences:

> I assure you, when he expresses an opinion about my schedule I take that as something more than just an expression of opinion. But if he tells me that he disagrees with a sentence I may have imposed, or a particular finding that I made, I don't pay much attention to it.

The President Judge sought to control sentencing in one area by prohibiting acceptance of "Acccelerated Rehabilitative Disposition" (ARD) in retail theft cases.[8] He failed, however, to achieve complete adherence. We witnessed his close friend grant ARD in a retail theft; the other criminal judge expressed to us his willingness to do so if a good argument for it were made out to him.

His sway in matters of scheduling was great. A court official familiar with the judges' interactions concluded:

> As far as a unified judicial policy, as far as judges affixing their signature to a particular document or scheduling or something like that, the President Judge dominates that. He's pretty much autonomous from the rest of the judges. . . . They can offer comments and suggestions. . . . But he has the ultimate say. All the other judges recognize that whatever the President Judge wants, the President Judge usually gets.

The President Judge's descriptions of his duties conformed to this view. Asked if he facilitated joint decisions or bore the responsibility for running the court and exerting strong leadership, he replied:

---

or difficult to talk to this judge informally with opposing counsel about the disposition of cases?" "What is your opinion of their willingness to be accommodating and helping you deal with the problems and pressures you face?" "To what degree can this judge be persuaded to change a decision or accept an argument initially rejected?" The judge referred to in the text had a score of -3.05 on responsiveness and -2.57 on involvement, both very low. For a discussion of how these scales were constructed, see Peter F. Nardulli, Roy B. Flemming, and James Eisenstein, *The Tenor of Justice* (Champaign-Urbana, Ill.: University of Illinois Press, 1987), Appendix II.

[8]Prosecutors could propose to the court that offenders without a serious prior criminal record arrested for a minor offense could be placed on ARD. Prosecution was deferred, and if the defendant fulfilled the conditions set forth, such as attending classes and avoiding subsequent arrest, the case was dropped and the defendant had no conviction added to his or her record.

> I think we have a little bit of both. I think like the saying, "The buck stops here." Somebody has to make the ultimate decision. That's the way it is. In other words, you receive all the input you can or should get or need. But eventually you're gonna have to make the decision.

He backed up his position with expressed willingness to meet direct challenges to his authority. What would you do, we asked, if a judge consistently violated the prohibition against granting ARD in retail theft cases. "I talk to him and try to understand," he replied. But what if the judge persisted? "You'd have to report to the judicial review board . . . if there is an established policy, I think the judge should adhere to it."

Thus, the chief judge in Erie acted much like the president of the United States — exercising strong executive leadership. But like the president, his ability to get his way by persuasion surpassed his ability to command and order. Even in matters of scheduling, his control sometimes failed. When the juvenile court judge refused to hear adult trials because of a backlog in his own docket, the President Judge backed down.

This description fails to convey adequately the personalities of the judges or the substantial differences among them. One judge earned a reputation, a prosecutor mentioned, as

> notorious for settling the case . . . leaning on the case or requiring a plea . . . in the conference before the trial, in the recesses during the trial, all the way through.

Prosecutors and defense attorneys ranked him very high in his "involvement" in determining how cases would be disposed and low in his "responsiveness" to the problems of attorneys. Another judge presented the opposite profile: reluctant to be directive in settling a case and highly responsive to attorneys' requests and needs. Nearly everyone commented on his reluctance to make decisions.[9]

If the Erie criminal court system benefited from its judges' experience, it also paid a price in interest and vigor. Some lawyers in the community believed that time had begun to pass the judges by. Our interviews picked up the loss of vigor. "I'm sort of winding

---

[9]The evaluations of prosecutors and defense attorneys confirmed what the interviews suggested. The first judge received a very high score on the "involvement" scale ($+3.26$) and a low score on responsiveness ($-.65$); the second scored $+.26$ on involvement and $+3.77$ on responsiveness.

down," one judge told us. "I'm getting closer to when I think I'll retire." Asked what he found satisfying and unsatisfying about his work, another replied:

> Well, I read a lot and I enjoy studying, and I did originally enjoy studying and writing opinions. I'll admit it's getting a little tedious now, but at first I did. And I liked trial work at first. I liked all those things. Now I'm getting to the point where I'm thinking about retirement, to be frank with you.

The relations of Erie's judges with other significant figures in the courthouse presented a mixed picture. Unlike those in our other two Pennsylvania counties, the judges relied heavily on the probation department, routinely requiring a presentence report on convicted defendants from it before they imposed sentences. The chief probation officer enjoyed the judges' confidence, and had a crucial role in recommending which inmates in the overcrowded jail could be paroled to make room for a fresh recruit. But relations with the County Executive and County Council were strained. Products of Erie's old political system, the judges got on well with the old system's governing board, the three County Commissioners. An individual who dealt with the new regime on behalf of the judges described the changes that came with the adoption of home rule in 1977:

> We're not dealing with three people any more. We're dealing with many more. . . . not only the County Executive, but his director of finance, his personnel director, and his director of administration. . . . Not only that, but we have to deal with seven county councilmen, because everything has to go before them.

A judge lamented, "They don't understand the operations of the courts, and I think there is a sort of resentment there. They think the judges are high and mighty. . . ." The resentment was mutual. "They always try to cut us once they have satisfied the needs of the other people," observed a court administrator. A showdown over the judges' hiring of additional courtroom personnel and probation officers nearly occurred, and tension lingered. But the court's operations did not appear to be greatly threatened, and self-restraint avoided an all-out public battle. One judge, reminded that in Pennsylvania the court had the power to issue an order to the county for needed funds, remarked: "But you don't like to be dogmatic. You have to be a little bit politician to get along with people."

The "home-town," "old-style politician" character of the judges produced strong links between the judges and the larger community.

They knew the county and its people well. Though they were somewhat isolated once on the bench, we got the impression that old ties
and lines of communication did not disappear. A prosecutor intri-
guingly depicted the judges' informal contacts:

> R: There is an awful lot of hearsay about it. But my understand-
> ing of it is that it will break itself down generally into a con-
> tact from someone along the way. That's a contact in terms
> of "We'll take a look at this," or "Judge, what can you do
> about this?" or "Judge, what can you do about that?"
>
> I: Are these attorneys or political figures?
>
> R: Oh, anybody. Anybody. Political figures, people who you
> might not want to call political figures, people who worked
> in campaigns, that kind of thing.
>
> I: So the telephone lines are open?
>
> R: Yeah.
>
> I: And they pay attention to it?
>
> R: Oh sure. The chambers are open, and that's a very difficult
> thing to have to deal with.

However you interpret phrases like "the chambers are open" and
"people who you might not want to call political figures," it is clear
that major participants in the criminal process believed that the
judges responded to outside influences on cases for reasons that went
beyond facts and law.

PROSECUTOR'S OFFICE

Erie's prosecutors contrasted sharply with the judges in almost every
characteristic. When the judges themselves were at equivalent stages
in their careers, most members of the office had not been born. Five
of its nine-member staff were thirty-one or younger, the oldest only
forty-one, and the DA himself but thirty-two. As a group, these eight
men and one woman had spent less than half their lives in Erie
County; in fact, five indicated that they had moved to Erie for
professional reasons. The judges counted three Republicans, one
Democrat, and one independent; the prosecutors had two Republicans, six Democrats, and an independent. The DA, elected just a
few months before our field research began, displayed a vigor, en-
thusiasm, and vision in his work that the judges did not. And if the
judges stood as remnants of the old political order with strong ties
to the community, the prosecutor came to office as an insurgent.

The story of the new DA's route to office illustrates how events and human values shape the life of a criminal court community. The highly regarded Democratic DA who hired him as a young assistant died suddenly in 1974. The judges appointed an experienced trial attorney in the office to replace him, and this individual, running as a Democrat, narrowly won a new term in 1975. Soon nearly everyone on the deceased DA's staff left, citing a litany of complaints about the new DA ("not giving a damn," "not bothering to delegate," "no organization," "no leadership"). The young assistant, who became a defense attorney after he quit, was increasingly dismayed at the deterioration of an office he felt had been a fine one. A combination of nostalgia and anger led him to challenge the incumbent's reelection in 1979.

Because both were Democrats, it meant a fight in the primary for the nomination. Anyone wise in the way of politics knows that challenging incumbents, especially in their own party's primary, usually results in failure. Established politicians counseled him to keep out; labor leaders refused to support him. Then the politically powerful mayor of Erie announced his support for a third candidate. But he stubbornly persisted, assembling a brain trust of politically experienced advisers, several of whom had also served with him in the deceased DA's office. They waged an aggressive campaign in the primary, criticizing the incumbent's loss of thirty-five cases for violating the speedy-trial rule, and hammering on the theme, "It's time to get tough." The incumbent suffered an astonishing defeat, receiving a paltry 10 percent of the vote. The results demonstrated how effective Erie's grapevine was in informing the community of the low regard in which he was allegedly held in the courthouse. Equally unusual was the insurgent's 20 percent margin of victory over the mayor's candidate.

The Republicans had a strong prospective candidate, the man who barely lost the DA's race in 1975. Personal problems, however, caused him to surprise everyone by declining to run, leaving the GOP with no candidate. The Democrats' insurgent candidate faced no opposition in the general election. Rebuffed by Democratic party and labor union leaders in the early stages of his campaign, bucked by the mayor of Erie, and not requiring anyone's assistance in the uncontested general election, he came to office with very few political obligations. Ironically, the new DA did face his potential GOP challenger, but in a different capacity. The Republican County Executive fired the longtime incumbent Republican Public Defender and appointed him to the vacancy. The absence of organized, politically effective groups such as the American Civil Liberties Union, civil rights organizations, and even business groups capable of pressuring the office also contributed to the freedom enjoyed by the new DA. In fact, when asked what organizations or groups impinged on the office, office officials identified only the local rape crisis center.

Motivated by the desire to restore the office to what he believed to be its former competence and performance, and unencumbered by political debts, the new Erie District Attorney came to office eager to make big changes. He began with a clear view of the potential his office offered, a view expressed when he was asked if the criminal court administrator could change the way in which cases were scheduled:

> He's not able to pull it off by himself. No. But the person who is, the guy who's got to be out on the point . . . is the district attorney — the combination lawyer, politician, administrator, social worker.

He started his initiatives before taking office, utilizing the general election campaign period to prepare an elaborate justification for increasing his budget. Initially rebuffed by the County Executive, he finally prevailed by lobbying the County Council to override the executive's veto of the increase. He consequently gained both an enhanced reputation for effectiveness and an additional $40,000.

The extra funds permitted basic restructuring of the office. Instead of five full-time assistants, he switched to three full-time and five half-time assistants. Only one attorney from the defeated incumbent's staff remained. His new full-time first assistant knew the criminal process well, because he had served as second assistant public defender. Two of the half-time assistants had also worked for the deceased DA, and a third had engaged in defense work for some time. The added half-timers gave the office some experienced "big guns" to handle the difficult cases and to help train the younger members of the staff who had never tried a case. The half-timers joined because of the new DA's leadership, not for the $12,000 salary. As one explained,

> I haven't been doing it for the money. It's a loss leader. It's a disaster. But it's fun. That's why you do it. That's why he has the staff that he has. It's an economic disaster, but you don't do everything for economic reasons in this world.

Several large changes in policy accompanied inauguration of the reinvigorated DA's office. And several of these flowed directly from the theme of the campaign, "It's time to get tough." The slogan reflected sentiment widely shared in the office, not merely campaign rhetoric. The office sought higher bail, especially in crimes of violence. "They oppose everything you do now," an experienced public defender complained. "You go in for a bond reduction and they oppose it, automatically." It became stingier in recommending lenient dispositions in less serious cases, including Accelerated Rehabilitative Disposition (ARD). The office's leadership felt the previous DA had agreed to plea bargains that reduced the seriousness of the charges "just for the sake of reduction." The new regime claimed it had stopped this practice, reducing charges only when the case was weak, a witness was missing, or the facts justified a lower charge. Finally, the office began writing what some referred to as "hate letters" to the probation department urging that its presentence reports to the judges recommend stiff sentences. Assistants also began appearing at sentencing to make their views known. A militant tenor about this practice arose from the interviews, as one assistant demonstrated:

> That's another thing that's happening that didn't happen before. The judges, under the old regime, were not asking the district attorney to comment at the time of sentence. They are now. We have a right to comment.

Despite widespread agreement among the staff on the need to "get tough," Erie's prosecutors did not appear from the interviews to be vindictive, "grind defendants into the dust" individuals. One administrator volunteered that he retained his belief in due process, and admitted he would find it difficult to sentence some defendants. As a group, Erie's prosecutors held less strong "belief in punishment" views and less negative attitudes toward "due process" than their counterparts in the other two Pennsylvania counties. They ranked seventh among the nine counties in "belief in punishment" and third in "regard for due process."

The leadership style of Erie's new district attorney flowed naturally from the composition of the office. Seven of the eight staff attorneys owed their appointments to the DA. Several part-timers helped plan election strategy, shared memories of the old office, and considered themselves close friends of his. The staff strongly ap-

proved of the changes in policy instituted. Its members also social-
ized in the evening. Both attorneys and secretaries, for instance, attended performances by a band in which one of the lawyers played.
A spirit of comradery and pride seemed to prevail. One assistant en-
thusiastically remarked, "He's assembled a hell of a staff. And that's
fun. It's always fun to be associated with competent people. It's interesting." Despite the youth of the office, it had much experience
in the criminal process and a high degree of self-assurance, as one
administrator's boast showed: "We know all the angles, we know the
ropes, we know the way the system works."

These factors encouraged an informal, loose management style.
No written rules or manual of office policies existed. No formal procedures for checking staff performance, such as auditing monthly
disposition statistics for each attorney, were employed. The DA and
the first assistant spent much time in the conference room; the proximity of the courtrooms made it easy to drop in on the inexperienced
assistants' performances; the grapevine filled in any gaps. The DA
gained familiarity with the cases by reviewing all new matters as they
came into the office.

The half-timers were former colleagues older than the DA, pre-
cluding a traditional "boss-employee" relationship. The degree of supervision thus varied depending on the assistant's experience. The
half-timers felt free to exercise discretion consistent with the DA's
views, as the comments of one suggest:

> He knows me and I know him. If there is a question of policy,
> I would go and ask him. But generally, if a deal is to be made,
> I in my own discretion would make the deal, and I know he
> would accept it, just because I've been around. . . . I think we
> think alike, we act alike, and we have probably very similar at-
> titudes on what law and order is and what justice is. . . . So con-
> sequently we really don't have any problems.

In fact, the DA did not always insist causes be handled as he would
handle them, even when he became aware of such differences. An
experienced assistant told us what happened when he discussed with
his boss a plea bargain he had reached:

> He told me he disagreed with it. And I said, "Well, I think I have
> some pretty good reasons for doing it. . . ." He said, "Well, okay,
> I'm not going to overrule you. It's your decision."

Rookie assistants received closer scrutiny and direction, but typically through informal means. One, asked if his plea bargains were reviewed by the DA, explained:

> He does monitor that. Probably not on a formal basis as far as keeping a list. He very much stays in the conference room and just sort of sits here and sees what's going on, and asks, like, "Why did you do this?"

They often assisted veteran attorneys on difficult and important cases as part of their training. "Post mortems" in the conference room after trial were another way to give rookies feedback.

If internal office management and relations presented few problems and challenges, the same could not be said of external relations. The successful effort to obtain a budget increase was a significant though difficult victory in dealing with the county government. Like most members of criminal court communities everywhere, however, Erie's prosecutors felt county officials had little knowledge of or real interest in the operations of the criminal courts. The DA did not enjoy a close relationship with the Republican County Executive, a political ally of the Public Defender. But he got on extremely well with the criminal court administrator, an employee of the judges who oversaw scheduling and other administrative matters pertaining to the criminal docket. In fact, everyone knew that the administrator participated actively in the DA's campaign. Good relations with the probation department also developed.

Interaction with several other organizations deserves brief mention. Relations with the news media seemed important to the office. One key office member, assessing the newspaper, strongly implied it favored the judges and the head Public Defender: "I've sensed that certain things will get printed and certain things won't get printed, and certain people get treated better in the media." The DA received better coverage from the broadcast media, appearing frequently on local television news programs. The office appreciated the cooperation the district justices showed, promptly forwarding copies of case documents after the preliminary hearing, but felt less happy about their refusal to toss out weak cases. Attitudes toward the police, as we have seen, varied from respect to disdain depending on the department.

Our description of the Erie DA's office would be incomplete without mentioning its desire to bring about a number of changes. It sought to enhance the office's investigative capabilities beyond the one county detective available, to institute a career criminal prosecution program, and to create a special unit to focus on consumer fraud, drug cases, and white-collar crime. The office's ambitious long-run agenda clashed with the bench's preferences. The judges engaged in almost no long-range planning. Major changes in the way things worked, indeed any changes, failed to excite them.

Our field research ended after the DA's first nine months, and so we could not assess his success in overcoming judicial apathy. His failure, however, to win the President Judge's approval of a change in the structure of the criminal calendar demonstrated the need for judicial cooperation, and suggested the formidable obstacles to success that he faced.

PUBLIC DEFENDER'S OFFICE

If Erie's judges contrasted sharply with its prosecutors, the public defenders displayed many superficial similarities. The Public Defender himself had also assumed control recently. Though slightly larger, with thirteen attorneys (counting the head) handling adult criminal cases, the office's average age of thirty-three nearly matched that of the prosecutors. The staff also had three full-timers, including the first and second assistants, with the rest, including the head, part-timers. The new leader felt extensive changes needed to be made, and took steps to bring them about. He fired several people and encouraged others considered "deadwood" to retire. By June 1980, only two part-timers with the office when he took over in 1979 remained.

Despite these obvious similarities, however, major differences could be seen. All but three of the attorneys had lived in Erie County almost all their lives. Despite the head's status as a partisan Republican, the office had four Republicans, four Democrats, and five Independents. Three women and two blacks worked there. The DA had one woman and no blacks. The PD's staff had much less experience in criminal law. The first assistant and the two holdover part-timers knew their way around criminal courts, though the first assistant won his knowledge in another state. But the other two full-timers were new both to the office and to criminal law, and five of the six other part-timers had served a year or less. The head PD owed his appointment to his political rather than legal activities. He practiced civil, not criminal law, and had worked as a Washington lobbyist. Prominent in GOP politics, and narrowly defeated for DA in 1975, he played a central role in the County Executive's campaign.

The office failed to achieve the esprit and social cohesion found in the prosecutor's office. The cramped third-floor offices provided space only for the full-timers. The others worked primarily from their private offices, appearing in the main office sporadically during trial terms. The PD called few staff meetings gathering everyone together. An assistant bothered by the lack of communication described several unsuccessful efforts to generate informal social get-togethers.

The head PD identified several long-range goals, including moving the main office out of the courthouse, establishing a student-intern program, and transforming the operation into a private corporation. Like the DA, he demonstrated considerable sophistication and political savvy in devising strategies to realize them. But he classified himself as a "short-run implementer" rather than a "long-range goal man."

Like nearly all supervisors we talked to in public defenders' offices, Erie's head PD believed his staff should be allowed wide autonomy in handling individual clients' cases.

> I am dealing with professionals and if they are good public defenders or good lawyers they have big egos. So that, to some extent, to get the best out of them, I have to take an equal or even a subordinate role in an individual case.

Some staff attorneys agreed that their discretion was not unduly limited. Asked what office policies influenced how he handled cases, one assistant public defender replied there were none. "And it's just like that person is a private client. I have complete latitude on the cases to do what I feel is in his best interest."

Several aspects of the head Public Defender's management style contrasted, though, with his expressed belief in autonomy. He believed strongly in "over-motioning," filing a whole series of pretrial motions as standard practice. Unlike the DA, he sought to implement and enforce this and other policies with formal written memos to the staff and a case file folder with places for the attorney to record every action taken. The data recorded there could then be used as a management tool. "I am not above evaluating lawyers and individual cases. That's one of the reasons I got this file-folder system," he

informed us. He also differed from the DA in avoiding informal socializing with the staff: "It's fine when you're one or two years out
of law school. But when you start fraternizing with people that you
have to tell how to do things, it doesn't work." He used salary-
increase allocations to reward some assistants, and gave no raises to
others. Everyone knew he had fired several assistants. An individual
who had served under the previous Public Defender summarized the
changes as "a more formal and standardized basis now." Holdovers
disliked his management style and some of the policies. One who
quit complained: "Now it's kind of they're looking over your shoulder all the time. And when I've tried as many cases as I have, I don't
need somebody looking over my shoulder."

Other stated policies contributed to the new regime's formal, strict
tone. The office prohibited part-time assistants from representing
paying criminal clients in their private practices, a common occurrence among part-time defenders in Montgomery County. It became
stricter in applying criteria to determine eligibility of poor defendants for representation, and began keeping records of those turned
down. It encouraged assistants to talk to defendants before preliminary hearings, tried to assign repeat clients to the attorney who handled the earlier case, and sought to provide a "continuous" or "vertical" defense (that is, have the same attorney represent the
defendant from the initial stages to final disposition or sentencing).
High turnover in the months just before our field research began,
however, made such continuous assignment extremely difficult.

The head PD's management style thus contrasted with the DA's
in his desire to establish and monitor compliance with formal policies, in his willingness to reward and punish assistants, in his rigidity,
and in his lack of informality.

Did the PD succeed in running a tight ship and achieving conformity to his policies? The answer is complicated somewhat because
assistants differed in their reaction to office policies. Acts that ran-
kled old-timers as unnecessary interference were a perfectly acceptable and normal way of doing things for newcomers. A further com-
plication arose from the head's spending relatively little time directly
supervising the office. He remained uninvolved in day-to-day operations, and delegated much of the task of direct administration to
the first assistant.

The first assistant employed a more informal and looser management style. He announced an open-door policy to assistants, espe-

cially the less experienced ones, and encouraged them to consult with him as equals in an atmosphere of low tension. He inserted memos in case files making suggestions to the trial attorney. "But," he told us, "I don't ever follow up to see if they do or not. It's none of my business." And he apparently failed to ensure that the head's wishes regarding "over-motioning" were met. One attorney said, "Each guy does as he sees fit—what he wants to do." The result was a public defender's office somewhat less tightly and formally run than the head sought, but also more formal and controlled than those in other counties.

Several features of the office's relations outside the court community deserve mention. The head PD's relations with the County Executive were very good, though no surprise given their close political ties. Like many aspects of life in other human communities, the effect of their ties on events, though powerful, was often quite subtle. For example, in January 1980, several assistant public defenders were, for various reasons, unavailable. Consistent with his desire to provide defendants with "continuous" representation by the same attorney, the head PD refused to reassign cases to other members of the office. The resulting disruption of the docket angered the rest of the court community, especially the judges. When we asked the Public Defender if his defiance of the judges might not lead to later trouble in the form of complaints from the judges to the County Executive, he replied it would not be a problem due to the "independence" of the County Executive from the President Judge. Left unsaid was the fact that in such a dispute the Public Defender would win the County Executive's support.

Like the prosecutor, the public defender received little pressure from the community. The private bar voiced few complaints about the office taking paying clients away from struggling attorneys, a situation the office attributed to its strict application of eligibility standards. The PD's law firm represented the newspapers, leading the prosecutors to claim that it received favorable coverage.

The office recognized the importance of district justices and probation officers, and sought to cultivate good relations with both. One policy the head PD pursued required cooperation by the district justices: disposition of minor charges at the preliminary hearing stage. Erie's public defenders sounded a frequent refrain in discussing lower judges: "Some of the district judges are excellent; some are just dumb."

The lack of the same social cohesion and esprit found in the DA's office led to a less coherent "office view" among Erie's public defenders. The relative inexperience among its attorneys also made it difficult to summarize their attitudes neatly. We can, however, draw two useful conclusions. First, the office felt it did a very good job. An experienced assistant boasted:

> I think we give our clientele excellent service. I think we give the taxpayers a lot for their money. I think our services are really very effective, and are just as much — if not more — effective than private counsel.

The management orientation produced an emphasis on statistical measures of success. An office supervisor rattled off figures on performance in jury trials as proof of effectiveness:

> The public defender's staff had nine guilties, seven splits, nine not guilties, one hung, for twenty-six jury trials. The private bar had eleven guilties, five guilty of lesser offenses, seven not guilties. So we beat them in every category . . . we compare favorably with the private bar.

Second, the office lacked a strong "defendant orientation" in the attitudes of its staff and its policies. Several assistants remarked that they could just as easily work for the prosecutor; one recent departee wanted to join the DA's staff. An assistant's answer to a question about his job's frustrations illustrated this attitude:

> Well, the frustration with being a public defender goes back to the fact that just basically our client is not what society is going to consider as an upstanding citizen by and large. . . . They don't really consider what they've done as wrong.

A recently departed assistant complained sentences were not harsh enough; another said he just got fed up with clients charged repeatedly with serious crimes lying each time about what happened. Public defenders in only one other county produced a higher mean on the "belief of punishment" measure, though they scored relatively high in "regard for due process." Finally, the office acquiesced in permitting defendants to accept a disposition entered in the records as "NPCOD," which stood for "Noll Pros (that is, dismissal by the prosecutor), Costs on Defendant." The office did not challenge the practice. And even though some defenders thought it was unfair for defendants to pay court costs when charges were dropped, they felt it was up to the defendant to accept or reject such a disposition.

ERIE'S PRIVATE DEFENSE BAR

In the first half of 1980, fifty different attorneys represented the 220 defendants who appeared on the arraignment docket in Erie's trial court. We had neither the time nor money to interview this many people as part of our research. Thirty-eight attorneys handled only one or two defendants, anyway. We did speak with five men who handled the cases of ninety-one defendants, more than 40 percent of those privately represented. Our information consequently is limited.

We found a few general characteristics of the defense bar. In the years just before our research began, several of the high-volume, established private defense attorneys began to cut back. Four of the five white male attorneys we spoke with had yet to reach their thirty-fifth birthdays. The gap in age between them and the fading group of old-timers interfered with the development of a cohesive defense bar, despite their familiarity with one another. One interviewee conveyed the tenor of relations among defense attorneys when he told us: "I'm not very active in the bar. I'm not crazy about most of them." Though a criminal rules committee of the Erie Bar Association met regularly, it wielded little influence with the President Judge. An assistant prosecutor's surprise when told it met regularly conveyed its minimal importance and status. In 1980, only ten women practiced among the three hundred lawyers in Erie; only the three assistant public defenders and an assistant prosecutor among them dealt with criminal matters. Except for several of the less active veteran specialists, the private defense bar enjoyed little status. Several had the reputation of benefiting their clients through, one prosecutor said, their "inexplicable access before certain judges" rather than through their legal ability. According to one judge, the top civil attorneys avoided criminal law.

Of course, the private defense bar had some communication and structure. As described earlier, a group of attorneys, including several currently handling criminal cases, joined in the effort to elect the new DA. They shared a common fate and interest. Several told us, for example, of widespread grumbling at the Public Defender's "slam" at the private bar when he hired an attorney from Pittsburgh to fill a vacancy.

STRUCTURE OF ATTITUDES

Our descriptions of the attitudes of court community members referred several times to scores on the "belief in punishment" and "regard for due process" scales. Derived from a set of thirty questions about criminal justice, they provide a useful technique for summarizing key decision makers' attitudes. They can also be used to compare the views of the group of prosecutors, public defenders, and judges within a county, and to measure the degree of consensus or disagreement among all three compared to those in other counties.

The manner in which we derived the average scores on the punishment and due process scales is described in Appendix One. It lists the questions used to obtain each scale, illustrates how people with very different scores answered the questions, and makes clear that the "average" for all prosecutors or public defenders conceals some disagreement among office mates. The sample answers are drawn from respondents in Erie. Readers' understanding of references to the scores on these scales both in this and subsequent chapters will improve with careful reading of the Appendix.

Figure 4–1 compares Erie's judges, prosecutors, and public defenders on the two scales. The direction and length of the bars represent the average of the scale scores for each group. The judges fall between the DA's and PD's office on "belief in punishment," but in keeping with their conservatism have more negative attitudes toward due process than the prosecutors.

SOCIAL AND WORKING RELATIONSHIPS IN ERIE'S COURT COMMUNITY

For the most part, encounters between the people who formed Erie's criminal court community on the surface displayed courtesy, cordiality, and cooperation. This pattern seemed especially prevalent in personal relations between rank-and-file members of the DA's and the PD's office. Referring to assistant prosecutors, a PD said:

Figure 4–1

Average Standard Scores on Attitude Scales, by Position in Erie

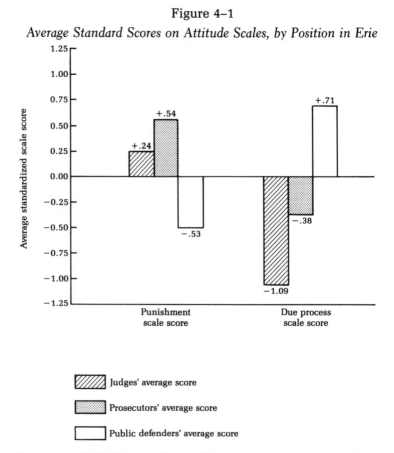

The average "belief in punishment" for prosecutors was higher than for public defenders. Erie's judges, in keeping with their conservative views, expressed attitudes closer to those of the prosecutors than the public defenders. Public defenders' "regard for due process" was positive, and the difference exceeded that seen for belief in punishment.

> They're nice guys, you know. They're professionally enjoyable and you can get them aside over a cup of coffee and quite frankly tell them that they're just full of crap and they'll just laugh about it.

A former assistant defender expressed a similar view.

> If you don't normally give the DA's office a rough time—by
> rough I mean by being unavailable or not around—you say,
> "Listen, I've got a real important civil matter this morning. Can
> I start it this afternoon?" They're going to accommodate you.

The stereotyped image of the friendly way of life in small communities, the avoidance of conflict in favor of cooperation, and the unwillingness to offend, held true much of the time.

Under the surface in most small towns, college faculties, workers in fast-food restaurants, and most other places where people gather, we find another pattern, with personality clashes, disagreements, grudges, and lack of cooperation. Erie's criminal court was no exception. Relationships between a few prosecutors and public defenders were less friendly. But more significantly, relations between the principal personalities in the community displayed considerable tension, criticism, and dislike. It would be impossible (and tedious) to describe these conflicts in full detail, but we will briefly summarize the crucial characteristics of relations among the leading members of the criminal court community to convey this feature of Erie's court community.

The judges' cohesiveness, mutual friendship, long joint service, and strong leadership from the President Judge produced a common outlook toward the DA and PD. They mentioned improvement in prosecutors' performances since the new DA took office, describing them as "better prepared," "more on the ball," "aggressive," "intelligent and scholarly." Nevertheless, all opposed his call for a change in the calendar, blaming the office for its failure to use the full two weeks of existing trial terms.

The judges expressed very different opinions about the public defender's office. "I'm not satisfied with the public defender," one judge revealed. "I think it's pathetic." He regarded its attorneys as "very inexperienced" and "incompetent." Resentment lingered over the office's failure to reassign the cases of PDs unable to work during the January trial term. The President Judge demonstrated his lack of confidence by taking over himself the job of deciding which private attorneys would represent homicide defendants, a task formerly delegated to the PD. The PD wanted to reacquire this power, but the President Judge refused.

Members of the prosecutor's office shared the judges' assessment of the public defender's office. Said one:

> It's really a sin what's happened up there in the last year. . . .
> They don't have a single experienced trial attorney on the staff.
> . . . He's picking real bad people. In consequence of doing that
> he's really destroying the reputation of the office that was good
> for a long time.

Another reported the common belief that the PD's appointment resulted from the return of a political debt.

> There may be some merit to it because he doesn't have any trial
> experience, doesn't have any criminal law experience, and
> doesn't have any administrative experience.

An experienced assistant summarized the office's view:

> As a generalization, by and large we don't particularly care for
> the public defender's office. We don't like the way they handle
> their office. We don't think it's administered well and we just
> don't think too much of how they handle their clients.

Part of the explanation for this tension and dislike can be attributed to the relationship between the heads of the two offices. Though they professed mutual friendship, their assertions lacked credibility. In fact, one complained to us that the other had lied a lot to him. The opinions expressed by their staffs reflected the tension between them. A member of the PD's staff observed that the "political stuff" between them was both messy and petty, and that they were "at each other all the time." A counterpart in the DA's office expressed views that revealed their rivalry. "There is bad blood between [the DA] and [the PD]. The [PD] is a political creature." Relations between assistants in administrative positions in the two offices showed similar tension. Prosecutors voiced other criticisms, such as, "they wait too long, or wait till the last minute to do much of their work."

The PD's office mirrored the DA's views in its assessment. An administrator charged the DA's office with lack of respect, failure to do its homework, and poor performance in trials. The public defenders considered a supervisor in the DA's office to be a poor trial attorney and a rigid, unreasonable administrator. They felt the DA's office had "gone overboard" in getting tough, refusing to plea bargain when it should have, backing out on tentative agreements, and generally being "inflexible," "unyielding," and "unbending."

We alluded to the attitudes of the prosecutor's office toward the judges. They blamed the early end of trial terms not on themselves, but on the pressures exerted by the judges to settle cases in order to avoid trials. Seven of the prosecutors we interviewed indicated in one way or another that they regarded the bench as a whole, and the two judges close to retirement in particular, as lazy. Immediately after stating that the aloof judge was "the only worker on the court," a prosecutor interjected:

> while the other ones are — classic example — today: President Judge is out to lunch at 11:15, back at 2:00, gone at 3:30, a month's vacation right during the middle of a court term.

They resented the President Judge's refusal to alter the calendar. The one judge labeled "the only worker" received praise for his sentences. But the others' sentences appeared "very lenient" to the DA's office, expecially the standard 11.5- to 23-month county jail sentences that frequently resulted in the defendant's release in a few days.

The public defenders said little about the judges. They neglected to complain about the harshness of sentences, an indirect expression of their apparent satisfaction. They shared the prosecutor's judgment that only one judge worked hard, that another was slow in making decisions, and that a third lacked much knowledge of criminal law. But administrators knew the judges did not think well of the office, telling us they got the idea the judges were displeased. This recognition, however, brought forth no efforts to modify the practices that aroused criticism.

AGE AND GENERATIONS
IN ERIE'S COURT COMMUNITY

Differences in the ages of judges, prosecutors, and public defenders in Erie and the prominence of "cohorts" were so striking that we used them in Chapter Two to introduce this characteristic of criminal court communities. Data on the average age of judges (60.4 years) compared to those of prosecutors and public defenders (33.1 years and 32.9 years respectively) confirms the size of Erie's generation gap. Only Kalamazoo's judges had a higher average age. Only Saginaw's judges had a higher average of years of service on the bench (12.8 versus Erie's 12.0). The ages of prosecutors and public defenders differed little from those in other counties, though as the earlier descriptions of the two offices imply, Erie's prosecutors were a little older than the average for all nine counties, and its public defenders about a year younger.

Comparing the differences in age of the judge, prosecutor, and either the PD or private counsel who handled each defendant's case provides a clearer picture of Erie's generation gap. Judges averaged more than 30 years older than prosecutors and 28.6 years older than defense attorneys, a larger gap than in seven of the eight other counties. In fact, the gap in three counties was only about half as great, about 15 years.

STRUCTURE OF INFLUENCE

In Erie, the judges set the tone and rhythm of the criminal court. The President Judge believed in exercising strong leadership, and he enjoyed the support and friendship of a cohesive group of three of the four other judges. The general policies of Erie's newspapers, and their relationship with the President Judge in particular, insulated the judges from criticism. The county's long tradition of strong President Judges reinforced his status. One important attorney in the community minced no words in describing his control: "This is a county, historically, that has had under-the-thumb kind of rule from the President Judge, from the incumbent as well as his predecessors." One subtle indication of his stature appeared in a prosecutor's response to a question about how the county officials on the first floor reacted when the judges came down from the second to request their budget:

> Well, the judges don't come down for their budget. I think that's a classic illustration of how it works. The second floor doesn't go down to see the first floor. The first floor comes up.

It was clear that his power had entered its final stages as retirement loomed. But his ability to prevail on issues like the structure of the calendar remained. Though the prosecutor began making speeches calling for change, he acknowledged that if the President Judge were to call him in and ask him to stop, he would have to comply.

The public defender exerted little influence within the court community. He lost the duty of assigning attorneys to homicide cases, had an inexperienced staff, and was regarded by judges, prosecutors, and the private bar as inexperienced in criminal work and highly political. Only his strong ties to the County Executive provided him with significant support. The new district attorney enjoyed a good reputation among the private bar and the judges. Though he established an ambitious agenda for change, only the initiatives that could be implemented within his own office succeeded in the early months of his tenure. The impending retirement of two judges, his vigor, and his access to the broadcast media augured well from a rise in the DA's influence. At the time of our research, however, the President Judge still dominated Erie's criminal court community. As one important community member said, "It's a one-horse county. It always has been."

SUMMARY

In Chapter Four we describe features of the criminal court community in Erie. The small size and extensive familiarity of the court community, which reflected characteristics of the county generally, contributed to the development of an effective grapevine, and to a tradition of informality and accommodation in interpersonal relations. The proximity of major participants in the courthouse facilitated informal interaction and exchange of information.

The principal characteristics of each of the three major sponsoring organizations — the judges, prosecutors, and public defenders — are described in some detail. For each, we look at the age and experience of its members, the content of policies and internal management styles, the degree of cohesion, the structure of attitudes, and the nature of relations with the newspapers, lower court judges, and others. Comparing attitudes, we found both judges and prosecutors adhering more strongly to a belief in punishment than public defenders did; the judges were surprisingly negative in their regard for due process.

We found tension in relations between the public defender's office on the one hand, and judges and prosecutors on the other. The prosecutors criticized the judges for their lack of hard work, their leniency, and their unwillingness to change the calendar. Continuing a long tradition in Erie county, the judges, and the President Judge in particular, exerted most influence over the operations of the court community.

A final significant aspect of the work of the court community remains to be examined in Chapter Five: the way in which it went about the task of reaching decisions in the cases of defendants who came to court.

Technology, Case Flow, and Defendant Outcomes in Erie

Analogies to games frequently appear in discussions of many significant social processes, as demonstrated by the often-used phrase, "the game of politics." Popular views of the most visible feature of the criminal process — the jury trial — easily accommodate "fight" imagery.[1] Two adversaries "fight it out" in public according to established rules enforced by a trained referee, and the winner is chosen by the jury. Though the public tends to equate jury trials with the sum total of the work that criminal courts perform, in practice trials are but a tiny fraction of what they do. The analogy to a game can be extended beyond the jury trial to less visible components, but the object of the game becomes less focused on "winning." From the perspective of the entire court community, the object is to dispose of each defendant sent from the lower court. The participants employ tactics according to established rules. Because new defendants keep coming to court, the game never ends. Procedures and techniques must be devised to accommodate and schedule the continuous influx of defendants to be disposed. In this chapter we explore how Erie's criminal court community went about disposing of the defendants sent to it. We begin by looking at the techniques for handling the flow of defendants.

THE ERIE COURT COMMUNITY'S TECHNOLOGY

The tools and procedures that Erie's criminal courts used to handle its caseload, its technology, resulted from the interrelated but independent decisions made by the judges and the offices of the district

---

[1] For a good general discussion of jury trials as a form of fight, see Jerome Frank, *Courts on Trial* (Princeton, N.J.: Princeton University Press, 1940), Chapter 2, "Fights and Rights."

attorney and public defender. Describing Erie's scheduling technology will provide a good illustration of how a court's technology shapes the rhythm and content of its work. As you know if you have tried to explain the rules of a game to someone completely unfamiliar with them, however, describing such things is a real challenge. The rules and procedures are complicated, especially for people with little or no knowledge or experience. In our description we first present the basic outlines of Erie's technology, and then examine how it affects the work life of the court community.

Rules imposed by appellate courts define a limited number of ways in which to dispose of a defendant's case. It can be dismissed completely, either by the prosecutor or the judge. Defendants also escape sentencing when a trial before a judge or jury results in a not-guilty verdict on all charges. Conviction can result from a guilty verdict on some or all charges following trial. The defendant can also plead guilty to some or all charges.

Pennsylvania's rules required that a defendant who did not plead guilty had to be brought to trial within 180 days of arrest, not counting postponements requested by the defendant. Otherwise, the defendant "won" by having all charges dismissed. The rules also afforded defendants an opportunity to file motions requesting a change in bail, challenging the legality of the evidence seized and procedures used, and raising various other legal or procedural issues. All such motions, as well as the final disposition, had to be decided at a prearranged time in open court in the presence of the defendant, his or her attorney, the judge, and the prosecutor.

As we explained in Chapter Two, the choices judges made about when they were available to hear motions, accept guilty pleas, or conduct trials established the basic rhythm to which everyone else danced. Erie used a rotating mixed system of docket assignments with periodic trial terms (see Table 2–1). All five judges presided over both civil and criminal trials, making it a "mixed" docket. Instead of fitting trials into the flow of work continuously, however, nine two-week periods beginning the second Tuesday of each month except July, August, and December were designed as trial terms. Rather than designating separate periods for criminal and civil trials, both were heard during each trial term. The judges took turns hearing only civil or criminal cases during any given term, though, making it a "rotating" mixed system. Usually three judges took only criminal cases and two civil cases. The President Judge draw up a schedule at the beginning of the year, assigning judges to either civil or criminal cases for each trial term.

Within this general timetable, the court administrator assigned cases to judges for trial as they become ready for disposition, making Erie a "master-calendar" rather than an "individual-calendar" county. As a result, attorneys usually did not find out which judge would preside until the day the trial began.

Judges also had to be available to hear pretrial motions, bail reductions, and other pretrial matters. In Erie, three judges took turns doing this work for a one-week stint as the duty judge presiding over "motion court," which was held each week except during trial terms. On the last day of each month, a judge presided over arraignment of all defendants sent up from the lower courts on the charges listed in a document prepared by the prosecutor's office known as an information. Usually, these charges were identical to those the defendant faced at the preliminary hearing.

The criminal court administrator, who worked for and was supervised by the judges, coordinated scheduling of attorneys' requests for hearings and motions. Therefore a defense attorney filing a motion alleging that the police had seized evidence illegally would argue it before the judge assigned to motion court during the week in which it was scheduled by the court administrator. The criminal court administrator performed two other important scheduling tasks. When defense attorneys came to inform him that their defendant would plead guilty rather than go to trial, he assigned one of the three duty judges to take the plea. The duty judges heard all pleas assigned to them one day each month. The judges instructed him to ensure that each took the same number of pleas. Cases not pled or dismissed went on the trial list for assignment by the court administrator to a courtroom during the trial term. He gave each judge a first case and compiled a list of the rest to be sent in sequential order to the next courtroom that opened during the trial term. The court employed a different procedure for assigning murder cases. The judge was designated shortly after arraignment to ensure that each of the five handled an equal share.

Separate and independent methods for assigning a defense attorney and prosecutor for each court appearance operated simultaneously. For the 46 percent of Erie's defendants who could afford to hire an attorney, the choice was theirs. But defendants unable to make bail automatically received representation from the public defender's office. The district justices instructed defendants who made bail to apply at the PD's office if they could not afford their own lawyer. The first assistant PD assigned a staff attorney to represent at the preliminary hearing both those found qualified and those unable to make bail. Because the office believed in continuous or vertical representation, this attorney was supposed to stay with the defendant at each stage. The first assistant sought to distribute cases evenly, but took into account his attorneys' experience, thinking of the case and the district justice hearing the case.

The DA's office employed very different procedures. Its four full-time and five half-time staff could not have attended every preliminary hearing in the seventeen district justice courts even during nontrial term periods. Prosecutors conducted preliminary hearings only in major felony cases, including all sexual assaults and homicides, in cases considered "sensitive," or when asked to do so by the police. Except for murder cases, the office made no effort to keep the prosecutor at the preliminary hearing on the case. The new DA had not firmly established procedures for distributing cases to his staff, producing in practice a discontinuous or horizontal assignment policy. Full-time assistants worked out most plea bargains. Cases set for trial went on just one list and were assigned shortly before trial at a staff meeting in the conference room. Of course, some trials and last-minute pleas in serious cases went to the experienced part-timers, the "big guns." But in most cases, no one really knew which prosecutor would handle what aspect of a case.

INFLUENCE OF CASE-SCHEDULING TECHNIQUES

The scheduling technology just described structured the work life of the entire court community in varied ways, similar to the way in which students' course schedules, with the infamous eight o'clocks and Saturday classes, shape theirs. We will discuss three of the most significant effects: the rhythm of work; the unpredictability; and the patterns of judge-shopping or "routing" of cases.

Rhythm of Work

Erie's technology established a very uneven work rhythm. The beginning of a trial term ushered in a period of intense activity and pressure for everyone, followed by a lull until the next trial term.

The September and January terms were especially hectic because they followed months with no trial term. Defendants usually appeared for arraignment about six weeks before the start of the trial term in which their disposition was scheduled to occur. As they were being arraigned, the previous batch of defendants arraigned the month before were only a few days away from their scheduled trial date. Work on preparing the cases of newly arraigned defendants, therefore, had to be postponed to get ready for the impending trial term. Erie's prosecutors in particular voiced their complaints about this arrangement. One said:

> That's nine months out of twelve . . . that you are supposed to run a court term that often and prepare this many cases that often, and get out of court and have two weeks to go before you go right into the next term. Which means you have absolutely very little opportunity to do any of the quality work that a prosecutor has to do.

Following the end of a trial term, the cases of defendants arraigned in the previous month received concentrated attention. The guilty pleas worked out during this period went to one of the three judges assigned to motion court. Some cases ended in dismissals or ARD, and some were continued to a later term. Those remaining went on the trial list for the upcoming term. Most on the trial list, however, ended in guilty pleas or were continued rather than actually tried.

Members of Erie's court community thought about their work in units of time defined by trial terms. They speculated on what the next trial term would be like. They also drew conclusions about how the term had gone upon its completion. The January 1980 term was remembered as a time of troubles. Shortage of personnel in the PD's office, coupled with its refusal to reassign the cases of absent assistants, disrupted the dispostion of many cases. The community remembered February as the month in which the President Judge took off for a Florida vacation.

The dynamics of each trial term as it unfolded also affected the life of Erie's criminal court community. The most serious cases came to trial first, and the mixture of convictions and acquittals shaped perceptions of how the rest of the term would go. Prosecutors and public defenders each traded information among themselves about which jurors served on acquitting and convicting panels. This exchange helped them decide whether these same people should be kept on subsequent juries. As days passed, the judges' energy and interest flagged. Perceptive attorneys recorded how the judges reacted, kept track of the kinds of cases they already had heard, and altered their tactics accordingly. An experienced former public defender explained how he did this analysis:

> First of all you want to look at which judges are sitting for criminal cases. . . . We have one judge who—he just wants to be busy constantly. . . . He doesn't care if you can't work it out. "Let's go try it. Come on." We've got some judges that are basically— I shouldn't say lazy. They love their work, but they want something that's gonna interest them. If they've had three burglary cases in front of them, you find out. . . . And if the lawyers are basically monotone-speaking, this judge is a bored judge. . . . He doesn't want to hear it. So he might say, "Well, will you plead to theft?"

In these circumstances, he would refuse a prosecutor's offer of a plea to anything other than theft, demand a trial, and wait for the judge to pressure the prosecutor. He offered several other examples of things that shaped outcomes:

> One of the factors determining how good a plea bargain you can get is . . . how busy the trial court is at that point in time. At the end of the term, if you have a marginal case, and it's weather like this—blue skies, balmy weather—the judges just don't want to be bothered with it. And they'll give you the sun, the moon, and the stars.

> If the district attorney's office has tried ten cases, and he's nine and one, your chances of getting a deal are great. If they're one and nine, they're going to be more reluctant to give you a super deal because obviously they look like losers this term.

The way in which Erie court community members looked at their world, then, depended very much on the technology adopted. In counties that assigned judges for a sustained period to conduct criminal trials and take pleas continuously, as Peoria and Montgomery did, court community members made very different kinds of assessments.

Unpredictability

Prosecutors and defense attorneys, like most other people, dislike uncertainty in their work. It raises anxiety, makes the work atmosphere less pleasant, and complicates planning how to meet the demands of tasks at hand. The President Judge's dominance over the court community, especially over the calendar and scheduling of cases, injected just such a sense of uncertainty for both. The prosecutor's office in particular complained about last-minute changes made arbitrarily at the whim of the President Judge. When the judge handling juvenile cases won the President Judge's approval to skip hearing criminal cases during a trial term, it reduced the number of trial judges. One official predicted that the office would unexpectedly be

> left with two judges, and one of them is the judge who is forum-shopped for all the time, you know, the liberal judge of the five. And how that will affect the quality of justice will be that a higher proportional number of cases will have to go in front of him this term — plea and trial — and people will get effectively more liberal sentences than from the other ones.

Other examples of unpredictability, such as the President Judge's taking a month's vacation in February during the trial term, were cited. Instead of being able to rely on a predictable environment, Erie's prosecutors and defense attorneys confronted a more erratic, unstable, and changing situation than that of their counterparts in the other counties.

Theory and Practice of Judge-Shopping

Research on criminal courts reveals disparities in the significance of which judge hears a case or imposes sentence. Clearly, how much influence the judge has varies from jurisdiction to jurisdiction. At least, some attorneys in every jurisdiction *think* that it makes a big difference. These comments by a full-time prosecutor typify the kind of judgments we heard from lawyers everywhere about their judges:

> You know [Judge A], under normal circumstances, is gonna give a prostitute probation. [Judge B] is gonna give a drunk driver probation. . . . Woe be to you if you happen to be a child abuser and you're in front of B, 'cause he'll send you away. A hates violent crimes, gun crimes. He screams about guns all the time.

Because lawyers know they cannot change most things that determine the outcomes of cases, they naturally seize upon what they can manipulate. Consequently, both prosecutors and defense attorneys devote much time and effort to discovering how they can steer their cases to some judges and away from others. The techniques used to schedule cases and assign them to judges determines how and how much attorneys shop for judges. Regardless of technique, efforts to judge-shop or "route" cases are made everywhere.

Erie was no exception. Like most judges using master calendar systems, Erie's bench tried to reduce opportunities for shopping. As mentioned, cases listed for trial were supposed to be assigned sequentially to the next available courtroom. The court administrator could assign one of three judges to hear a guilty plea, but was required to see that each handled an equal number. Like lawyers in most master calendar systems, Erie attorneys employed varied tactics to circumvent the obstacles to shopping.

Public defenders and some private attorneys learned when which judges were scheduled to conduct motion court. By delaying or speeding up a case, they changed the odds of getting specific judges. They would file motions when they calculated that their favorite judge was scheduled for motion court. Sometimes, the duty judges would accept a plea after motions had been argued rather than referring the case to the court administrator for assignment as they were supposed to. Both prosecutors and regular defense attorneys knew who among the judges would hear criminal cases during upcoming trial terms. They sought continuances or went ahead so that the case was scheduled for a term when a judge they wanted to avoid heard civil trials, or a judge they sought was assigned to criminal trials.

How much routing of cases occurred in Erie? Probably no one could give a precise count. Our research suggested several general conclusions, however. Some attorneys either did not know how to shop or felt the judges did not differ enough in their treatment of many cases to bother. An official in the PD's office, discussing case assignments during trial terms, told us:

> You don't know which one is going to be your judge that day. And judge-shopping can't be done in a community this size with the court administrator running things the way he does. . . . [I]f we don't have the DA's help we can't judge-shop.

A defense attorney implied that trying to shop was just too much work. "I had so many cases I just kind of rolled with the punches and took whoever they gave me, to tell you the truth." One attorney explained his lack of interest in shopping by telling us: "I don't care if it's before the Pope. There are certain standard characteristics that are gonna deserve some sentence or other. . . . The judges don't vary that much." Furthermore, the procedures designed to stop shopping clearly restricted its scope. Nevertheless, a number of attorneys indicated that routing mattered in at least some cases, and went on to describe how they steered defendants to some judges and away from others. Though not universal, case routing was a common occurrence in Erie.

Most routing involved cases ending in a guilty plea, and required cooperation by the court administrator. Although every month he had to equalize the number each of the three judges received, he could maintain balance by exercising discretion in cases wherein neither side requested a specific judge. When the attorneys explicitly requested a specific judge, the court administrator went along. In other cases, the procedure was subtler. "It's sort of understood that maybe we're gonna ask for that judge," observed a public defender. How would it be understood, we asked?

> The DA will just say, "There's nothing wrong with him pleading to that. You know _____ isn't going to put him in jail," or "Judge _____ will only give him county time."

Evidently, the court administrator did not always require agreement between the attorneys. An experienced public defender told us the court administrator "will go along with what you say." A private defense lawyer said he would "just go in and give him a hard time until he schedules you in front of the judge you want."

Routing a trial (as opposed to a plea) to a specific judge proved much more difficult, but not impossible. An assistant prosecutor described intricately how the office played the game:

> If we're trying to manipulate a case in front of Judge _____ , what we do usually is when _____ opens up, tell [the court administrator] that this case is the one that's ready to go. There's no other one ready to go. . . . He'll say, "What about these other cases?" We'll say, "Witnesses aren't here." The defense attorney meanwhile will use his game, which is, "I can't find my client. I can't go right now. I'm in the middle of a closing." Now the court administrator's either gotta put the heat on him through himself, or go to the judge and have the judge's secretary call the guy and say, "Look, I don't care what you have. You're in this courtroom."

Whether the court administrator would accommodate such requests depended on who did the asking. We asked the assistant prosecutor just quoted why the administrator wouldn't pressure the DA's office rather than the defense attorney. "Because he's pretty good friends with [the DA]. I mean it, that's it." Our interviewer countered that many defense attorneys were good friends with the administrator too. "I was just gonna say he'll do the same thing for a defense attorney that he's real good friends with." Indeed, we talked with a defense attorney who claimed precisely the same ability to choose his trial judge:

> R: I say, "_____, this case is gonna go to trial. Give me Judge _____."
> I: What if he asks, "Why?"
> R: Because I want a fair trial. He says, "I'll see what I can do."
> I: He'll do that?
> R: Yeah. I don't know if all the lawyers get away with that or not. I've had good luck with him.

That not everyone could do this choosing was proven because the defense attorney quoted above who routed pleas by giving the administrator a "hard time" admitted he found it "very difficult" to shop for a trial judge.

How effectively members of the court community could route cases, then, depended in part on the quality of their relationships with other members of the criminal court community. The DA's office believed that its close relationship with the court administrator gave it an advantage, especially in influencing which case went first to each judge at the start of a new trial term. But other established attorneys also benefited. In fact, mutual accommodation and cooperation provided the basis for working out case assignments.

HOW ERIE'S COURT COMMUNITY DISPOSED OF CASES

How did Erie's criminal court community dispose of defendants' cases? We employed two techniques for learning about these dispositions: interviewing members of the community and analyzing data from official records. Only by interviewing could we discover the technologies employed, the policies key participants followed, and the dynamics of their interaction. Court records alone could not reflect crucial characteristics of the disposition process, such as the judges' insistence on presentence investigations for convicted defendants, or agreements in plea bargains that the prosecutor would remain silent at sentencing.

There is a problem with relying solely on interviews, however. The descriptions of community members reflect their perceptions of what is memorable and significant. The average, the routine, and the boring are not talked about much. Much as college faculty tell one another about their very best and very worst students, people in court communities focus on the extraordinary. Consequently, what they tell researchers about what "usually" happens often reflects the exception rather than the rule. To learn what the typical plea bargain involves or how harsh sentences are, we must look at our data on case outcomes.

Our research design permits us to combine information from both techniques. Again an analogy to baseball is apt. Reading a box score conveys only the bare outlines of what happened. More detailed information in a scorecard fills in many details. To truly understand and appreciate the game, however, you need to watch it. At the same time, just watching and describing from memory also has its limitations. Summary statistics on hits, runs, and errors and other aspects of the game also contribute to understanding it.

Initial Charges and Bail Outcomes

The criminal process for defendants begins with their arrest, arraignment on the charges initially lodged, and the setting of bail. In the following paragraphs we describe what Erie's defendants experienced as their journeys to court began.

Figure 3-4 shows that only about one defendant in seven faced charges involving a serious crime of violence. More than one fifth answered to charges of drunk driving, a relatively less serious offense not even handled in Michigan's and Illinois's trial courts. The level of the most serious charge was the most important attribute determining what happened to defendants. Our analysis throughout this book returns to it again and again. That many defendants in Erie faced relatively minor charges like drunk driving shaped the overall process in many ways, including bail decisions, the mode of disposition employed, and the severity of sentences imposed.

Another characteristic of the charges defendants faced stemmed from police agencies' practice of filing separate arrests for similar or closely related crimes. A gentleman who passed six bad checks was charged with six crimes. When the charges came from the district justice following the preliminary hearing, the Clerk of Courts assigned six consecutive docket numbers to them, rather than combining them in one case with six identical counts. Erie reported receiving six cases to Pennsylvania officials, but handled them simultaneously. When recording information from the case files, we combined multiple cases against the same defendant that arose from the same or a related incident.

Data on the number of counts that defendants in our sample faced showed the average number of charges at arrest to be 1.87, second highest among our nine counties. Neither the district judges at the preliminary hearings nor the prosecutor's office in drawing up the informations upon which defendants were arraigned made many changes. The average number of charges per defendant after the preliminary hearing dropped only slightly, to 1.79. Nearly half (48 percent) of defendants had multiple charges lodged against them in the information filed by the prosecutor, second only to Montgomery county. Figure 5–1 shows the distribution of the number of charges lodged at arrest for defendants ultimately convicted or pleading guilty. We will use these data later when we look at the number of charges upon which they were convicted.

Bail outcomes for defendants are a major component of any jurisdiction's case processing. Anyone who has visited a county jail, or better still, lived in one, will attest to the quality of life there. Much research has established that in many jurisdictions defendants in pretrial detention suffer more than just the unpleasantries of poor food, occasional homosexual rape, boredom, and other consequences of jail. Jailed defendants more often are convicted and are sentenced more severely.[2]

Both absolutely and in comparison to the other counties, judges in Erie made lenient bail decisions. Almost 60 percent of its defendants received "release on recognizance," or "ROR," freeing them in return for a promise to show up for court hearings. All three Pennsylvania counties gave defendants ROR much more often than did the other six jurisdictions, in part reflecting the presence of many drunk-driving cases. In Erie, 90 percent of defendants facing such charges got ROR. But Erie's release-on-recognizance rate surpassed

[2]See, for example, the discussion of the effect of pretrial detention in Roy B. Flemming, *Punishment Before Trial* (New York: Longman, 1983), Chapter 2.

Figure 5–1

Number of Charges at Arrest for Erie Convicted Defendants: 1980

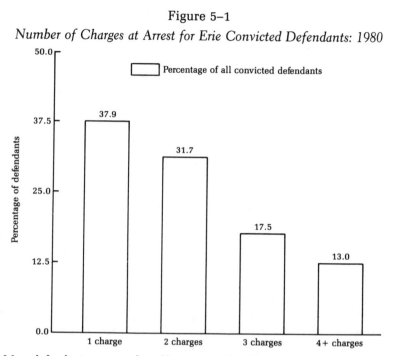

Most defendants — more than 60 percent — faced more than one charge. In fact, almost one-third (30.5 percent) had three or more charges lodged against them.

Source: 1980 sample of Erie defendants who were convicted.

those of the other two Pennsylvania counties, as did its proportion of defendants released before final disposition (84 percent).[3]

The principal determinant of bail is the seriousness of offense. But the defendant's prior criminal record, the second factor that repeatedly shapes how criminal cases everywhere are handled, also was

[3]Other evidence of Erie's lenient bail policies is available. Defendants in Erie and Dauphin charged with armed robbery who had to post a bail bond had the lowest median amount among the nine counties ($5,000). See James Eisenstein, Peter F. Nardulli, and Roy B. Flemming, *Explaining and Assessing Criminal Case Disposition: A Comparative Study of Nine Counties,* report submitted to the National Institute of Justice, Washington, D.C., April 29, 1982, Chapter 5.

influential.[4] Figure 5–2 shows this relationship to hold both in Erie and in the counties described in Chapters Six and Seven. It also provides additional evidence of Erie's relatively lenient bail policy.

How and When Defendants' Cases Ended

What happened to defendants who appeared in Erie's trial court? Our analysis of defendants' case files allows us to present a scorecard on how many were convicted, how long it took to dispose of each case, and how severely convicted defendants were sentenced. Figure 5–3 shows that 85 percent were convicted, and that most of the convictions resulted from the defendant's plea of guilty (53.2 percent) or obtaining accelerated rehabilitative disposition (ARD) (26.0 percent). We combine ARD with pleas in Figure 5–3 because the ARD defendant implicitly admitted guilt and incurred costs similar to those borne by people who formally pled guilty. The ARD program for drunk drivers assessed fees of several hundred dollars, compelled attendance at classes on drinking and driving, and required that participants avoid subsequent arrest for a specified period or face reinstitution of the initial charge. These requirements differed little from those imposed on defendants who received a fine and probation.

Data on time elapsed between arrest and final disposition showed that half the cases in Erie took about five months or more to end. One fourth of its defendants finished in less than 110 days, about three and one-half months. Only 10 percent of defendants' cases lingered more than eleven months. In Chapter Six we will compare these figures with comparable data from Kalamazoo and Du Page (Figure 6–5).

THE GUILTY-PLEA PROCESS

Eighty percent of Erie's defendants neither went to trial nor escaped conviction by having their cases dismissed. Instead, they entered pleas of guilty. Any evaluation of how well courts adhere to the basic

[4]We produced a general measure of how serious defendants' prior records were by using the number of prior arrests, convictions, jail commitments, and penitentiary commitments. A statistical procedure (factor analysis) allowed combining them into one measure, which we then used to separate defendants into the three categories used in Figure 5–2. For a more detailed description of our measure of prior record, see Peter F. Nardulli, Roy B. Flemming, and James Eisenstein, *The Tenor of Justice* (Champaign, Ill.: University of Illinois Press, 1987), Chapter 3.

Figure 5–2

Percentage of Defendants Released in Erie, Du Page,
and Kalamazoo Counties, by Seriousness of Prior Record

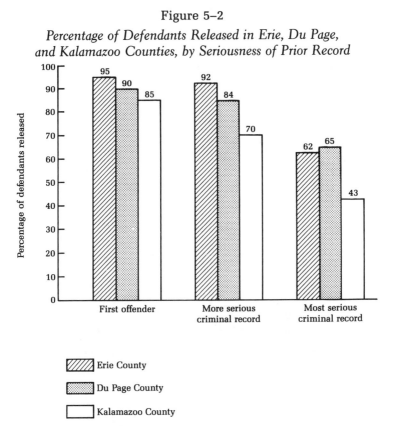

Most defendants did not stay in jail until the disposition of their cases, as the overall height of the bars indicates. Defendants with more serious records, however, less frequently won release regardless of county. Erie's defendants were more likely to be released at each level of seriousness of prior record than defendants in Kalamazoo and for all but defendants with the most serious records in Du Page.

Source: Defendant samples

principles of fairness, consistency, and justice inevitably must focus primarily on guilty-plea cases.

Traditionally, the term "plea bargaining" has been applied to these dispositions. We consciously employ a different phrase, the "guilty-plea process," to indicate that guilty pleas do not always result from explicit give-and-take bargaining. Rather, some result from the de-

Figure 5–3

Method of Disposition for Erie Trial Court Defendants, 1980

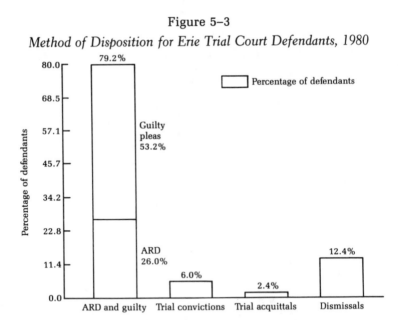

Most defendants' cases ended with a conviction by a guilty plea or its equivalent, ARD. Adding the small number (6 percent) convicted after trial, 85 percent were convicted. Those escaping conviction usually did so by dismissal (12.4 percent) rather than acquittal (2.4 percent).

Source: Erie case sample

fense's accepting the standard disposition, the "going rate." They take the sentence that forms part of the consensus on how defendants with given criminal records should be sentenced for a given offense.

One student of criminal courts nicely explained the difference between the two notions of how pleas come about by comparing the give-and-take haggling customers use to arrive at the prices they pay in a Middle Eastern bazaar to the way in which we shop in a modern supermarket, where we accept the posted price.[5] In a later chapter we discuss the relative frequency of guilty pleas that result from bargaining (the "concessions" model) as opposed to accepting the going rate (the "consensus" model).

[5]Malcolm Feeley, "Perspective on Plea Bargaining," 13 *Law and Society Review* (1970), p. 462.

Regardless of whether a defendant bargains for concessions or merely enters a plea, several crucial elements are common. The defendant surrenders the right to a trial before a judge or jury. In return, he or she gains benefit of some sort of concession. Guilty-plea systems differ in the content of the benefit. Some reduce the *number* of crimes charged; others reduce the *seriousness* of the charges; still others reduce both the number and seriousness of counts. Pleas can also include explicit agreements on the sentence to be imposed. Though they can be concrete ("If you plead, you will get probation"), sentence agreements may involve only an understanding about what the prosecutor will say at sentencing or even merely an expectation of what the sentence will be. Pleas can also include agreement on which judge will hear the plea. Together, these concessions are the principal elements that can appear on plea agendas.

These components of guilty pleas can combine in varied ways in any given court to form a distinctive plea agenda. Furthermore, the techniques used to arrive at pleas and their timing vary considerably among court communities. The result is that guilty-plea systems display significant differences from one another.

Our interviews in Erie's criminal court community revealed the general outlines of its guilty-plea system. Many less serious charges that nevertheless made it to trial court ended with the defendant being granted ARD. Thus, for many cases involving minor crimes and first offenders, the "going rate" was ARD. Next to no "bargaining" in the normal sense took place, and little doubt ever arose about how the case would end.

In less routine and more serious cases, Erie's court community normally avoided pleas that included an agreement on sentence that bound the judge. In Chapter Two we quoted an Erie judge's vigorous rejection of such practices. Others in Erie confirmed the potency of the judges' dislike for such pleas. "I can recall one time years ago," said a prosecutor, "when they were beginning here to make recommendations on sentencing. The judge said, 'Hey, listen. You can plea bargain the case, but it's up to the court to sentence.'" Thus agreement on sentences did not appear on Erie's plea agenda.

The pleas Erie's judges accepted routinely included reduction in the *number* of charges to which the defendant pled. "That kind of plea bargain is what I allow," a judge told us. "And they don't even try anything else with me, because I've told them I don't want it." The judges looked much less favorably on reductions in the *seriousness* of the top charge:

> If you've got a man charged with five burglaries and he wants
> to plead to two, I don't see any harm in it. If he's charged with
> burglary and wants to plead to unlawful entry, I don't approve
> of that. . . . I don't want real burglaries knocked down.

The district attorney's office supported the judges' policies. It sought to eliminate what it claimed had been the previous DA's tendency to reduce the seriousness of charges routinely as part of plea bargains. One official starkly described the new policy: "I won't reduce it unless there is a mitigating circumstance such as 'I can't prove my case,' and that's just about it." Prosecutors expressed no desire to engage in sentence bargaining. "I'm not really sure we're in a strong enough position, with the records available to us," a young assistant DA said, "in evaluating what the proper sentence would be." Prosecutors across the state in Montgomery county felt no such modesty about their ability to decide what sentence was proper.

The avoidance of sentence bargains received support and reinforcement through the judges' practice of postponing sentence until the probation department prepared a presentence investigation. As the statement by a judge quoted above suggests, they placed great confidence in the probation department and relied upon the information in the presentence reports.

Because we know that passionate statements about the policies that allegedly control behavior may conceal substantial exceptions, we asked judges if on occasion informal, indirect, off-the-record discussions of pleas and possible sentences might not take place in chambers. One judge interrupted as we asked the question: "I do not participate in bargaining at all. I refuse to be part of it, you know, informally prior to its being presented. I want it in open court, on the record." Interestingly, prosecutors and defense attorneys confirmed that this judge really did not involve himself in trying to influence how cases ended. He received a very low score on the "judicial-involvement" scale derived from the Q-sort evaluations of judges made by prosecutors and defense attorneys. Another judge answered differently. He initially told us, "I think here judges don't participate until it's brought into court." When we described the informal discussion about sentences that we learned took place elsewhere, however, he qualified his assessment:

> I'm not saying that that doesn't in some instances happen here.
> . . . It is not the regular practice, but during a term of court it

might. Somebody might come in and say, "If this fellow were gonna get Mercer [a regional low-security prison] rather than the penitentiary, he might plead."

An attorney described just such a practice with this man:

> I can go to this judge and say, "Judge, this is what we got. I know you don't like it on the record, but I've got a skittish client, and if you tell me off the record what you're gonna do, I will tell that to the defendant and tell him that your word is good." And we do that.

An experienced former assistant public defender confirmed that the judge quoted earlier as refusing to participate was "never involved," and that others were. He described what one judge might say in such a situation:

> "Well, unless there's something more that I don't know about, I don't think I'll find him guilty of anything more than third-degree murder from what you tell me." Now that's not really involving yourself in a plea bargain, but he's basically telling you.

He want on to tell us that discussions in chambers took place in "most kinds of cases." "You usually want to try to familiarize the court a little bit with the case and get a feel for what they're gonna do."

These descriptions begin to reveal the complexity of the guilty-plea process. Substantial differences arose on just one aspect of it — whether judges discussed sentences before disposition. Not only did this behavior vary by judge, but also by the attorneys involved. A very young public defender tried to approach the same judge the experienced former public defender described as discussing sentences in "most kinds of cases." The judge refused to discuss the case with him.

The timing of such discussions in chambers also varied. One judge earned the reputation of actively seeking to settle cases scheduled for trial after the first few days of the trial term had passed. He observed that the pretrial conference held before the jury was picked served as "a very good time to pressure the district attorney to accept a reasonable plea bargain." An attorney described just how this judge would exert subtle pressure to encourage pleas:

> Maybe the implied threats go to the district attorney in saying that, "Well, it's really not gonna matter that much whether it's

an aggravated assault to a misdemeanor or aggravated assault as a felony. And I don't see why you can't let the boy plead to a misdemeanor. Why don't you want to do that?"

The "judicial involvement" of this judge was $+3.26$; the next highest judge's score in Erie was only $+0.26$.

Of course, many defendants pled guilty before the trial term began. We described earlier the intricacies of the case assignment system. The ability to include in a plea agreement tacit understanding of which judge would take the plea; that is, to "route" the case, was an essential element on the plea agenda in Erie. So too were reductions in the number of counts. When pleas resulted from explicit discussions between the opposing attorneys, a third element sometimes appeared—agreement that the prosecutor would "stand mute" at sentencing rather than review the defendant's record and describe his or her crime. Thus, the picture we assembled from the interviews about content of discussions on pleas between prosecutors and defense attorneys had three elements: reductions in the number of counts; mostly unstated agreement over which judge would take the plea; and standing mute at sentencing.

The analysis of data drawn from the case files can reveal nothing about routing or standing mute at sentencing; such information does not appear in court files. But we can examine what happened to counts. The frequency with which defendants in Erie faced more than one charge at arrest, depicted in Figure 5-1, made it possible to reduce the number of counts in most cases. Analysis of case outcomes provided strong confirmation of the interview descriptions. Drops in the number of counts took place frequently. In fact, nearly three of every five defendants saw a drop in counts when they pled guilty, more than in any other county. Furthermore, the data show that very few defendants pled to a less serious primary charge. Only 8.6 percent of Erie's guilty pleas saw a drop in primary charge; the ratio of such drops in primary charges to all reductions, including those in the number of counts, was much larger in every other county.[6]

[6]In Erie, only about one reduction in seven involved lowering the primary charge rather than just reducing the number of counts. Du Page ranked next at one in 4.3. In contrast, almost half the cases with changes in four counties (Peoria, Dauphin, Oakland, and Kalamazoo) involved lowering the primary charge. For further discussion of the guilty-plea patterns in the nine counties, see Chapter 9 and Nardulli, *Tenor of Justice*, op. cit., Chapter 8.

Defendants pleading guilty to fewer counts with no change in the most serious charge get little break in their sentences. This conclusion grows from much prior research. Judges rarely impose consecutive jail sentences for additional counts (i.e., sentences to be served after the term for the primary offense has passed). Our research found the same thing. Only reductions in the seriousness of the primary charge affected severity of sentence significantly.[7] Why then did so many defendants in Erie plead guilty? Before addressing this question, we need to examine a final aspect of case outcomes — sentences.

SEVERITY OF ERIE'S SENTENCES

Assessing the harshness of a court community's sentences poses as many challenges as deciding whether crime in a community is "serious." The terms "lenient" and "harsh" convey no inherent meaning, but rather depend on human judgment. Punishment that strikes a college student caught driving home intoxicated from Saturday-night relaxation as severe may be regarded as lenient by the mother of a child killed by a drunk driver.

Comparison of courts' sentences provided some information about *relative* severity, but deciding how and what should be compared quickly gets complicated. Unless summary measures such as median and average are used, we soon become overwhelmed by a barrage of numbers that no one can keep straight or remember. But just as a team batting average disguises performances by very poor and very good hitters, so too do measures of median or mean sentences conceal meaningful information. Deciding what cases or defendants to compare also poses dilemmas. If we look at all defendants, our summary measures can produce misleading conclusions. Suppose that in an identical twin to Erie County, the system meted out the same sentences to an identical set of cases and defendants. If the second county disposed of its drunk-driving cases in the lower court, the trial court's caseload would be small and a higher proportion of its defendants would be charged with serious crimes that brought long sentences. Therefore, the average and median sentences for all defendants disposed of in the second county's trial court would be

[7]Ibid., Chapter 8.

higher, even though the entire group of defendants received the same outcome. Erie would look more lenient, but only because the mixture of cases used to compute the average sentence in the trial court included drunk-driving cases that in the second county were disposed of in the lower courts.

Other problems arise in deciding what cases to use in comparing courts' sentences. Only convicted defendants are sentenced. If one court dismisses many defendants that a second convicts, but punishes severely, its average sentences for the few though dangerous people convicted will exceed the second court's. Is the first harsher in overall punishment just because sentences are longer, even though it lets more defendants go without punishment? What if the dismissed defendants should not have been charged in the first place, and would not have even made it to the second court?

Even something seemingly straightforward like the proportion of defendants incarcerated leads to difficulties. Suppose County A convicts just 50 of 100 robbery defendants, but sends 45 of those convicted to prison. The "percentage of convicted defendants imprisoned" (45/50) is 90. County B also has 100 robbery defendants, but convicts 80 of them. If B also sends 45 of the convicted to prison, it equals County A in the rate of *all* defendants incarcerated. If we compute County B's "percentage of *convicted* defendants incarcerated," however, it is 45/80, or 56 percent, much lower than County A's 90 percent rate on the same measure.

It makes little sense to conclude that County A is harsher than B. We do not know, however, why as many as 50 of County A's 100 defendants escaped conviction. Perhaps County A had no choice thanks to weak cases brought by a poor police department. Alternatively, County A may just be reluctant to convict. Because we don't know why the conviction rate is 50 percent, the fact that a higher proportion of convicted defendants in County A go to prison cannot be ignored.

Finally, the sentences imposed may mean different things in practice. Even among counties in the same state, the degree to which fines imposed are actually collected and the time defendants actually spend in the county jail before being paroled varies widely.

Our discussion of sentence severity in Erie and the other counties reflects the problems just discussed. A variety of measures need to be utilized. The diversity in case-processing systems and the difficulty of finding a way to identify truly equivalent categories of comparison preclude coming up with one measure of severity.

We begin describing Erie's sentences with a fact already presented. Eighty-five percent of Erie's trial court defendants were convicted. What percentage of them received the most serious punishment — incarceration? The answer is 30 percent, placing Erie in the middle of the nine counties, which ranged from 51 percent to 20 percent. The proportion of *convicted* defendants going to jail or penitentiary is about 42 percent, again somewhere in the middle of our counties. Figure 5–4 depicts the proportions of convicted defendants sentenced to the penitentiary, to the county jail, to probation (often with an accompanying fine), and to ARD.

We know that the mixture of charges Erie's defendants faced differed in major respects from other counties, raising many of the problems of comparison discussed above. We can gain a better view of sentencing by looking at what happened to defendants charged at arrest with similar offenses.[8] Figure 5–5 presents such data for four crimes: armed robbery, burglary, larceny, and serious offenses involving hard drugs (possession and sale). To account for differences in conviction rates, the figure shows in the left bar the percentage of defendants arrested for each crime who were convicted, the percentage of defendants arrested who were incarcerated in the center, and the proportion of just those convicted who went to prison on the right. For example, 35 percent of defendants arrested for larceny *and* convicted went to jail or prison. But because 76 percent of larceny arrestees were convicted, the proportion of all arrested for larceny incarcerated, represented by the middle bar, fell to 27 percent. As we show later, Erie consistently incarcerated fewer of its defendants for all four charges than Kalamazoo, but its rates compared to Du Page's showed no consistent pattern for the four offenses.

Figures 5–4 and 5–5 say nothing about the length of the jail and prison terms given to convicted defendants. To avoid entanglement in the problems arising from differences in the mixture of crimes for which defendants were convicted, Figure 5–6 depicts the median months of the minimum expected sentence length for the same four

---

[8]It is better to use the most serious charge at the arrest rather than the offense convicted upon to define similar groups of defendants because police charging practices vary less than plea-bargaining patterns that alter the offense convicted upon.

Figure 5–4

Distribution of Sentences Imposed on Convicted Erie Defendants, 1980[a]

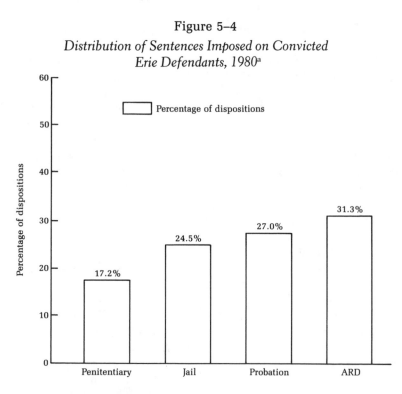

[a]Includes ARD as convictions.

Most convicted defendants did not go to state prison. In fact, adding that proportion (17.2 percent) to those given an Erie county jail sentence (24.5 percent) produced an incarceration rate of just over 40 percent. Almost 60 percent of convicted defendants, therefore, received probation or ARD.

Source: Erie case sample

crimes listed in Figure 5–5. Of course, as mentioned in Chapter Three, defendants sentenced for prostitution and other lesser offenses to the Erie County jail often served only a few days before being released. Thus, Figure 5–6 shows that of the fifteen defendants arrested for armed robbery and given jail or prison terms, the "middle" defendant (ranked eighth among the fifteen) got a minimum 22.5-month sentence. Compared to the other nine counties, Erie ranked sixth in median sentence for armed robbery, tied for fifth on burglary, for second on larceny, and for fifth on possession of hard drugs.

Figure 5–5

*Incarceration Rates on Selected Arrest Charges
for Erie Defendants, 1980*

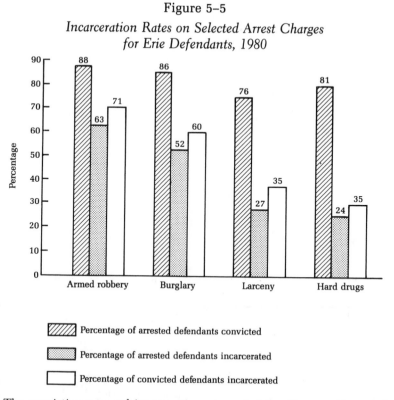

Percentage of arrested defendants convicted

Percentage of arrested defendants incarcerated

Percentage of convicted defendants incarcerated

The conviction rate and incarceration rate varied by offense, with armed robbery defendants most often convicted and incarcerated. Burglary defendants received dispositions almost as severe. Conviction rates, however, represented by the first bar in each grouping, varied only from 76 percent to 88 percent, a range of 12 percent. The proportion of those arrested who were incarcerated, the second bar in each grouping, went from 24 percent to 63 percent, a range of 39 percent.

Source: Erie case sample

As mentioned, Erie's prosecutors believed sentences were too lenient, but defense attorneys characterized them generally as "fair." Clearly, the actual length of time defendants sentenced to the county jail served (which meant any sentence with a minimum of 11.5 months or less) often fell far short of what the judge imposed. The minimums therefore may actually overstate the severity of the sentences. It is also possible, though, that defendants who elsewhere

Figure 5–6

*Median Minimum Expected Sentence in Months Imposed on Erie
Defendants Incarcerated for Selected Arrest Charges, 1980*

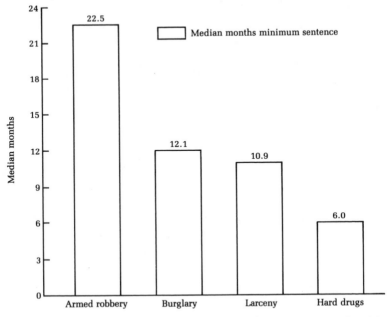

Among defendants arrested for armed robbery who were convicted and incarcerated (15 in number), the "middle" defendant; that is, the one with the
eighth-longest sentence, received a minimum effective sentence of 22.5
months. The comparable sentence for those arrested for burglary and robbery was about a year. The median incarceration sentence for drug defendants was half a year, only about a quarter of that for armed robbers.

Source: Erie case sample

would have received probation instead got a county jail sentence with
immediate parole. A former assistant defender described Erie's policy in handling young defendants.

> You sentence him to jail. The kid gets that immediate shock,
> spends the night upstairs, and then the next morning they cut
> him loose. That is much more effective than giving a kid five
> years' probation.

GOING RATES, TRIAL PENALTIES,
AND GUILTY PLEAS

We now return to the question posed earlier. Why did so many Erie defendants plead guilty when all that most of them got in return was a drop in the number of counts? The practice of paroling defendants from the overcrowded Erie jail far short of the formal minimum term imposed may help explain why defendants pled guilty in Erie in the face of the mainly symbolic but substantively meaningless count drops that most guilty pleas entailed. The analysis of sentence severity showed that, compared to the other counties, Erie did not punish with especial harshness. More sophisticated analysis of sentence length for convicted defendants, counting ARD, fines only, and probation as zero months, and controlling statistically for differences in the mixture of offenses and defendants' prior criminal records, placed Erie in the middle of the group of nine counties.[9]

Defense attorneys' discussions with their clients on the advantages of pleading guilty benefited from predictions of sentences that would follow a plea. Because the certainty that sentence bargaining provides rarely arose, the ability of defense attorneys to predict sentences accurately could serve as a partial substitute. Attorneys who could route cases increased their ability to predict sentences. The widely known and much-followed going rates based on the defendant's prior record and the content of the charges also enhanced predictability. When we tested to see how well we could predict convicted defendants' sentence length, knowing just the offense and prior record, our statistical analysis revealed fairly strong going rates. In only two counties were going rates much better established. Erie and Kalamazoo tied for third. We could predict more than a third of the differences in sentences knowing only offense and record.[10]

Finally, perceptions of a "trial penalty," that is, the practice of sentencing more severely defendants who insist on a trial rather than pleading guilty, also encouraged guilty pleas. We heard various opin-

[9]For a discussion of relative severity of sentences in all nine counties, see Chapter 9. See also Nardulli, *Tenor of Justice*, op. cit., Chapter 10.

[10]Peter F. Nardulli, James Eisenstein, and Roy B. Flemming, "Sentencing as a Sociopolitical Process: Environmental, Contextual, and Individual Level Dimension," Chapter 5, graph 5.3. Report submitted to the National Institute of Justice, June 30, 1983.

ions from court community members in Erie on the existence of such a sentence penalty. Some believed that it existed, but only when defendants took the stand and lied. One claimed, "often the judges will say it: 'Not only did you do this, but it's my conviction that you lied under oath.'" Others, like the private attorney quoted below, insisted that defendants were punished even if they did not testify falsely:

> I'll tell the guy, "If you go to trial and are found guilty, you're gonna get a hell of a lot more time than if you just plead guilty." I'll tell them that, and it's true. There's no question about it.

But some, including an official in the prosecutor's office with experience as a public defender, did question its existence:

> So I would *like* to tell [clients insisting on trial], "Listen, if you go to trial and lose, you're going to get banged." But you couldn't really say that to them because more often than not the judge really didn't bang you.

Our data permitted a statistical test to see if going to trial increased sentences, holding constant the seriousness of the charges faced. It revealed that defendants going to trial in Erie apparently received a somewhat longer sentence, but other factors, such as the strength of evidence and number of motions filed, accounted for most of the difference.[11] Thus, some attorneys *believed* that a trial penalty operated. This belief undoubtedly contributed to some pleas. If a stringent sentence penalty had been consistently applied to defendants going to trial, however, our analysis would have detected it. Of course, it is possible that the penalty was so effective and certain that few bothered to risk going to trial on a case that everyone considered inappropriate for trial. Did this happen? Probably not, for the interviews did not reveal a clear and strong agreement on the point. But it is difficult to know for sure.

EFFECTS OF STATE-LEVEL FACTORS

What difference did it make that Erie's court community nestled in the northwest corner of Pennsylvania rather than in some other state? As we argued in Chapter Two, communities reflect the cultural, po-

[11]Nardulli, "Sentencing," ibid., Chapter 6, graph 6.4.

litical, and social characteristics of the larger environment in which they exist. A complete analysis of the ways in which the criminal court community in Erie was molded by forces from outside the county would be a book in itself. Our discussion will be brief and narrow, focusing on the most significant factors associated with the state of Pennsylvania.

The methods used to recruit judges conformed to Pennsylvania's long tradition of partisanship. Judges ran for their first ten-year term in a contested, partisan election. District justices ran in their local constituencies for election and for reelection in partisan contests every six years. Both engaged in some campaign activities at least, and usually knew and had worked with party officials and politically relevant organizations. Though the President Judge of each trial court had formal authority to supervise the district judges who presided over the lower courts scattered throughout the jurisdiction, these lower judges gained considerable autonomy from the fact that they owed their offices to their home constituencies.

The political process in each Pennsylvania county chose and influenced the district attorney and public defender. The DA ran for a four-year term in a partisan election. Though his salary was set by state statute, he depended on the county government to provide space, set the size of his professional and clerical staff and their salaries, and provide the money for all expenses and supplies. The public defender's office also received all its financial support from the county. Its head, though, was appointed by the county government, and could be fired by it at any time.

The state government set and paid judges' salaries, and provided a portion of the money needed to run the courts.[12] Judges, too, depended on the county government for most of their budget, though they retained the seldom-used power to issue a court order requiring the county to release funds to them. Judges' control over the hiring of clerical personnel provided them with a significant amount of patronage. Unlike their colleagues in other states, Pennsylvania judges did not control the offices that provide crucial support services. The Clerk of Courts, charged with maintaining official criminal case files

[12]In fiscal year 1978, for example, the state of Pennsylvania provided 36 percent of local expenditures for the criminal justice system. U.S. Department of Justice, Bureau of Justice Statistics, *Expenditure and Employment Rate for the Criminal Justice System, 1978.* (Washington, D.C.: U.S. Government Printing Office, 1981), table 1, p. 30.

essential to the court's work, won a four-year term in a partisan election, as did the official, called the Prothonotary, who maintained records and papers relating to civil litigation; the Recorder of Deeds; the Controller; and the County Treasurer. (In Erie, the new Home Rule charter gave the County Executive the power to appoint many of these officials.)

The details of how key personnel came to office, who provided their budget, and how much control they had over others who affected their work all point to a significant conclusion: in Pennsylvania, criminal court communities found themselves enmeshed in the local political system. The fact that in all but the largest counties they shared the same building with other county officials and fed into a common grapevine further tied court communities to their environment.

In form, Pennsylvania had a "unified" court system. The State Supreme Court exercised general administrative authority and supervision over the entire court system. It appointed a State Court Administrator to head the Administrative Office of Pennsylvania Courts (AOPC). He held the power to appoint the court administrator for each trial court. The AOPC, President Judges, and county court administrators shared the responsibility for supervising the district justices. As we have seen, the state provided judges' salaries and provided a substantial portion (more than one third) of the money needed to run the courts.

In practice, however, Pennsylvania's court system operated in a much more decentralized fashion than its formal structure suggested. The independence that district justices gained due to their election from their own small constituencies was reinforced by the cumbersome and ineffective procedure for disciplining them. Though the state provided funds, it failed to use this support to exercise control.[13] The State Court Administrator delegated selection of local court administrators to the local judges. The Supreme Court did not appoint or remove President Judges, but decreed that in small

[13]After describing a general trend toward greater financing of courts from state sources, a student of court budgeting observed that "Only in Pennsylvania has an increase in the breadth of state financing been used to decrease the burden on county treasuries without a simultaneous increase in budgetary authority of state judicial administrators." Carl Baar, *Separate But Subservient: Court Budgeting in the American States* (Lexington, Mass.: D.C. Heath, 1975), p. 119.

courts, the judge of less than seventy years of age with the longest service would automatically serve till retirement, and that courts with eight or more judges would elect their President Judges for a five-year term. In general, the Supreme Court drew back from trying to exercise tight control. Further, neither the Supreme Court nor the state court administrator enjoyed the respect and confidence of local officials that would have enabled them to exercise influence.

If state officials exercised less influence over local courts like Erie's than they might have, state-level factors nonetheless exerted a constant and profound effect. The processing of cases depended in part on the *Pennsylvania Rules of Criminal Procedure* issued by the Supreme Court. The "180-day rule," which required dismissal of cases not brought to trial within 180 days of the defendant's arrest, not counting delays requested by the defense, affected scheduling of cases, pressure felt by judges and prosecutors, and content of plea bargains in cases approaching their 180th day. Unlike those in Michigan, police in Pennsylvania did not need prior approval from a prosecutor before formally lodging charges. This system prevented prosecutors from screening weak or petty cases before they got into the system. The structure of many scattered lower courts conducting preliminary hearings, and the reluctance of district justices to throw out charges, eliminated another technique for washing out cases. Prosecutors regained some control over charges after the preliminary hearing by their control of the information listing the charges, which replaced, at each county's option, indictment by a Grand Jury. The availability of ARD dispositions, initiated upon the prosecutor's recommendation and approved by a judge also partially compensated for the difficulty of screening cases.

Few restrictions were imposed on plea bargaining. A Pennsylvania Supreme Court decision forbade judges' participation in negotiations leading to a plea, though as described above, it was not always strictly adhered to. Plea bargains had to be taken in open court with a statement of its terms and conditions. A judge who accepted a plea that included a specific agreement on the length of incarceration or a sentence of probation had to adhere to its terms when sentencing.

The entire structure of sentencing in Pennsylvania, as elsewhere, depended upon the criminal code. As we show in a later chapter, in 1980 Pennsylvania's penal code provided for less harsh sentences and greater judicial discretion than Michigan's or Illinois's. It established maximum sentences for first-degree murder, three degrees of felonies, three degrees of misdemeanors, and summary offenses.[14] Judges could not impose a minimum exceeding half the maximum. Probation could be given in most offenses. Sentences carrying maximums of less than two years had to be served in the county jail. Maximums of more than five years meant the defendant had to go to a state prison. At the time of our research, the state prison system had not yet reached capacity, allowing judges to sentence defendants to state prison without having to worry about overcrowding. The notoriously bad conditions in the state prisons, though, made some judges reluctant to send some defendants there.

Our research did not investigate whether Pennsylvania had a distinctive "state legal culture." But we know that judges, prosecutors, public defenders, and established private defense attorneys attended statewide conferences, read the same publications, and shared experiences and perceptions of appellate court judges and state court administrators. It is likely that some convergence in attitudes toward sentencing and appropriate administrative technologies resulted. For example, most courts we know of in Pennsylvania (including the three we studied) used master rather than individual calendars. And on a number of measures, such as average length of prison sentences and size of the prison population per 100,000, Pennsylvania ranked as less punitive than either Illinois or Michigan.

SUMMARY

We begin Chapter Five by describing how the Erie court community organized to dispose of the cases sent to it. The five judges rotated, presiding over civil and criminal cases during the nine two-week trial terms scheduled each year. Three judges shared responsibility for handling criminal matters during other times, including rotating as duty judge to preside over motion court for one-week stints. The sequence of a burst of intense actvity at the start of each trial term, followed by a lull till the next one, dictated the rhythm of work and

[14]For example, robbery and burglary were first-degree felonies, which carried a maximum of more than ten years in prison. Second-degree misdemeanors carried a maximum of more than one but less than two years. Simple assault and petty thefts (involving $50 to $200) were classified as second-degree misdemeanors. Substantial revisions in Pennsylvania's penal code were made after our research ended.

the outlook of the entire community, and contributed to uncertainty about what each trial term would be like. Elaborate techniques for routing guilty pleas allowed most attorneys who so desired to influence which judge would impose sentence; determining which judge presided over a trial proved much more difficult, but not impossible.

In most of the chapter we concentrate on the characteristics of the cases and how they ended. More than 60 percent of defendants faced more than one charge; 84 percent won release from jail before their cases ended, most by release on recognizance. Only one defendant in seven escaped conviction, mostly by dismissal of all charges. Almost four of every five pled guilty or accepted ARD. The guilty-plea process relied heavily on going rates that dropped the number of counts but not the level of the most serious charge. Pleas did not include explicit understanding of what sentence would be imposed in most guilty-plea cases. Most defendants spent no time incarcerated after sentencing. Only 17 percent went to state prison. The conviction rate and incarceration rate varied according to the offense charged. Compared to other counties, Erie's sentences proved moderately lenient.

We conclude the chapter by examining how state-level factors shaped the court community's structure and behavior. These included methods of recruiting key participants, funding mechanisms, provisions for supervision by state officials, content of the criminal code, procedures established by appellate court decisions, and state legal culture. This discussion provides a springboard for description of Kalamazoo's court community, which we begin by examining similar state-level factors in Michigan.

CHAPTER SIX

Kalamazoo's Criminal Court

INTRODUCTION

Our exploration of the contours of justice required studying courts that varied in meaningful respects. Many of the common features of criminal courts in the United States alluded to in Chapter One and presented in our lengthy description of Erie can be passed over, allowing us to focus on how Kalamazoo differed.

Kalamazoo, an "autonomous" county, displayed social, economic, and political characteristics very different from those of Erie. We begin our description of Kalamazoo by asking the same question that ended Chapter Five: What difference did the state in which the court was located make?

STATE-LEVEL FACTORS

Michigan's court structure reflected the state's flirtation with the political reforms and spirit of the progressive era. Its formal court structure exhibited many features of the centralized, management-oriented approach associated with the "good-government" ethos. Though Pennsylvania also had a unified court system in form, Michigan's went further. Its Supreme Court enjoyed greater formal powers than Pennsylvania's, including the authority to assign additional judges to courts experiencing backlogs. It appointed a State Court Administrator, whose staff of eighty performed various administrative and record-gathering duties, and it issued detailed rules for the lower courts' administration and case processing.

Michigan rejected partisan elections for judges both in the lower court, called the District Court, and the trial court, called the Circuit Court. Instead, it chose both for six-year terms in nonpartisan elections. Circuit judges seeking another term faced not a mere retention election, but another contest in which they could face opposition. Michigan sought to ensure selection of better-qualified lower-court judges by requiring that they be lawyers, unlike Pennsylvania, where nearly all district magistrates lacked a law degree.

Like Pennsylvania, however, Michigan's court system showed less unity and central direction in practice than in form. District court judges enjoyed considerable de facto independence from the circuit court chief judges. The fact that they were elected and enjoyed a tradition of autonomy insulated them from tight control. Similarly, the circuit courts operated with little interference or supervision from above.

Michigan court communities probably were not as consistently and deeply enmeshed in local politics as those in Pennsylvania. The differences, however, were not large. Judges faced election more often, though they rarely saw opposition when seeking reelection. Prosecutors ran for four-year terms in partisan elections like their Pennsylvania counterparts. Both depended heavily on county governments for funding.[1]

Between the two states, several significant differences impinged on court communties' operations. The advantages that Michigan prosecutors enjoyed were especially important. Police in Michigan could not formally charge a defendant without obtaining a prosecutor's prior approval. Whether additional investigation would be done, what the charges would be, indeed whether any charges resulted at all fell under prosecutors' control. Provisions of the criminal code strengthened their hand in plea bargaining. A general "attempt" charge could be added to almost any offense. It carried a penalty of one half the actual offense, providing a convenient formula for guilty pleas. To a defendant charged with burglarly, the prosecutor could offer a plea to attempted burglary. Judges could not accept pleas to lesser offenses or new charges without the prosecutor's agreement, allowing the DA to veto pleas offered by defense

---

[1]For a more thorough discussion, see James Eisenstein, Peter F. Nardulli, and Roy B. Flemming, "Explaining and Assessing Criminal Case Disposition: A Comparative Study of Nine Counties," Report submitted to the National Institute of Justice, Washington, D.C., 1982, Chapter 10.

attorneys that appealed to judges. Further, the criminal code contained provisions allowing optional enhancements in sentence severity for habitual offenders. Threats to add and promises to dismiss such enhancements were often part of the plea agenda in Michigan jurisdictions.

A generally more stringent criminal code constituted a second major difference. At one time, Michigan judges enjoyed wide discretion in sentencing, with probation an option in most instances. But in the years before 1980, provisions were added that: (1) imposed a mandatory two-year prison sentence on defendants charged with possession of a firearm during commission of a felony; (2) imposed mandatory prison sentences for defendants convicted of some drug offenses; (3) eliminated "good time" credit in calculating when defendants convicted of some eighty crimes were eligible for parole; and (4) tightened bail provisions by allowing "preventive detention" of repeat offenders and those charged with serious crimes of violence. We will examine Michigan's relative severity again in Chapter Nine. In general, more defendants in Michigan went to prison and for longer periods. Predictably, its state prisons had reached capacity in 1980.

Michigan law also required that criminal cases be concluded within 180 days. Instead of dismissing charges when a case passed the deadline as in Pennsylvania, Michigan mandated only that defendants still in jail after 180 days be released.

A miscellany of less consequential differences deserve brief mention. Michigan imposed no uniform procedure for providing poor defendants with an attorney. Consequently, its counties were free to use varied techniques to ensure that indigents received representation. Because district judges were attorneys, they were a natural source of aspirants to positions on the circuit court. Most Michigan trial courts used individual rather than master calendaring systems. Its chief judges owed their office to their fellow judges, being elected for two-year terms. Though changes designed to enhance their influence came into effect during our field research, Michigan's chief judges had fewer powers than their counterparts in Pennsylvania. Michigan offered the equivalent of Pennsylvania's accelerated rehabilitative disposition (ARD) for defendants between ages seventeen and nineteen, the Youth Training Act (YTA). A YTA disposition could be granted for a wider variety of offenses, but in other respects was much like an ARD. Older defendants could have imposition of sentence deferred for a year, with dismissal of charges upon good behavior during that time provided the prosecutor concurred.

Finally, Michigan's political culture supported the notion of an active government. Many of the changes listed above resulted from citizen initiatives passed in statewide referendums. At the same time, the voters turned down proposals to cut taxes. A vigorous, statewide political elite fought the tax-limitation proposals, and felt responsible for undertaking on its own actions that seemed warranted. It enlarged and modernized the prison system in the years preceding our research, without which the higher incarceration rates and longer prison terms we found in Michigan could not have come to pass.

THE COURT'S ENVIRONMENT AND WORK

General Characteristics

Situated in the gently rolling hills of southwestern Michigan, Kalamazoo County exhibited a few similarities to and many differences from Erie County. Its population of 212,378 put it in approximately the same category as Erie, which had about 67,000 more people. Both grew slowly between 1970 and 1980, about one-half of 1 percent. Kalamazoo's black population, though larger (7.5 percent vs. 4.4 percent), was still quite small. Both counties had only a handful of incorporated localities, ten in Kalamazoo and fourteen in Erie; the major city in each contained about 40 percent of the population and most of the blacks.

One newspaper company and a television station served the city of Kalamazoo and surrounding territory. A newspaperman's description of the *Kalamazoo Gazette*'s character could apply just as well to Erie's morning and evening papers:

> Kalamazoo really has this positive self-image and it has a lot of good reasons for it. The newspaper, to a certain extent I think, has helped foster that feeling in the community and is very proud of it. They are perhaps more reluctant because of that to rock the boat, even when it knows there's a problem.

Kalamazoo's diversified economy, concentrated around the paper and chemical industries, had prospered compared to Erie's. Its per capita income of $7,769 exceeded Erie's by almost 17 percent; unemployment in both 1979 and 1980 was lower. While the Erie Standard Metropolitan Statistical Area (SMSA) lost the equivalent of 4.2 percent of its population because more people moved away than in, the Kalamazoo SMSA actually gained 2.2 percent. The physical appearance of the city, including its still-vigorous downtown shopping area, reflected its relative prosperity. The city still had its problems, including a slightly higher rate of people on public assistance than Erie, but overall enjoyed better economic health.

Kalamazoo's political tendencies reflected its greater prosperity, favoring the Republican party. The Republicans held a solid majority of eleven of the seventeen county commission seats. Democratic votes came mostly from the city of Kalamazoo, but were not numerous enough to offset GOP support in suburban and rural areas. Democrats had not had a victory in a county-wide race since 1934. The county consistently supported Republicans for state legislative offices as well, and gave large majorities to state-wide and national GOP candidates. Thus, the Republican candidate for governor in 1978 captured 65 percent of its votes; in 1980, Ronald Reagan won 58.8 percent. Overall, Kalamazoo's voting patterns made it a solid Republican county. One exception to this pattern was the U.S. congressman from the area, a Democrat, who won a series of tough, close races.

Our measure of ideology, which looked at voting patterns and representatives' roll-call votes, and which identified Erie as moderately liberal, placed Kalamazoo in the middle of our nine counties as moderate. The newspaper also took a middle-of-the-road line on most issues. When other Michigan communities experienced strong anti-tax movements, Kalamazoo's county commissioners voted for increased taxes to support its criminal justice system with a single dissenting vote, and its electorate approved the increase in a referendum. The presence of a cohesive, conservative, but civic-minded group of local business-owning families and three institutions of higher learning also contributed to Kalamazoo's moderate atmosphere.

Crime in Kalamazoo

In 1980, the Part I rate of serious crime per 100,000 reported to the FBI by the police reached 5,217, considerably above Erie's 3,420. As expected, 90 percent of these reported crimes involved property offenses. Kalamazoo's violent-crime rate of 411 per 100,000 far outstripped Erie's 297.9. The city contained only 37.5 percent of the county's population, from which came 77 percent of the reported violent crimes; property crimes showed a more even distribution, though the city of Kalamazoo still contributed more than its share, with 54 percent of the property crimes.[2] Just as Erie's rate of reported serious crime fell far below that found in Pennsylvania's major city, Philadelphia, so too did Kalamazoo's fall below that of Detroit. Detroit's serious crime rate was 10,642 per 100,000. Kalamazoo's rate also was about 20 percent below that of the state as a whole, which reported 6,676 per 100,000. Nevertheless, compared to Erie, Kalamazoo faced a fairly serious crime problem, as measured by crimes reported by the police to the FBI. When we looked at the ten-year average of FBI figures, Kalamazoo ranked third in the rate of reported personal crimes and first in property crime among the nine counties.[3]

We cannot compare reported crimes and arrests as we did for Erie because budget cuts in Michigan ended the publishing of arrest data. We have information on changes in the rates of reported crime, however. Reports of murder, rape, assault, and robbery showed some large swings, with a sharp increase from 1978 to 1979, and an even larger decrease for 1979 to 1980. Property crimes showed a similar pattern.

Cases and Defendants

Figure 6–1 displays the most serious charge at arrest for the sample of defendants in Kalamazoo. As in Erie, serious crimes against people were only about a quarter of the caseload. Erie's most common charge, drunk driving, practically never appeared in Kalamazoo. In Michigan, the lower courts disposed of such charges. Reflecting the high levels of property crimes reported, burglary, larceny, and other property crimes accounted for 55 percent of the charges in Kalamazoo.

Kalamazoo's defendants resembled Erie's in sex (85 percent vs. 86 percent male), and race (32.3 percent vs 29.2 percent black). The ratio of black defendants to their proportion of the county's population was 6.5 to 1, still high, but below Erie's 9.7 to 1. The absence

[2]For a discussion of patterns of crimes and crime rates in Kalamazoo (and the other eight counties), see Peter F. Nardulli, Roy B. Flemming, and James Eisenstein, *The Tenor of Justice* (Champaign-Urbana, Ill.: University of Illinois Press, 1987), Chapter 4.

[3]Ibid.

Figure 6–1

Composition of Kalamazoo County's 1980 Caseload:
Most Serious Charge at Arrest

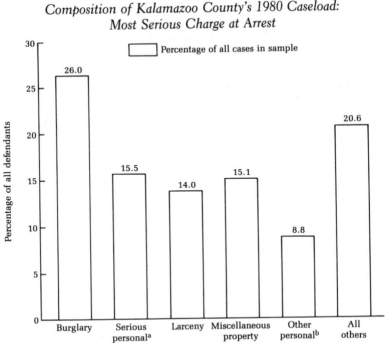

[a]Includes murder, manslaughter, rape, robbery, attempted robbery, aggravated assault.

[b]For example, simple assault.

In Kalamazoo, defendants charged with burglary formed the largest group, more than one-fourth of the caseload. All property crimes (burglary, larceny, and miscellaneous) accounted for more than half the caseload. Property crimes dominated, as in Erie; defendants charged with serious personal crimes were relatively infrequent.

Source: Kalamazoo sample of disposed cases

in the trial court, however, of defendants charged with drunk driving, who often are older and married, produced lower figures in Kalamazoo both for age and for the proportion married, which was about 15 percent. This difference may also help explain the sharp difference in the proportion of defendants who had no prior arrest. In Kalamazoo, only about one defendant in four (26.3 percent) was a first offender; in Erie, the rate was almost one in two (47.4 percent).

Our related measure of prior record, which combines data on arrests, conviction, and imprisonment, places Kalamazoo at the top among the nine counties in the seriousness of defendants' past criminal behavior. We will need to recall this fact during discussion of sentencing severity in Kalamazoo. Information on employment status for Kalamazoo indicated that only 45 percent of defendants had jobs.

COMPOSITION OF THE COURT COMMUNITY

The Defense Bar

Because there is no uniform system of county public defender's offices in Michigan, each county devised its own techniques for providing poor defendants with representation. Kalamazoo County signed a contract with a consortium of five experienced white male attorneys. They agreed to provide representation in at least 900 cases in return for $545,000, and to represent defendants after the first 1,100 for $545 a case. The signatories maintained separate practices in different firms, joined formally only by the contract and informally by their past association and friendship. Five other attorneys associated with them had been approved by the judges to share this work. The ten contract attorneys took weeklong turns representing all eligible defendants who appeared in the lower court during their week, and continued with these defendants throughout the case. Consequently, no matching of defendants or charges to the experience or skills of the attorneys took place.

These ten attorneys represented just under 80 percent of defendants in Kalamazoo. District judges determined eligibility, and their ill-defined and elastic standards had pushed estimates of the number of indigents needing representation during the two-year contract to about 1,500. The proportion of defendants who had publicly paid attorneys in Kalamazoo ranked first among our nine counties.

Because they handled so many cases, these ten attorneys' characteristics were significant in determining the criminal court community's composition and dynamics. Though somewhat fewer of them were hometown boys than Erie's public defenders, as a group these men had spent 60 percent of their life in the county, versus 81 percent for Erie. One of them specialized in criminal work; the rest devoted from 40 percent to 70 percent of their time to civil practice. But they had extensive experience in and knowledge of the criminal process. They averaged seven years in private practice; their average age of thirty-six topped that of public attorneys in every other county. Seven had served as assistant prosecutors, one as chief assistant.

Kalamazoo's contract attorneys' thorough knowledge of recent court history shaped their outlook and behavior much as it did for those in the Erie DA's office. In 1974, Kalamazoo replaced its old practice of appointing counsel for indigents from a roster of private attorneys with the contract system. The people we interviewed in 1980 cited a number of problems that plagued the group of attorneys who had won the first contracts in 1974 and 1975. They apparently provided a vigorous, careful, deliberate, and aggressive form of representation. A signatory of the 1979–1980 contract expressed his admiration for one of the original group's members, but added: "[H]e has a different philosophy. This may not be fair, but it's perceived as getting in bed with his client." A judge concurred, stating that the original group was

> going beyond what I felt a defense attorney owes his client. . . . They were hardworking, aggressive, but they were turning over rocks, filing every possible legal motion that could be filed in every case, and to some extent contributed to our backlog.

Others also attributed the backlog of cases that plagued Kalamazoo to the first group's style of practice. Another judge complained: "The first group we had, it took a day and a half to draw a jury, and we never recovered from it." The reluctance of that group to plea bargain also drew comment from this judge:

> I don't think they were representing their clients any better because they wouldn't plea bargain because it was contrary to their philosophy: "Every person is entitled to his day in court; therefore, we won't plea bargain." The present ones will plea bargain and get their client off on a better deal. . . .

One organizer of the current group of contract attorneys described what happened to the previous group. He claimed that their propensity to file motions led to personality conflicts with the prosecutor's office, causing the DAs to stiffen on plea bargains, and contributing to backlog. He commented that "[T]he judges, of course, were sick and tired of listening to those flakey, crappy motions—a lot of paper, a lot of time. Nothing ever got done—a terrible backlog." The judges let it be known to county officials that they were displeased and would prefer that another group seek the contract.

The new group clearly understood the financial implications that flowed from the first group's time-consuming tactics:

> The short of it is, they got burned on the contract. Either they didn't negotiate for enough dollars, or they spent too much time chasing rabbits. . . . And they went belly up financially. . . . So we sat down informally, over a few drinks, and got a list together of people we thought we could live with, and chatted with them, and came to the conclusion, "Yes. If the dollars are right, we'll do it. But we ain't doing it to do the county no favors." . . .
>
> So we negotiated what I felt was a pretty fair contract. It cost them double the money. We put an escalator in there. . . . We had a reputation for getting the job done, not too much fucking around, and we would handle it professionally. They took the gamble, and I think it's worked out for them.

Thus, the new group approached the job of representing four out of every five of Kalamazoo's defendants, keenly aware that the judges inspired replacement of the previous group because of its slowness in disposing of cases, inability to resolve cases by pleas, and contribution to the case backlog. They clearly resolved to avoid the financially disastrous consequences of locking themselves into representing a set number of defendants for a fixed fee, and then spending too much time on each case. Strong incentives to move cases joined with their knowledge of the consequencs of failing to do so. They felt they knew what to look for in police reports, knew when to waive preliminary hearings, knew how to avoid wasting time filing nitpicking motions, and knew how to maintain good relations with police and prosecutors. As a result, Kalamazoo's contract attorneys waived more than 60 percent of preliminary hearings, far more frequently than attorneys in the other counties.[4] They believed their style not only helped the county, the docket, and the judges, but also provided their clients with better representation.

Clearly, ideological convictions about the nobility of providing vigorous representation to the poor did not explain why Kalamazoo's publicly paid attorneys plied their trade. Their interest in financial

---

[4]For a discussion of the frequency with which defense attorneys waive preliminary hearings, and their reasons, see Roy B. Flemming, "The Client Game: Defense Attorney Perspectives on Their Relations with Criminal Clients," *American Bar Foundation Research Journal* (forthcoming, 1987).

rewards, coupled with their background as prosecutors, provided a self-evident explanation for their expressing strong belief in punishment and low regard for due process. The problem with this explanation is that they did *not* exhibit such attitudes (as Figure 6–3 will show). Their average "belief in punishment" score fell below that of Erie's public defenders, and below those of public defenders in four of the seven counties with an identifiable core group of such attorneys. Furthermore, they ranked approximately in the middle in their "regard for due process," just below that of Erie's defenders.

Kalamazoo's Judges

It is no surprise that some similarities appeared between the judges in Erie and Kalamazoo. Both found themselves enmeshed in the political system as they sought county funding to run the court and votes to win their job. These relatively superficial similarities, however, provided only a small counterweight to the many contrasts found between the two groups. Our brief depiction of Kalamazoo's bench revolves around the theme of contrast.

Kalamazoo's bench consisted of four older men, but three assumed the post late in their careers. Their average age of almost sixty-four exceeded that in the other eight counties, including Erie's relatively high 60.4 years, but only one, with ten years' experience, had served more than one six-year term. The bench averaged only a little more than six years' tenure, about half of Erie's figure. Two judges had come in 1974 and another in 1977. Though one man previously sat six years as a district judge and another twelve years as probate judge, the other two came directly from private practice. Unlike Erie, none had served in the district attorney's office. Four people served as court administrator between 1970 and 1980, including one regarded as incompetent and another who antagonized the County Board of Commissioners. In place of a chief judge who exercised strong control over a fairly cohesive and experienced bench, Kalamazoo had weak leadership and substantial internal conflict among its older but less experienced judges.

The lack of cohesion among Kalamazoo's judges deserves special emphasis, for it affected the entire character of the court community's operations. These differences stemmed not from partisan differences, for all four were Republicans, but from personal conflict. Procedures used to schedule and process cases provided a striking example. The court administrator scheduled the civil docket for two judges, but the other two insisted on doing their own scheduling. Two judges conducted pretrial conferences in criminal cases, bringing the opposing attorneys together to discuss the case. Two did not. Two held sentencing conferences in chambers with the attorneys prior to formal imposition of the sentence. Two did not. Finally, the pair who agreed that pretrial conferences should be held disagreed about the wisdom of sentencing conferences. Disagreement among the four judges on these two questions was complete. Evaluations of the four judges' operating styles by prosecutors and defense attorneys confirmed these sharp differences.

The two judges elected in 1974 not only disagreed on many questions affecting their work, but also clashed personally. Both sought to claim the grander of the two courtrooms to which their joint seniority entitled one of them. One felt the other was "prostituting" himself by participating in sentence bargaining. When it came time to seek a new term in 1980, they could not campaign as a team. One said:

> I don't want to campaign against him, nor does he want to campaign against me. And still, we're so different, we're not sure we want to make it as a slate either. . . . I would antagonize someone that he might not, and vice versa.

Both faced opponents, the first time in thirty years incumbents had been challenged, and one went down to defeat.

The chief judge in 1980 had assumed the post recently, and tried to grapple with the many problems of the court. He provided strong support to the court administrator, who in turn achieved some success in strengthening his office and repairing the court's reputation and working relationship with other government officials. He openly campaigned for passage of a tax hike proposed by the County Commissioners in order to build credibility with them. He identified nine objectives for the court, and sought to involve both the bar association and the other judges in achieving them:

> What I'm doing is making each one of those guys a part of answering the problems as we go along, rather than just saying, "Okay, here's what we're going to do." They participate in, and help make, the decisions. So in a sense, it's a consensus thing. Now, sometimes I've got to say, "This is the way it's going to be." But not very often.

His ability to impose decisions, in any event, fell short of that of the Erie President Judge. Kalamazoo had no strong tradition of leadership. The chief judge was elected, and for just a two-year term. He himself had come to the bench only three years before.

An attorney familiar with the court's dynamics summarized for us the status of relations among the judges:

> There is no singleness of purpose on our circuit bench. For a long time there has never been an instance where one judge would say, "I don't agree with it, but for the good of the whole, I will suppress my desires and go with the majority." Never!

The lack of cohesion led to difficulties for the court. The judges could not achieve common policy in controversial matters. A series of cases arose from a highly publicized investigation of homosexual conduct in a public restroom along U.S. Highway 131. Each of the judges faced the question of whether videotapes could be introduced as evidence. Rather than adopting a uniform policy, each judge issued an individual opinion at a different time. They split two to two on the question of admissibility. Nor could the court deal effectively with its backlog of cases, a problem that had persisted since at least 1976. Its powerlessness to reduce the backlog drew private criticism from the bar and public scolding from the District Attorney.

Three of the judges filled out the attitude questionnaires. Despite the conservatism of Kalamazoo, their average score on the "belief-in-punishment" scale fell below that of the Erie judges. Indeed, it was the lowest among all nine counties. Their average "regard for due process" surpassed the relatively low score of the Erie judges. Despite their persistent docket problems, it is interesting that only one other county's judges ranked lower than Kalamazoo on another scale measuring "concern with efficiency" in processing cases.

Prosecutor's Office

The district attorney's office in Kalamazoo exercised dominance equivalent to that of the judges in Erie. The DA realized influence aspired to but not yet acquired by Erie's prosecutor. In one sense, Kalamazoo's elected prosecutor also was a newcomer. He had moved to the county in 1969 to join the prosecutor's office, after serving in the Sheriff's Department in Wayne County (which includes Detroit). Promoted to chief assistant, he won the office in his own right in 1976 when his boss declined to seek reelection.

Several attributes of the office contributed to its strong influence. Though Kalamazoo County had fewer people, its DA's office employed nineteen full-time attorneys, compared to Erie's combined total of nine part- and full-timers. Ten experienced assistants, all white, nine male, primarily handled felony cases. A staff of twelve provided clerical and administrative support. Salaries started at a modest $14,000, but rapidly jumped. Trial attorneys received a minimum of $22,000; attorneys with five years' experience made more than $32,000. The high salaries helped explain why the average tenure in the office exceeded five years, considerably above the 3.7 years for all prosecutors in our study.

A vigorous "management" tradition characterized the office. An office policy and procedure manual first appeared in 1969. The first assistant assumed responsibility for reviewing guilty pleas in 1972. At a time the DA's office in Erie unsuccessfully struggled to make a newly purchased computer work, Kalamazoo had been using a computer-based case-management system for several years, and had a well-functioning word-processing operation. Scrutiny of assistants' work occurred regularly as a matter of established tradition. Office forms and procedures facilitated such review. Case files included a form asking for a "ranking" from one to ten of the case's strength by the attorney handling it at each stage. An administrator's description of the case-ranking system illustrates well the centralization and management orientation that characterized its entire operation:

> Since we rank them periodically, I'd take a look. At the time it was issued it's been ranked on a scale of one to ten, let's see where it lies. At the time of the preliminary examination, the bindover, it's ranked again. At the time of certification, it's ranked by another attorney. And then at the time of disposition, it's ranked by the attorney who wrote the disposition. So basically, if I'm looking at a seven, eight, and nine, and all of a sudden it's a four, there better be some specific data as to why it all of a sudden turned to garbage. . . .

Recruitment patterns reflected the office's management orientation. Despite the overwhelmingly Republican leaning of the county, the office did not make partisan loyalty a condition of employment. The ten felony assistants included a Democrat, four Republicans, and five Independents. Nor did assistants need to be "home towners." In fact, the ten felony assistants had spent an average of only

22 percent of their lives in Kalamazoo county, tied for lowest with Du Page among the nine counties.

The structure of the office also contributed to its formal atmosphere and centralization. Four categories or ranks for assistants, each carrying progressively higher pay and greater responsibility, presented a stable and established career ladder to new personnel. Attorneys rotated among several defined assignments weekly: reviewing police requests for arrest warrants; conducting preliminary hearings; conducting internal review of cases going to trial, called "certification"; and handling cases scheduled for trial. This arrangement meant the office, as in Erie, used discontinuous deployment of its assistants to cases. Some matching of attorneys' experience and skill to cases occurred when defendants were scheduled for trial. Defendants identified as career criminals or charged with consumer fraud were assigned to prosecutors assigned to units specializing in such cases.

As a consequence of these factors, Kalamazoo's DA exercised much tighter control over his assistants than Erie's prosecutor, and this supervision came through formal as well as informal channels. His assistant in charge of the trial division checked to see that the policy guidelines described below were followed. The trial chief approved settlements in all cases scheduled for trial. A top official described the trial chief's role colorfully: "He's the lightning rod. There's no question about it. The defense bar dislikes him. The judges dislike him. Cops dislike him because many times on warrant screening he handled it."

Because the office had long engaged in tight supervision of its staff, many accepted it as a fact of life. But like attorneys everywhere, some were resentful that professionals like themselves were so closely supervised, like this assistant:

> You'll find people here that are somewhat irked, and I am at times, by having my professional judgment second-guessed or not having the discretion I think I should have. But I knew that when I started here. It's not that he doesn't trust me or is in some way out to affront me. It's just that he feels that's the best way he can serve the public.

At the Kalamazoo prosecutor's office, substantial resources for innovating were augmented by aggressive pursuit of additional funding. A successful application to the federal government provided money to establish a Career Criminal Prosecution Unit. The office persuaded the county to take over funding when the federal grant expired, allowing it to keep the prosecution unit. It also had a Victim/Witness Assistance Unit and a Citizen's Probation Authority to run a diversion program. A federal grant to establish a Consumer and Commercial Fraud Unit still funded that program in 1980. Erie's prosecutor wanted to establish similar special units, but had no money for any of them.

The DA's office mobilized its personnel in a conscious effort to implement a package of explicit policies. The abbreviated description below is focused on the two policies that count most for our analysis: screening of warrants and guilty pleas.

Kalamazoo's DA took full advantage of the opportunity Michigan law gave him to decide which of the defendants the police wanted to charge would in fact be prosecuted, and for what crimes. All assistants rotated on warrant duty for one-week stints. The primary standard the office wanted them to apply was "trial sufficiency." As an assistant described it:

> We feel that we require more than probable cause to believe the defendant committed this crime, which is all the police have to operate on. . . . [W]e aren't in this business just to convict and have great conviction rates. So we don't issue just on cases that we feel will result in conviction. . . . [T]he boss's philosophy would be that we go on what's called "reasonable probability of conviction." And that is, if everything goes the way it looks like it should go in the police report, this person should be convicted of this crime.

In other words, cases which *might* produce a conviction by a plea but which also might end in acquittal if taken to trial would be declined for prosecution. This is the most stringent standard that can be applied, and contrasts sharply with the total absence of any opportunity for prosecutor screening at arrest in Erie.

A second guideline used at the warrant stage was meant, in the view of one official, to implement the prosecutor's goal of

> providing differential treatment to the people who commit crimes instead of focusing on just the crimes themselves. It recognizes that there are different classes of individuals who commit crimes and, in order to be effective, the prosecutor must tailor his response to the types of individuals that he prosecutes. Hence, the approach of diversion for the first-time offender and career criminal for the patterned recidivist.

Many first offenders committing less serious property offenses were screened immediately by referring them to the office's diversion agency, the Citizen's Probation Authority (CPA). These defendants accepted "voluntary probation" for four months to a year under the office's supervision. They paid a program fee ($70 to $100) or engaged in volunteer work, and made restitution. In 1979, the CPA successfully handled 141 individuals, reducing the caseload by roughly 15 percent. Most of the cases diverted to the CPA in Kalamazoo would have produced a full-blown case in Erie — arrest, arraignment, preliminary hearing, and trial court appearance — ending in Pennsylvania's form of diversion, ARD.

Accuracy of charges was a third element in warrant policy. The office wanted defendants charged with crimes that could be proven. It disavowed the practice common in many jurisdictions called "overcharging," that is consciously charging a more serious crime than the facts warranted (such as attempted murder rather than assault) in anticipation of a plea agreement down to the lower offense. The office policies on pleas described below could not have been implemented without accurate charges.

A final component of the warrant process impinged on plea agreements. The assistant authorizing a warrant also established a "bottom-line" plea that could not be lowered by assistants handling the preliminary hearing without explicit approval. A new bottom line, based on the increased information available after the preliminary hearing, was determined for the trial court stage. These bottom lines built an additional administrative control into the office's supervision techniques.

Warrant policies produced several significant consequences. First, many cases that would have gone to Erie's trial court left the system at the arrest stage in Kalamazoo. Records compiled by the prosecutor's office for 1974 through 1978 showed an average of 21 percent of the warrant requests were referred to the Citizens Probation Authority and 36 percent were denied outright. Only 43 percent survived and entered the system. Second, the caseload in Kalamazoo's trial court had a higher proportion of serious crimes than in Erie. Third, most defendants faced only one charge. Figure 6-2 illustrates the sharp differences between Kalamazoo and Erie in the number of counts charged that resulted from their charging practices. The data for Erie are the same as depicted in Figure 5-1. Other information about charges shows the same pattern. Only 16 percent of

Figure 6–2

*Comparison of Number of Charges at Arrest in Erie and Kalamazoo
for Convicted Defendants, 1980*

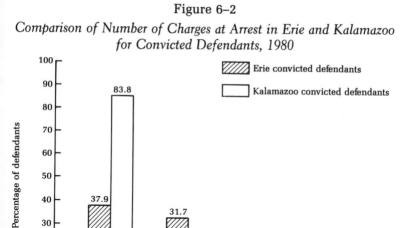

Unlike Erie, convicted defendants in Kalamazoo almost always faced only
one initial charge. Just 16 percent had multiple charges, nearly one-fourth
the frequency of multiple charges in Erie. Charging practices differed radically.

Source: 1980 case samples of convicted defendants

defendants in Kalamazoo had more than one charge, 5 percent lower
than the next county (St. Clair), and only one third the level of Erie's
48 percent. The average number of charges was only 1.21, also the
lowest and far below Erie's 1.87.

The office's policy on plea agreements flowed naturally from the
DA's commitment to "credibility."

> I guess it goes back to my background as a police officer and
> the concept of people being held accountable. The prosecutor
> can either take a plea to a lesser charge and then not get in-
> volved in the sentencing ... or the prosecutor can establish
> somewhat of a hard line, which I believe gives the criminal jus-
> tice system, not just the prosecutor's office, credibility in the
> community. . . .

He clearly felt that a hard line meant charging and convicting people for the crime they actually had committed, regardless of sentence. He recognized the importance of sentences, but believed the public especially disliked charge bargaining. He obviously responded to the belief:

> An elimination of plea bargaining [here, count bargaining] in some respects is cosmetic. Yet it's something that the public sees and they say, "Okay, good. Those guys are doing their job because this is what we want."

The goal of striving for "on-the-nose" pleas thus precluded routine bargaining over the seriousness of charges. The practice of charging most defendants with a single offense, of course, eliminated the possibility of dropping the number of charges most of the time. Refusal to reduce the seriousness of the charge as a matter of policy produced a perspective on sentence agreements that was the direct opposite of Erie's. A prosecutor worked through this logic for us. He acknowledged that "nobody likes to lose," requiring a "save-face philosophy" in dealings with opposing attorneys:

> The defense attorney's got to get something for his client. He just can't go in there and lay down and roll over dead. Maybe once or twice, but he'll get you later on. So you've got to give him something. You've got to give the defendant something. And so we give them bond recommendations, sentence recommendations, restitution, no restitution, six months in jail, two days in jail, expungement, a whole host of things.

Thus, Kalamazoo's prosecutors saw nothing wrong with sentence agreements, and felt none of the hesitation in making judgments about what punishment was most appropriate that their counterparts in Erie did. Instead, they avoided bargains reducing the seriousness of the charges. Given their role in shaping sentences, the content of beliefs about punishment become particularly important. Interestingly, despite the fairly high crime rate, Kalamazoo prosecutors and judges held moderate views compared to those of other counties. Prosecutors in only one other county, St. Clair, held less punishment-oriented attitudes. On the "regard for due process" scale, Kalamazoo's prosecutors ranked sixth. In keeping with the office's management orientation, its members average on the "concern for efficiency" scale proved to be considerably higher than any other county's.

Geography, Influence, and Relationships in the Court Community

More than 400 attorneys comprised the bar in Kalamazoo County. The criminal court community's core at the trial court level, however, consisted of just twenty-four people—four circuit judges, ten prosecutors, and ten contract attorneys. Even adding the seven district judges, court administrator, and other personnel, the core group was quite small. So little business remained for private attorneys that few could get enough clients to become regulars. The same newspaper reporter had covered the courts for·twelve years, and enjoyed the confidence of and access to judges and prosecutors. In effect, he became a regular member of the community, and engaged in little criticism or in-depth analysis. Clearly, the members of the core community were very familiar with one another.

In Erie, the courthouse sat on the fringes of a declining downtown business district. In Kalamazoo, it faced a beautiful park in the center of the city, surrounded by a still-vigorous business district. The city hall, steepled churches, municipal auditorium, and other noncommercial buildings also bordered the park.

The layout of the courthouse helped shape the court community's interactions. With no office in the building, the contract attorneys' communications with one another depended on encounters during their frequent appearances representing clients. The prosecutors used a separate elevator, causing them to enter and leave the courthouse lobby without running into other regulars. Interestingly, their offices occupied the top floor, above the judges. The arrangement of the judges' chambers mirrored and contributed to the splits among them. The offices were paired at either end of the same floor. The two who did not get along shared one end, helping isolate both from the other two. Unlike Erie, with its justice courts scattered throughout the county, the district court that served much of the county outside the city of Kalamazoo occupied the first floor, ensuring that news of its decisions rapidly entered the courthouse grapevine.

The contract attorneys formed the core of experienced, established insiders defending criminals in Kalamazoo. They lacked the zeal of the legal purists who had previously held the contract. They had neither the inclination nor organizational cohesion to mount major challenges to existing procedures. They experienced none of the attempts to impose policies or controls from above that Erie's public defenders did. The comments of one in response to a question about client control summarized nicely the attitudes of Kalamazoo's contract attorneys toward their role:

> So I think that client control is a key. . . . I tell them that I'm not gonna be their friend. . . . I'm charged with defending them on this charge, and I will fight for them and I will be honest with them. I don't know whether I'm gonna get them off or not, and that's what the ground rules are and they understand it.

The judges, old but not experienced, split among themselves, suffering strained relations with the County Commissioners, and the object of criticism from the bar for failing to solve their docket problems, exerted far less influence on the court community's operations than did their brethren in Erie.

The weakness of the judges and the contract attorneys' lack of organization and motivation left the field open to the prosecutor. He seized the opportunity to implement a series of policies. His easy reelection victory in 1980 strengthened his position. The prestige of the office also contributed to its dominance over the community. It served as a stepping-stone to other important positions. In 1980, former members of the office held these positions: the county's appointed executive; the county's director of management and budget; the head of the criminal justice commission; the county probate judge; the newly elected circuit judge, who defeated an incumbent in 1980; and a newly elected district court judge.

Analyzing the differences in age among judges, prosecutors, and defense attorneys showed as large a gap between the judges and the other two positions as in Erie. Neither prosecutors nor contract attorneys could approach the judges as contemporaries. Clearly, huge turnover loomed not too many years in the future. The average age of the prosecutors and defense attorneys who opposed one another in our sample of cases was identical, however. They dealt with each other as generational equals. Differences in overall influence stemmed from other sources.

The distinctive position of the prosecutor's staff appears clearly from the comparison of their attitudes toward punishment and their regard for due process to those of the judges and contract attorneys. As Figure 6–3 shows, they expressed views in conflict with both the judges and defense attorneys.

Figure 6–3

Average Standard Scores on Attitude Scales, by Position, in Kalamazoo

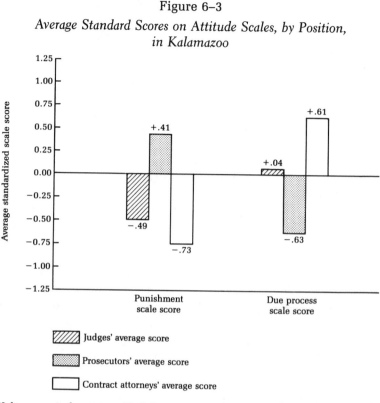

Kalamazoo judges resembled the contract attorneys in their "belief in punishment," but fell between them and the prosecutors in "regard for due process." The contract attorneys and prosecutors differed among themselves sharply on both measures.

THE COURT COMMUNITY'S TECHNOLOGY

Kalamazoo employed too few judges to permit specialization in their docket assignments. All four presided over a mixed docket of civil and criminal cases. They conducted trials only during designated weeks, with each judge taking only civil or criminal cases during any one trial period. In basic structure, then, Kalamazoo joined Erie as a "mixed-docket" "periodic-rotating" trial term system (see Figure 2–1).

Kalamazoo used a pure individual calendar system, with cases as-

signed to judges using a random-draw procedure at the preliminary
hearing stage, and the prosecutor's office deciding when each judge's
cases would be heard. At an earlier time, the judges had followed a
predictable pattern. In 1976, two judges heard criminal cases for a
three-week period, and the other two took other matters at five times
during the year. The two judges each spent fifteen weeks on criminal
trials. By 1980, regularity disintegrated. Each judge determined how
many weeks he would hear criminal cases and which weeks they
would be. The court administrator took over the task of docketing
cases assigned through the random draw, but had to accommodate
each judge's decision on which weeks were available. The more serious the charge and the older the case, the higher in the queue the
court administrator positioned it.

Because of continuing backlogs, the purity of the individual calendar had to be compromised in June 1980. The court administrator
began to shift cases from the courtroom to which they had been
assigned through the random draw based on the availability of another courtroom in the classic mold of master-calendar technology.
If this system was not complicated enough, recall that two judges
allowed the court administrator to schedule their civil work, two did
not.

Prior to this reform, Kalamazoo's case-assignment system left no
room for interplay of personalties, cajoling of the court administrator,
or routing of pleas to a specific judge that led to guilty pleas in Erie.
Uncertainty about what judge would hear a plea ended after the preliminary hearing at the time the defendant was arraigned in the trial
court, months before Erie defendants knew this information. To the
extent that the judge's identity shaped attorneys' behavior in assessing the content of pleas, it operated early in the life of a case. We
have no information about any changes induced by the court administrator's new procedures.

The contract attorney providing publicly paid representation to
poor defendants stuck with his client throughout the life of a case.
As we saw, however, the prosecutor's office shifted responsibilities.
When cases reached the point where they were set for a specific
week in a courtroom, they were handled by the prosecutor assigned
to take all cases that appeared in that courtroom during the week.
Thus, unlike Erie, where last-minute assignments of prosecutors to
cases set for trial sent different people into a judge's courtroom during a trial term, Kalamazoo prosecutors stayed in the same place for
a week waiting for cases to come to them.

DISPOSITION OF CASES IN KALAMAZOO

Figures 6-1 and 6-2 depicted two major characteristics of the cases that came to Kalamazoo's trial court, the number and content of charges. Burglary, larceny, and other property crimes accounted for more than 55 percent of the cases. As in Erie, one in seven cases involved serious crimes of violence. Defendants typically faced only one charge.

Bail decisions in Kalamazoo proved to be considerably more stringent than in Erie. Erie released more than twice as many defendants on their own recognizance (ROR) at the initial bail hearing (58.7 percent vs. 24.6 percent). In its place, Kalamazoo district judges imposed 10 percent deposit bonds. Defendants able to come up with 10 percent of the amount of the bond recovered most of their deposit in a refund. Almost half of Kalamazoo's defendants had the opportunity to post the 10 percent deposit. The less frequent use of ROR helps explain Kalamazoo's lower rate of release. In Erie, 84 percent of defendants ultimately won release at some time before their cases ended, the highest rate among our counties. Kalamazoo released only 64 percent, a shade above the lowest rate of 63 percent in Peoria. As Figure 5-2 shows, fewer defendants won their pretrial freedom in Kalamazoo than in either Erie or Du Page for three categories of seriousness based on prior record. The dollar amount of bail was higher than Erie's for three of four selected offenses.[5]

Figure 6-4 summarizes how cases ended in Kalamazoo. The overall conviction rate of more than 90 percent exceeds Erie's 85 percent slightly. As we saw, prosecutors at the preliminary hearing already had a bottom-line plea established at the time the office authorized the warrant. Two policies of the DA's office encouraged preliminary hearing pleas. A defense attorney described one — making plea offers less attractive after the preliminary hearing:

> R: Not all the time, but frequently, if you have an exam [preliminary hearing], the price goes up.
> I: You mean in terms of what the office wants for a plea?
> R: Yeah. If you want to plead now to attempt, fine. If you want to go through the exam, the deal's off. We have no deal.
> I: Will they stick to that?
> R: Oh, yes.

[5]See Eisenstein et al., "Explaining and Assessing," op cit., Chapter 5. For example, the median bail set for armed-robbery defendants in Kalamazoo was $24,900; in Erie it was $5,000. For theft, Kalamazoo's median was $1,278, whereas it was close to zero in Erie (that is, most theft defendants were released without having to meet bail).

Figure 6–4

*Comparison of Method of Disposition for Erie and Kalamazoo
Trial Defendants, 1980*

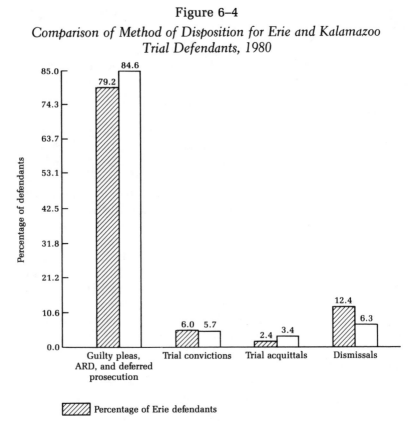

Percentage of Erie defendants

Percentage of Kalamazoo defendants

Conviction rates in Kalamazoo, as in Erie, were very high. Only minor differences in the disposition pattern appeared, with a few more convictions and a few less dismissals in Kalamazoo.

Source: Erie and Kalamazoo case samples

The second, an "open-file" policy, worked in tandem with the first. According to one defense attorney:

> They have an open-file policy. What they usually do is just give us their file, everything in it. Even their evaluation. Now what that does is two things. It gives us a clear evaluation of the case at the outset. It does away with the necessity of having to file

discovery motions. And it also clears up a lot of preliminary examinations that we used for discovery purposes only.

Thus, several factors contributed to the low 6.3 percent rate of dismissal. Warrant screening and the prosecutor's presence at the preliminary hearing washed out most poor cases before they got to circuit court. Eliminating other cases by early diversion and guilty pleas obtained at the preliminary hearing allowed the office to devote more attention to the cases that remained.

Frequent mention of the case-backlog problem suggested that cases would take a long time to be resolved. Our case-file data make it possible to compare disposition times across courts. Figure 6–5 presents these data for Erie, Kalamazoo, and Du Page, in the form of a "box-and-whiskers" diagram. To produce it, we ranked all cases according to their length from arrest to disposition and determined the age of the case that ended faster than 75 percent of all cases. That figure, 110 days in Erie, 33 days in Kalamazoo, and 113 days in Du Page, forms the left side of the boxes. The time elapsed for the case ending quicker than 25 percent of all cases forms the right side. The case that took the median amount of time defines the midline. The "whiskers" extending from the left and right show how quickly 10 percent and 90 percent of the cases took. For example, in Kalamazoo, 10 percent of the cases thus took more than 415 days.

Figure 6–5 does not confirm that Kalamazoo disposed of its whole caseload in an especially tardy fashion. In fact, it was quicker than either Erie or Du Page in several respects. Many cases ended quickly, before the preliminary hearing, drawing the bottom of the box down. The median case ended somewhat sooner as well. Some cases took longer, however. One-quarter of them took longer than 277 days in Kalamazoo, compared to 256 in Du Page and 239 in Erie. In fact, the overall speed of Kalamazoo depended on the cases disposed of very early. Once cases got past the preliminary hearing to arraignment in trial court, the median time to disposition jumped to 147 days and the slowest 25 percent of them took at least 275 days. These data suggest that indeed Kalamazoo's trial court did take a relatively long time to complete the processing of defendants. In fact, it was the slowest, as measured from the time elapsed between arraignment in the trial court and final disposition.[6]

[6]See Roy B. Flemming, Peter F. Nardulli, and James Eisenstein, "The Timing of Justice in Felony Trial Courts," *Law and Policy* (forthcoming, 1987).

Figure 6–5

*Days from Arrest to Disposition
for all Cases in Du Page, Kalamazoo, and Erie*

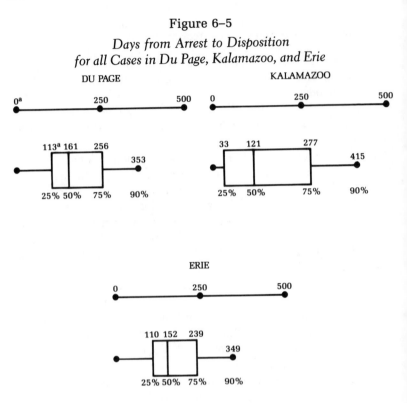

^ain days

Kalamazoo disposed of one-quarter of its cases within 33 days, much quicker than Du Page or Erie; its median case length of 121 days also fell below the other two counties. But it took longer to finish those cases that did not end quickly. Dispositions varied in complex ways among the three counties.

Kalamazoo's Guilty-Plea System

With nearly 85 percent of trial court defendants pleading guilty, Kalamazoo's guilty-plea system obviously succeeded in avoiding trials. How did it work?

Like Erie's guilty-plea system, the answer requires describing a fairly complex and subtle process. In most respects, the patterns we found in Kalamazoo differed sharply from those in Erie. Table 6–1 summarizes the principal differences. In our brief description of Kalamazoo's guilty-plea system that follows, we will translate the entries in Table 6–1 into an understanding of the dynamics of its court community's day-to-day operation.

Random assignment of cases to the individual calendars of the four judges provided few opportunities to alter the luck of the draw. That which Erie's technology made possible and its traditions made common simply did not exist in Kalamazoo. Introduction of provisions for moving cases between courtrooms in the midst of our field research in 1980 opened the possibility that attorneys would develop methods of routing. But discussions over which judge would hear a plea and impose sentence had not yet become part of the guilty-plea system we studied.

Erie judges publicly expressed their horror at being told what sentences should be imposed, and most of them privately stuck to this position. Discussions between prosecution and defense about what agreed-upon sentence would be recommended usually did not occur in Erie. When they occasionally did, they typically involved not specific recommendations but agreements to stand mute or at most indicate no objection to probation. In Kalamazoo, where agreements

Table 6–1

Features of Guilty-Plea System

	Kalamazoo	Erie
1. Is "routing" part of plea agreements?	Almost never	Very often
2. Do prosecutors recommend sentences agreed upon with the defense?	Often	Rarely
3. Is judge participation in plea negotiations considered legitimate?	Split	Mostly no
4. Are the number of counts charged lowered as part of agreements?	Rarely	Very often
5. Is the seriousness of the primary charge lowered as part of plea agreements?	Rarely	Rarely

between prosecution and defense on what sentence recommendation would be presented provided the driving force for the guilty-plea system, the judges took a different view.

Analysis of court records could not detect the presence of sentence recommendations, but it did confirm the *absence* of both types of count bargaining. Only 15.8 percent of the guilty-plea cases involved any type of reduction, a sharp contrast to Erie's 59.1 percent. Drops in the *seriousness* of the prior charge occurred in neither jurisdiction very often, 12.8 percent in Kalamazoo and 8.6 percent in Erie. Drops in the *number* of charges, however, accompanied 12.2 percent of Kalamazoo's guilty pleas and more than 59 percent of Erie's. As a Kalamazoo prosecutor quoted earlier observed, the defense had to be given *something,* and the "something" that remained involved sentence recommendations.

Guilty-plea systems that rely on prosecutor-defense agreement on sentence recommendations depend on the judges to follow the recommendations. Defendants would be understandably displeased if they entered a plea, heard the prosecutor tell the judge he and the defense attorney agreed that probation would be appropriate, and spent the next three years in the state prison. The interviews suggested what logical analysis predicted: the judges by and large imposed sentences at or close to what was recommended. A defense attorney's discussion of the practice expressed a common view:

> I think that when a recommendation is part of a plea bargain, the judges in this county know that obviously you've worked it out. I think the last time I saw the prosecutor's fancy statistics on that, through his computers, something like 96 percent of the cases when a recommendation was part of the plea bargain, the judge went along with it or was more lenient.

Not all guilty pleas included an understanding on what the prosecutor's recommendation would be, especially in more serious cases. Depending on who the judge was, alternative ways of affecting sentences could be used. As we saw earlier, two judges routinely held pretrial conferences. They provided an opportunity for judicial participation in bargaining. It is difficult, though, to know precisely how far these judges went, and how often, in indicating during such conferences what sentence they would impose. A judge who refused to hold them and considered the practice improper presented one view of how they worked:

> Well, in sentence bargaining here, the judge doesn't say, "Look, I'll give you two to five." His bargain is, "Well, if everything is equal, it looks to me for this kind of an offense that you probably will get two to five unless the presentence report indicates something else." But, you know, that is the kind of thing attorneys are really counting on.

Many people indicated, however, the judges rarely engaged in such "ball-parking" of sentences. One judge who held pretrial conferences told us: "I have on rare occasions, but I have never said, 'Okay, if you'll belly up on this charge, then I'll sentence this.' I don't think we do it here as a practice."

The other described his role in more detail:

> On plea bargaining I touch base. Now the judge should not ethically get into the negotiating of plea bargaining. But, on the other hand, I think the judge can ask about it. . . . At the bottom of my form letter I draft for criminal pretrials, I would put in whether or not the court expressed any proposed sentencing. I don't use that very often, but I did use it. . . .

The sentencing conferences that two judges conducted in chambers before pronouncing punishment in open court on convicted defendants offered defense attorneys another alternative to explicit agreements with prosecutors. They could enter a straight plea without any understanding with the prosecutor on sentence recommendation, relying on their credibility with the judge to argue for an acceptable sentence during the conference. A defense attorney described what sometimes took place:

> We have sentence conferences in chambers and I prefer that because you can really do a lot better for your client than if you have to get up and put on a show in front of the judge. You can say, "Judge, yeah, this guy has got problems. He may be a jerk, but you shouldn't send him to prison. And I'll be honest with you—give him thirty days in the slammer." And quite often if you maintain that credibility, you find over a period of time that you start getting more of what you want from the judges.

Two other features of Kalamazoo's guilty-plea system merit a brief note. First, both judges and contract attorneys encountered strong incentives that encouraged pleas. The judges' lingering case backlog made the trial time saved by pleas especially valuable. The contract attorneys received the same compensation whether they pled or engaged in a lengthy trial; quick pleas produced the same income and more time to engage in their private practice.

Second, the DA's practice of requiring the approval for guilty pleas of the trial division's chief magnified his importance in the guilty-plea system. He held strong law-enforcement views, and was the ideal person to implement the DA's hard line in sentencing. The DA deliberately injected the trial chief into negotiations as a strategy to stengthen the office's position. One administrator explained:

> One of the basic tenets of negotiation is: never send anybody to negotiate who has the ultimate authority to make decisions. That way, the people who negotiate always have the option of saying, "Well, hey! I'm still your friend and I like you, and we got to continue to negotiate, but let me take it back to the bastard who [approves bargains]."

If the DA sought to make the chief of the trial division a lightning rod for criticism, he succeeded nicely. "We have a third-in-command up in the prosecutor's office," a judge told us, "a nice guy, good lawyer, but he has a very tough attitude." An exasperated defense attorney was less circumspect:

> I can't begin to explain [him]. He's okay to go out and have a beer with. But time after time he takes this bull-headed, unreasonable approach.... And we've got a major case backlog in Kalamazoo. But it's not true. We don't have any backlog. What we have is [the trial chief] being unreasonable in accepting pleas.

Indeed, the trial rate in Kalamazoo, though low in absolute terms at 9.1 percent of dispositions, ranked second highest among the nine counties.

Severity of Sentences

Kalamazoo seemed to face a more serious crime problem than Erie. The defendants who came to the trial court more often had a prior criminal record. As we show in Chapter Eight, Michigan's criminal code called for harsher sentences than Pennsylvania's, and its prison capacity was larger. The county's residents were conservative, but not rigidly so. The prosecutor and his administrators had earned reputations as hard-liners. The case backlog and the method of providing defense counsel to the poor, however, provided incentives to end cases through pleas, and the attitudes of both judges and prosecutors displayed less belief in punishment.

Some of these characteristics point to harsh sentences, but others predict leniency. What actually happened to convicted defendants in Kalamazoo?

To facilitate comparison to Erie, we present again the information on Erie's sentences with data from Kalamazoo added. Figure 6–6 shows the distribution of type of sentences. The proporitions show what happened to those defendants who not only got to the trial court, but were convicted. Clearly, Kalamazoo incarcerated convicted defendants far more often, especially in the penitentiary.

The sentences depicted in Figure 6–6 accurately depict differences in how trial-level defendants fared. But we must recall that in Kalamazoo, defendants who would have gone to Erie's trial court only to receive ARD were diverted to the Citizen's Probation Authority at the warrant stage, or in drunk-driving cases, disposed of in the lower court. Differences in the type of sentence therefore would not be as sharp if the comparison group were all people who come to the atttention of the police.

Figure 6–7 avoids the problems posed by differences in the mixture of defendants and charges by looking at incarceration rates for the four crimes listed in Figure 5–5. That table provides information on conviction rates, and the proportion of arrestees and those convicted who were incarcerated. To avoid too complicated a chart, Figure 6–7 compares Erie and Kalamazoo on just one of these measures—the proportion of convicted defendants incarcerated for each of the four offenses.

Kalamazoo consistently sent a higher proportion of its convicted defendants to prison, particularly for larceny and drug charges. Data on the percentage of defendants convicted for these four offenses, not shown in Figure 6–7, also found higher rates for Kalamazoo in each case. The same is true for the proportion of arrestees incarcerated.

Figure 6–8 compares the length of the median expected minimum sentences for defendants who were arrested for the four crimes and who were convicted and incarcerated. For the less serious charges involving theft and hard drugs, the sentences defendants received

Figure 6–6

*Comparison of Distribution of Sentences Imposed on Erie
and Kalamazoo Defendants, 1980*

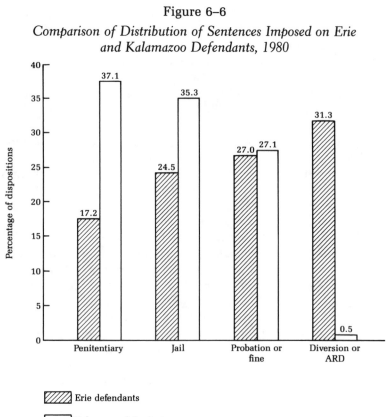

Kalamazoo treated convicted defendants much more harshly than Erie did,
sending substantially more to the penitentiary (20 percent) and to the county
jail (11 percent). Kalamazoo practically never gave defendants Michigan's
equivalent of ARD, an option given to almost one-third of Erie's convicted
defendants.

Source: Erie and Kalamazoo case samples

differed little; Erie imposed a median sentence longer by four months
on larceny defendants sent to jail, though often the actual time spent
in the Erie County jail was much less. For defendants arrested for
armed robbery and burglary, however, Kalamazoo defendants faced
significantly longer prison terms. For burglary, the difference

Figure 6–7

Comparison of Percentage of Convicted Defendants Incarcerated for Four Selected Arrest Charges in Erie and Kalamazoo, 1980

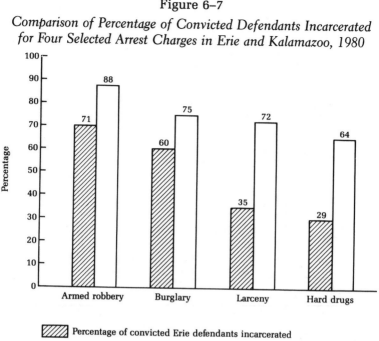

Kalamazoo consistently incarcerated a higher proportion of convicted defendants initially charged with each of four separate common offenses than Erie. The discrepancy was especially great for larceny and hard drugs.

Source: Erie and Kalamazoo case samples

amounted to almost a year; for armed robbery, three years and three months.

Other summary measures of sentence severity mentioned in Chapter Five confirm the severity of Kalamazoo's dispositions. The satistical analysis of sentencing, taking into account differences in the seriousness of offenses and prior criminal records, which placed Erie in the middle of the nine counties, identified Kalamazoo as the harshest. If we examine only sentences imposed on defendants with prior records, Kalamazoo's lead as harshest punisher increases. As we saw in Chapter Five, both Erie and Kalamazoo exhibited fairly

Figure 6–8

*Comparison of Median Months of Minimum Sentence Given
to Erie and Kalamazoo Defendants Incarcerated
for Selected Arrest Charges, 1980*

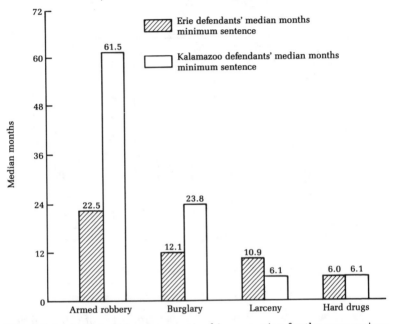

When defendants in Kalamazoo received incarceration for the more serious offenses of armed robbery and burglary, the length exceeded that imposed in Erie by substantial margins, more than three years and about one year respectively. For larceny and hard-drug defendants, the differences were much smaller. Recall from Figure 6–7 that the chances of getting a prison or jail sentence upon conviction were also higher in Kalamazoo. Thus, Kalamazoo defendants were more likely to be incarcerated, and when incarcerated, more likely to get a longer sentence.

Source: Erie and Kalamazoo case samples

well-established and equally strong "going rates," as measured by the ability to predict sentence using offense seriousness and prior record. Our analysis did not, however, uncover any trial penalty. Kalamazoo was the only county in which convicted defendants opting for trial rather than pleading guilty did not receive longer sentences once differences in the mixture of serious crimes were taken into account.

SUMMARY

Adding a second county to our study of criminal court communities provides the basis for going beyond mere summary to begin the task of describing the contours of justice. Despite the brevity of our description of Kalamazoo, which condenses into one chapter material covered in three for Erie, it reveals a number of differences.

General conclusions about which are most significant, what accounts for them, and what their implications are must wait until information about all nine counties is presented. We can, however, highlight some of the principal elements in the topography of court communities revealed by contrasting Kalamazoo and Erie.

Though the basic purpose of disposing of defendants brought to court was identical, the composition of the caseload and the characteristics of defendants varied. A number of factors interacted to produce these differences, and their presence demonstrates the links between court communities and the larger environment. For instance, the rate of crimes reported by the police to the FBI in Kalamazoo exceeded Erie's by a substantial margin. A characteristic of Michigan's procedures, the assigning of drunk-driving cases to the lower court, led to one difference in caseload. A second provision of Michigan law, the requirement that police obtain the prosecutor's approval before formal arrest and initial arraignment, produced another significant difference. Kalamazoo's prosecutor seized the opportunity to implement a diversion program for first offenders and to scrutinize the number and level of charges. The diversion policy lowered the number of minor cases and defendants with no criminal record who came to the trial court. The charging policy, pursued to facilitate the office's desire for on-the-nose pleas, resulted in few charges per defendant, but charges that could better be sustained through to conviction. Erie had no effective screening mechanism. The prosecutor had to accept the mixture of defendants and charges sent by the police and lower courts. Many Erie defendants faced more counts but on less serious charges.

Comparing the two counties suggests that different techniques can be applied to produce similar results. The technology employed to schedule cases and assign personnel to handle them differed. Kalamazoo's use of contract attorneys to represent all indigents for a set fee instead of a traditional public defender's office like Erie's is especially noteworthy. That some of these differences affected the community's work should not obscure the simple and easily overlooked fact that both courts accomplished the task of bringing together judges and attorneys to dispose of cases. The basic pattern of dispositions also displayed congruity. About nine of every ten defendants were convicted, most by guilty pleas. In Kalamazoo, however, prosecutors included understandings about sentence recommendations and rarely reduced the number of charges, but in Erie sentence bargaining was rare, though changes in the number of courts pled to were common.

Of course, we saw some significant variation in outcomes of cases. The proportion of defendants whose cases were dismissed in Erie exceeded that in Kalamazoo slightly (12.4 percent vs. 6.3 percent), probably in part because Erie lacked prosecutor screening. More significant were the differences in sentences. Kalamazoo imposed considerably tougher sentences, and not just because it dealt with more defendants with criminal records charged with more serious offenses. Holding constant the offense at arrest, Kalamazoo incarcerated more defendants and generally gave them longer terms, especially for armed robbery and burglary. A partial explanation for differences in the ongoing rates in the two courts rests in the generally harsher criminal code and larger prison capacity in Michigan.

The portraits of the two courts also revealed differences in attitudes toward punishment and due process held by judges, prosecutors, and public defenders. A striking lack, though, was a direct link between attitudes and cases outcomes. Kalamazoo's judges exhibited much less "belief in punishment" and more "regard for due process" than Erie's, yet their sentences meted out more punishment for the same crimes. Kalamazoo's contract attorneys scored low on "belief in punishment" and fairly high in "regard for due process." The vigor of the defense they provided their clients, however, was not especially impressive. Both findings suggest that attitudes do not automatically translate into decisions. Evidently a number of factors, some associated with the specific facts of a case, others stemming from the nature of the court community, its technologies, and its guilty-plea process, intervene to suppress the influence of attitudes.

Several other differences in the two counties' court communities warrant attention. First, judges do not always occupy the position of unchallenged influence and very high status that the legal metaphor accords them. Kalamazoo's judges lacked cohesion and experienced some intense personal rivalries. Their perceived inability to get their house in order and reduce the case backlog attracted considerable criticism from others in the community. Second, the geography of the community and the courthouse interacts with other factors to shape the life of the court. The Kalamazoo judges who did not get along were paired in adjoining chambers and isolated from the other two. All of Erie's judges could reach each other in a few steps. Third, the sequence of political events in the community, as demonstrated by the history of the Erie DA's office, and the age distribution of community members, as seen in the clustering of judges in both places in their sixties, exemplified the subtle effects of court community characteristics ignored in the legal metaphor's approach to criminal courts.

We now turn to our last application of the metaphor to the task of understanding a criminal court. In Chapter Seven, we examine a more populous and prosperous suburban locale, Du Page County, Illinois.

Criminal Courts and Communities in Du Page County

INTRODUCTION

Our description of Du Page's criminal court community, its technology, and the case outcomes it produced will impart only the basic outlines. Rather than present a complete portrait of the community and the dynamics of its work life, we focus on its contrast with the two counties described in the preceding chapters.

Located about fifty minutes west of downtown Chicago via Interstate 90, Du Page contained thirty-nine incorporated communities, the largest of them, Wheaton, accounting for only 6.5 percent of its population. Du Page was three times the size of Kalamazoo, but its 658,835 residents in 1980 included few blacks (1.2 percent) and fewer Hispanics. Unlike Kalamazoo or Erie, Du Page's population grew noticeably between 1970 and 1980, at the rate of 3.0 percent; between 1960 and 1970, the increase was even higher, 4.4 percent. This growth helped transform it from a collection of sleepy semi-rural communities to a major commuting suburb of Chicago with its own developing shopping centers and industry. In 1980, fully one third of its population had lived elsewhere in 1975, sharply contrasting with the stability found in Erie, where the comparable figure was only 10 percent. No other county among our nine came close to Du Page in the rate of population influx.

Du Page differed in other vital respects. It was much wealthier, economically healthier, more conservative, and more Republican. Per capita income in 1980, at $10,473, was one-third higher than Kalamazoo's and more than 50 percent above Erie's. Erie and Kalamazoo's public assistance exceeded Du Page's by a factor of more than seven. Its 1980 unemployment rate of 5.6 percent was lowest among our nine research sites, and contrasted with Kalamazoo's 7.9 percent and Erie's 9.1 percent. Overwhelmingly Republican, Du Page (like Kalamazoo) had elected few Democrats to a county office in recent memory. The twenty-three-member county board contained only one Democrat. In every election for U.S. Senator, U.S. Representative, or president between 1972 and 1980, a majority of the county's votes went to the Republican candidate. Republicans running for president in 1964, 1968, 1972, and 1980 received an average of 68 percent of the vote. Our summary measures led us to classify it as "strong Republican" and "conservative."

Du Page's wealthy, Republican, socially homogeneous composition, however, did not eliminate political conflict. People vigorously contested elections for the position of Republican precinct committeeman. Because few precinct committee persons held political jobs, ideological and policy matters formed the basis for intense conflict. A split between the longtime inhabitants and the many upwardly mobile and affluent newcomers was another line of cleavage within Republican ranks. These conflicts assumed greater significance because statewide Republican candidates needed a large plurality of GOP votes from Du Page. Furthermore, its leaders played a vital role in state party affairs.

Du Page's proximity to a major city produced several characteristics not exhibited by Kalamazoo and Erie. It lacked the sense of community found in the other two counties. In part, this difference resulted from rapid growth, influx of outsiders, and absence of a major population center. So too did the lack of a Du Page-oriented television station or a newspaper with wide circulation that focused on county affairs. Chicago newspapers, radio, and television blanketed Du Page, but provided little coverage of its affairs. Crime and courts in particular failed to attract the media's attention, competing poorly with stories on these topics arising in the big city. The few community newspapers in Du Page had limited circulation and could afford to provide little coverage of the courts. This lack of attention, coupled with Republican domination of elections, led to low visibility and relative isolation of the court community and its activities. Few paid much attention to or knew what was going on in the courts.

Despite the absence of a strong sense of community in the county, some common attitudes were found, and these shaped how the court community operated. The proximity of Chicago, poor, filled with minorities and Democrats, provided a negative reference point. People in positions of importance in Du Page shared a desire to be "not like Cook," the county in which Chicago is located. One judge said,

> We have always taken tremendous pride in that we are not like Cook County and that we are not going to get like Cook County. We are going to be honest; we are going to be hardworking; we are not going to have a backlog. This sort of dominates people's thinking in these areas, especially judges and lawyers and even politicians.

Congruent with this attitude was a commitment to professionalism in the conduct of public affairs that was at least as strong as Kalamazoo's. Both the clerk of courts and the prosecutor's office employed computers extensively in 1980. Du Page had one of the few full-time court administrators in Illinois. County offices employed large staffs of competent professional people chosen on merit rather than by patronage appointments, as in Chicago. The ideological cast to politics and the robust economic health of the county reduced incentives to dispense and seek patronage. The strong government ethos drew grudging praise even from the few Democrats we encountered:

> I'll say this, though, once they're in office—you know to get there they have to kowtow to the Republican people—but once they're in office they treat everyone impartially, whether they're Republican or Democrat. Now sometimes you'll find that in Chicago a fellow with a little clout would get superior service in some of the offices, but that's not the case here.

CRIME AND DEFENDANTS IN DU PAGE

The rate of reported "index" crimes in 1980 placed it nearly as far above Erie's rate as it did below Kalamazoo's. But the composition of crimes reflected the wealthy, middle-class character of Du Page's small communities. The police reported crimes such as murder, manslaughter, armed robbery, and rape to the FBI at the rate of 165.5 such offenses per 100,000. As Figure 7–1 shows, the comparable figure in Erie was 297 and in Kalamazoo 411. In fact, no other county in our study reported a lower personal crime rate. Property crime, however, exceeded Erie's by a considerable margin, though only one other county had a lower rate than Erie. Compared to Illinois as a whole, Du Page reported only one third the rate of violent crimes,

Figure 7–1

Comparison of Reported Crime Rates for Erie, Kalamazoo, and Du Page

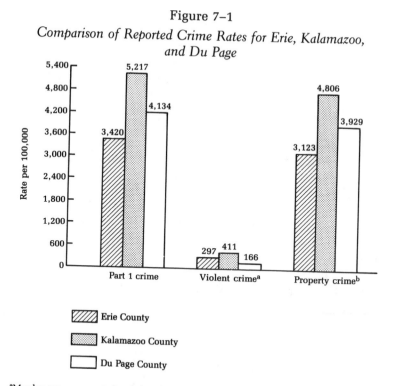

^aMurder, rape, aggravated assault, robbery

^bLarceny, burglary, auto theft

Rates of reported crime vary substantially among the counties. Du Page's overall rate (represented in the first set of bars) exceeded Erie's but not Kalamazoo's. Its violent crime rate, however (the second set), fell substantially below even Erie's, and its property crime rate (the third set) fell between Erie's and Kalamazoo's.

and its property crime rate came in at 18 percent below the statewide figure. Its reported crime clearly was "not like Cook's," which had an overall rate of 6,583 per 100,000.

Recent trends in reported crime rates covering 1976 through 1980 also pointed to a relatively mild crime problem. Property crime rates actually declined during that period. Du Page was the only county in our sample where this reduction happened. Furthermore, the rate of reported crimes against persons remained fairly stable during this period.

The composition of the defendants whose arrests passed prosecutor screening and whose cases did not end at the preliminary hearing stage reflected the relatively nonserious nature of crime in Du Page county. First offenders constituted over half the Du Page defendants, the highest proportion among the nine counties. Our composite measure of criminal record for all defendants placed Du Page last in overall seriousness. Bail decisions reflected the frequency of nondangerous defendants charged with nonserious crimes. Du Page released over a third of its defendants on their own recognizance, and nearly all the rest had 10 percent deposit bonds set. Only one defendant in twenty was denied bail or had to post a cash or surety bond, compared to one in three in Erie. Nearly as many defendants ultimately won release before final disposition of their cases (82 percent) as in Erie (84 percent), far above Kalamazoo's 64 percent. If we look just at the relatively few defendants with serious criminal records, the amount of bail set still fell below that in Kalamazoo, though it exceeded Erie's level by a considerable margin.[1]

Figure 7–2 provides another demonstration of the nonserious composition of Du Page's caseload. Only 5 percent of its defendants faced a serious personal offense as the most severe charge lodged at arrest. Burglary, larceny, and other miscellaneous property crimes accounted for more than half the most serious arrest charges. Figure 7–3 compares data on charges from Figure 7–2 with similar information from Erie and Kalamazoo, clearly demonstrating the substantial differences in the overall mixture of crimes court communities must deal with.

Data on the number of charges at arrest attested to the aggressiveness of Du Page's prosecutors. Erie's police, free of control by the prosecutor's office, lodged far more charges against defendants

---

[1]When we compared the median bail amount for defendants with different levels of seriousness in their prior record, we found that those with the worst prior records were given a median bail amount of $7,447 in Kalamazoo, $7,219 in Du Page, and $4,457 in Erie. For a more thorough treatment of bail outcomes, see James Eisenstein, Peter F. Nardulli, and Roy B. Flemming, "Explaining and Assessing Criminal Case Disposition: A Comparative Study of Nine Counties," Report submitted to the National Institute of Justice, Washington, D.C., 1982, Chapter 5.

Figure 7–2

Composition of Du Page County's 1980 Caseload: Most Serious Charge at Arrest

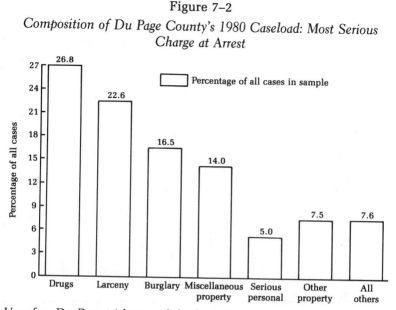

Very few Du Page trial court defendants faced charges involving serious crimes against the person. Drug charges accounted for more than a quarter of the cases, and crimes against property nearly all the rest.

Source: Du Page sample of disposed cases

than Kalamazoo's prosecutors allowed. The striking differences between the two counties originally displayed in Figure 6–2 appear again in Figure 7–4. Though prosecutor screening may have increased the number of single-count cases, Du Page's prosecutors still permitted considerably more multicount cases than Kalamazoo. These data reflected charges brought against convicted defendants. If we look at all defendants, the changing policies of Du Page and Erie converge, and show sharp differences from Kalamazoo. The proportion of defendants facing multicount indictments was 45 percent in Du Page and 48 percent in Erie, but only 16 percent in Kalamazoo. The average number of counts at arrest was 1.87 in Erie, 1.82 in Du Page, and 1.21 in Kalamazoo.

Figure 7–3

*Comparison of Most Serious Charge at Arrest for Trial Court
Caseloads in Erie, Kalamazoo, and Du Page*[a]

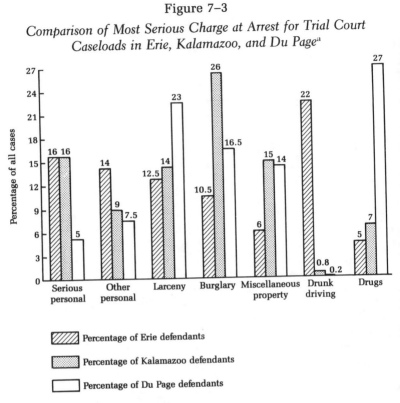

[a]Percentages shown are rounded. "Other" crimes not among
the categories listed are not included.

Huge differences came out in the "mix" of crimes faced by defendants in
the court communities of Erie, Kalamazoo, and Du Page. Du Page saw fewer
defendants charged with serious crimes against persons, but many more with
drug charges. Erie had fewer property crimes, but a substantial proportion
of drunk drivers. Kalamazoo nearly matched Erie in personal crimes and
slightly exceeded Du Page in property crimes, especially burglary, but handled fewer cases of other kinds.

Source: Case samples

Figure 7–4

Comparison of Number of Charges at Arrest in Erie, Kalamazoo, and Du Page Counties for Convicted Defendants, 1980

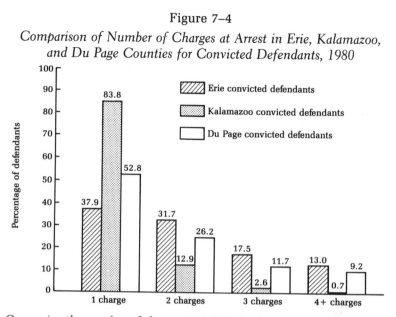

Comparing the number of charges initially lodged against convicted defendants illustrates the distinctiveness of Kalamazoo's charging policies, which resulted in less than one-fifth with more than one charge. By contrast, more than three-fifths of defendants in Erie, where police decided initial charges, faced multiple counts. Du Page, where the prosecutor's screening of arrests was not as stringent as Kalamazoo's, fell between Kalamazoo and Erie.

THE COURT COMMUNITY IN DU PAGE

Prosecutor's Office

In Illinois, head prosecutors were called state's attorneys. Unlike their counterparts in Pennsylvania, they represented the county government in some civil actions. They depended on the county for the full support of their operations, except for their own salary, which the state provided. They owed their position to the voters, who elected them to a four-year term in a partisan election.

In 1980, the state's attorney in Du Page reached the end of his first term. Like Erie's DA, he came to office as a political insurgent. In 1976, he brought to an abrupt end a long Du Page tradition whereby the choice of the Republican party organization swept to victory in the primary and coasted into office in the general election. Independently wealthy, and with extensive prosecuting experience at the federal level, he ran a well-financed, hard-hitting campaign and won a narrow primary victory. The scars from the battle still festered in 1980. Established party people resented the intruder's victory. His first actions did little to help. He eliminated part-time assistant prosecutor's positions, leading to the resignation of nearly all the senior assistants from the previous regime. He chose other outsiders to staff the supervisory posts in the office. They shared his hard-line, law-and-order perspective, and helped implement a series of changes.

Several of these changes were especially significant. First, the office initiated a system in which the prosecutor screened arrests. Each of the fourteen assistants in the felony division spent two days each month authorizing charges, handling arrests made after hours over the phone. Second, the office ended the practice of disposing of many cases at the preliminary hearing by offering the defense a guilty plea to a misdemeanor. Third, it abandoned the previous practice of assigning assistants to judges. Instead, assistants handled cases assigned to them after the preliminary hearing, and followed the case to its designated courtroom. This procedure led to scheduling difficulties for the judges. Fourth, assistants had to prepare a "prosecutor's memo" on each case. It could not be completed until all police investigative reports and the defendant's official criminal record arrived, a process that often consumed many weeks. The "pros memo" summarized the facts, evidence, weaknesses, defendant's record and social characteristics, and proposed the terms of a plea bargain that the assistant recommended the office adopt.

Twice each week, an indictment committee composed of the state's attorney, first assistant, and heads of the civil and criminal division reviewed each pros memo and decided upon the official "bottom line"; that is, the most generous or lenient plea permitted. Office policy prohibited any plea bargain that included concessions below the bottom line. Systematic checks to ensure that trial attorneys conformed to the bottom line were part of the office's routine. The very tight formal control over assistants' discretion that these arrangements produced contrasted sharply with the informal and loose supervision found in Erie, and probably constricted autonomy even more than in Kalamazoo.

Several other characteristics of the state's attorney's office were notable. It was large, with forty-four attorneys, a substantial clerical staff, seven investigators, four paralegals, a trial technical-support division, and a victim-witness unit complete with its own van for transporting witnesses. The attorneys received good salaries. The fourteen felony assistants had a median salary of $26,000; supervisors were in the $40,000 bracket.

Perhaps most noteworthy was the prosecution-minded character of the office's hierarchy and felony assistants. The felony assistants' mean "regard for due process" score ranked fourth highest among prosecutors, at −.58. They ranked in a tie for seventh on the "concern for efficiency" scale. No other set of prosecutors came close to Du Page on the "belief in punishment" scale. Their average score of +1.37 topped the next highest mean, Peoria's +1.01, by a substantial margin. All but two prosecutors surveyed displayed a high "belief in punishment."

What accounted for these strong views toward punishment? One possibility rests in the people recruited by the office. It sought prosecution-minded professionals, caring less about party affiliation or long-term residence in the county. Though none claimed to be Democrats, five trial assistants said they were independents, six "weak" Republicans, and only two "strong" Republicans. The felony assistants and supervisors we spoke with had spent an average of only 20 percent of their lives in Du Page. The office asked new assistants for a three-year commitment. Many stayed longer, leading to a fairly experienced staff by 1980. In contrast to most young assistant prosecutors in the United States, Du Page prosecutors did not view their position as a convenient and short-lived stepping-stone to private practice. More than half indicated that they hoped to be employed in the public sector in some capacity in the future.

Their commitment to prosecution and their punishment orientation conformed to the sharply drawn picture defense attorneys painted of a cohesive group of "vindictive, crusader" types accused of showing little concern for justice. Private defense attorneys especially offered impassioned criticism of the Du Page State's Attorney's Office felony assistants and administration. A former prosecutor told us:

> I was taught and I taught everybody that I ever trained that I'm there to do justice. . . . Those fellows, in my opinion, or some of them (I think most of this problem starts at the top and works its way down) have no concept of justice, absolutely none.

Defense attorneys provided examples of prosecutor "heavy-handedness" in most phases of the disposition process. A defense attorney offered as an example of overcharging an incident in which an estranged husband, drunk and with a beer bottle in hand, entered his former house to retrieve presents given his wife. Arrested initially for battery and burglary resulting from the fracas that ensued with the wife's new boyfriend, he was rearrested and charged with armed violence, a class X felony with a six-year minimum jail term. The dangerous weapon with which he was alleged to be armed was the beer bottle. Defense attorneys asserted that prosecutors complied slowly and as minimally as possible to motions for discovery. Unlike their counterparts in Kalamazoo, they volunteered next to no information. Many defense lawyers charged that the office was rigid and uncompromising in plea discussions, and blind to mitigating circumstances.

The Defense Bar

An official in a previous state's attorney's office discussed one effect of this perceived heavy-handedness:

> I've never seen anything like this. It makes me feel good to be a defense attorney. Up until they came in there, I think I was just kind of doing my job and making a few bucks here and there. I knew what had to be done. I really believe that a prosecutor's office like this helps me to realize what a defense attorney's role in society is.

The fifteen private defense attorneys we interviewed scored very low on the "belief in punishment" scale even though more than half had been prosecutors. They expressed uniformly negative attitudes toward the prosecutor's office. Those who had served previously in the prosecutor's office objected especially to the lack of respect and trust accorded them by suspicious and cold assistants. As a result of their outrage at the policies instituted and the treatment they received, a group of private defense lawyers banded together to form a defense-attorneys' organization shortly after the new state's attorney took office.

The diffuseness of Du Page's defense bar prevented it from mounting a cohesive and effective challenge to the prosecutor. A number of factors contributed to this diffuseness. First, a number of clients were available, for the public defenders handled just 45 percent of the cases. By contrast, Kalamazoo's contract attorneys accounted for 80 percent of a much smaller caseload. Second, in Illinois, only Cook County had more lawyers, reducing the familiarity conducive to taking united action. Third, many of them had moved into the county as adults, and lacked the family and school ties with one another found in Erie and most other counties in our study. Fourth, they worked in the small communities that dotted the county. No concentration of lawyers' offices surrounded the courthouse as in Erie or Kalamazoo. This dispersal further inhibited integration and communication. Finally, the number of attorneys handling criminal cases in our sample exceeded three hundred, and most of them took only a few cases. In fact, the fifteen among them who most often appeared represented only 11 percent of the defendants in our sample. By contrast, the top fifteen private lawyers in Erie handled 27 percent.

Only the public defender's office had the potential to confront the state's attorney's office. Its structure and personnel prevented it from doing so, however. It differed from the state's attorney's office in a number of ways. Its nine felony assistants all engaged in private practice. Assigned to judges rather than cases, assistant PDs pursued their private work when their judge was occupied with civil cases or criminal defendants were represented privately. The $15,000 to $19,000 salary provided a nice cushion upon which to build a growing private practice. Consequently, these positions attracted politically well-connected individuals. The office simply threw out the hundreds of applications from out-of-county lawyers. It functioned much as a patronage operation. Five of the ten office members we interviewed said they were "strong Republicans," the rest "average Republicans," giving it a more partisan cast than the state's attorney's office. One assistant claimed that nearly everyone had either a political sponsor or good connections: "You know, we've got the governor's nephew, the judge's son, the judge's girlfriend, and all kinds of other people with contacts." Not surprisingly, the conflicts found within the county's Republican ranks were reflected in the office. Individuals associated with different factions felt little inclination to identify with each other or with the office.

The head public defender, an eleven-year veteran with broad experience, amiable disposition, and strong ties to the Republican party, was the epitome of the Republican establishment. The judges selected him and could remove him at will, ensuring his responsiveness to their interests. In return, he enjoyed strong support from the judges, and benefited from generous appropriations from the county. Among its unusually abundant resources, the office counted eight secretaries, six investigators, and computer facilities. If his adversary ran a tight ship on the prosecution side, he presided over an extremely decentralized, laissez-faire operation. Even members of the office described confused lines of authority, administrators with nothing to do, and a lack of organized effort to counteract the state's attorney's aggressiveness. Internal resentment based on fears that other members of the office were getting a better deal reinforced divisions created by assistants' affiliations with rival party factions. Because assistants came to the office with strong political support, they could not easily be fired or disciplined for poor performance. One assistant's performance was so poor that no judge wanted that person in their courtroom. The result was that this assistant did practically no work, leading a colleague to complain that, "The worse you are the better off you are."

Thus, the highly disciplined, aggressive, and cohesive group of prosecutors faced a public defender's office that lacked cohesion, that was internally divided and rent with jealousy, and that could or would not discipline poorly performing assistants. Its members stayed longer than most assistant PDs elsewhere not because they felt an ideological commitment to the defense of criminals or because they wanted to learn the ropes. Rather, they enjoyed the security and income base their position offered. It was an ideal situation in which to pursue their primary interest — building their private practice. The office gave off the aroma of lethargy and its members exhibited considerable professional malaise. As a group, Du Page's PDs ranked nearly at the bottom of public defenders' offices in our study in their "regard for due process" and third highest in their "belief in punishment." The private defense attorneys expressed much more negative views toward punishment.

Du Page's Judges

Du Page's bench consisted of twelve circuit judges at the trial level and thirteen associate judges staffing the lower courts. Illinois law provided its trial judges with formidable resources in order to exercise effective supervision of lower-court judges. Circuit judges elected associate judges for four-year terms, and could refuse to reappoint them.

Du Page's larger trial bench led to an elaborate internal structure. The court established a number of committees, including one that chose and oversaw the work of the public defender, and several divisions that assumed responsibility for different kinds of cases. Six circuit judges plus an associate judge, who heard all preliminary hearings, staffed the "general" division. The six circuit judges handled a mixed docket of both civil and criminal cases, but scheduled them continuously rather than during designated trial terms as in Erie and Kalamazoo. Cases went to judges on a random-assignment basis at the time of the preliminary hearing. Illinois law allowed a defense attorney to make one request for a "substitute" judge as a matter of right. Thus, the defense could avoid taking the case before the judge initially assigned in the random draw. Additional substitutions and routing to a specific judge, however, could not occur without showing cause.

Du Page's judges faced a heavy workload. The county's population growth meant its allocation of judicial positions based on the 1970 census left it understaffed. The temporary assignment of two judges to appellate work and the illness of a third further strained judicial resources. We interviewed the associate judge handling preliminary hearings, and seven circuit judges. The eight included six "strong" and two "average" Republicans. All were white, one was female. As a group, they had spent almost three-fourths of their lives in Du Page, far higher than the public defenders or especially the prosecutors. Their average age was just over fifty years, significantly lower than the comparable figure in Erie and Kalamazoo. Given the conservatism of the county, the judges expressed surprisingly moderate attitudes. They produced a slightly negative average score on the "belief in punishment" scale, lower than the judges in all but two of the other nine counties, and they ranked third in their "regard for due process."

As in Kalamazoo, Du Page's judges displayed neither the cohesion nor the warm personal friendships found in Erie. Divisions within the Du Page Republican party, founded on personal loyalties and past incidents, formed the basis for factions among the judges. Thus, it was not ideological stance or policy positions, but rather unfathomable personal factors that produced these splits. As a result, the judges could not easily arrive at common policies or work effectively to implement them.

Relationships in the Court Community

The principal feature of Du Page's criminal court community in 1980 becomes clear in the foregoing discussion. The state's attorney's office generated both change and conflict, upsetting existing arrangements and importing aggressive newcomers to the criminal process. The distribution of attitudes toward punishment and due process summarize nicely the alignment of the judges and public defenders as the embodiment of the old style opposed to the prosecutors' office. Figure 7–5 depicts clearly the deviant position of the prosecutors. We included average scores from the "concern with efficiency" scale because they provide additional evidence of the isolated status of the prosecutors and confirm assertions made in the interviews that they worried much more about "professionalism" than efficiency. The addition of a bar representing attitudes among private defense attorneys would have strengthened the picture of prosecutor isolation presented in Figure 7–5.

As Figure 4–1 shows, in Erie the public defenders found that their attitudes differed from those of the judges and prosecutors. Kalamazoo's pattern (see Figure 6–3) resembled Du Page's on the surface. The prosecutors' attitudes opposed those of judges and the contract attorneys. The differences were less in Du Page on due process and greater on belief in punishment, however. More important, Kalamazoo's prosecutors set the tone and won the rest of the court community's approval in a way that Du Page's prosecutors did not.

The divisiveness caused by the state's attorney's office joined other factors working against the establishment of a small, intimate, and stable criminal court community. Twenty-three Du Page judges and prosecutors handled criminal cases in the trial court, consisting of six judges, fourteen assistant prosecutors, and three of their supervisors. In Erie, the equivalent figure was twelve (three judges, nine prosecutors) and sixteen in Kalamazoo (four judges, twelve prosecutors). The large number of defense attorneys especially reduced cohesiveness in Du Page's criminal court community. The fifteen private attorneys who most frequently appeared in our case sample and all the public defenders together represented fewer than 60 percent of all defendants in Du Page. In Kalamazoo, the comparable

Figure 7–5

Average Standardized Scores on Attitude Scales,
by Position, in Du Page

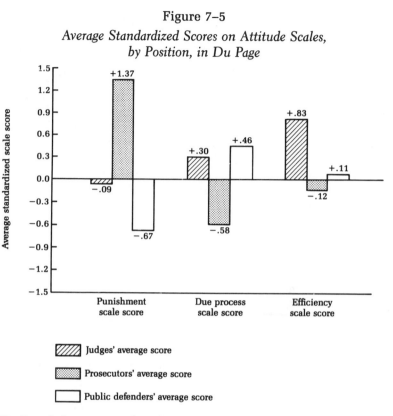

Du Page judges expressed moderate views on punishment and regard for due process. The prosecutor's hard-line views were clear — they held lower regard for due process and much stronger propunishment attitudes, and differed from both judges and public defenders on all three scales reported in the graph.

group of twenty-five people accounted for 90 percent of defendants. The twenty-nine defense regulars in Erie were not far behind, at more than 80 percent.

Not only was the number of people involved greater, but their familiarity with one another was low because they lacked home-town and precollege ties. They also interacted less frequently because of geographic dispersion than did defense lawyers in the other two counties. Of course, some interaction took place. We described how some defense attorneys had formed their own organization, and how they shared distaste for the state's attorney and his staff. Like nearly everyone else, the defense bar shared the conservative, Republican orientation of the county and the desire to "not be like Cook" County. The grapevine did appear to be less vigorous and important, though. The public defenders' isolation in a separate building across town and their part-time status made them less available. The hostility many felt toward the hierarchy of the prosecutor's office also inhibited chatter in the courthouse. Internal divisions among the judges and the scattering of their chambers throughout the courthouse further blocked communication. These factors reinforced division among formal roles; the grapevine seldom bridged the gaps.

The lack of a strong sense of community within the courthouse, coupled with the factors just mentioned, made people guarded in conversation and reluctant to share information. Consequently, familiarity, consensus, and interdependence among criminal court community members in Du Page fell short of their level in Erie or even in Kalamazoo.

It is instructive to relate briefly what happened to the State's Attorney after our field research ended. He managed to win his first reelection try in 1980. In 1984, however, he lost to the man he had defeated in the Republican primary in 1976. This individual had served as the first assistant in the regime prior to the defeated incumbent's tenure. Thus, ultimately the insurgent outsider was sent packing by a representative of the old regime.

CASE OUTCOMES

The information we have presented so far provides conflicting indications on the severity of case outcomes. Du Page exhibited conservative attitudes of the sort likely to support harsh treatment of criminals. The prosecutors especially expressed very strong "belief in punishment," and they were tightly controlled by the hardnosed indictment committee. On the other hand, the low frequency of serious crimes and defendants with long criminal records were characteristics associated with light sentences. Furthermore, the courts' low visibility and insulation created the conditions necessary for allowing great latitude in the court community's way of disposing of cases.

General outcomes for the defendants who came to Du Page's trial court differed little from those in the other two counties. In fact, the dismissal and guilty-plea rate for Kalamazoo differed by just a few percentage points. Figure 7–6 summarizes outcomes for these three counties.

Guilty pleas in Du Page resembled Erie's and contrasted with Kalamazoo's. As in Erie, Du Page's prosecutor cared little whether cases ended with on-the-nose pleas or not. More than half the pleas involved some sort of reduction in charge. But like Erie, it rarely involved reducing the primary charge. Instead, Du Page offered defendants reductions in the number of counts charged, a practice

Figure 7–6

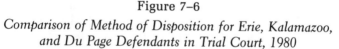

Comparison of Method of Disposition for Erie, Kalamazoo, and Du Page Defendants in Trial Court, 1980

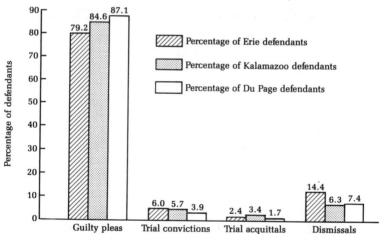

Erie, Kalamazoo, and Du Page defendants' cases ended very similarly, with the overwhelming proportion entering a guilty plea or accepting its equivalent in a diversion program. Less than 10 percent in each county went to trial. Small differences in the proportion of defendants dismissed exist, with Erie dismissing about twice as many as Du Page and Kalamazoo.

Source: Case samples

facilitated by the frequency of multiple counts charged.[2] The sparing use of reductions in the primary charge suggests that if the system compensated for overcharging, it had to do so at the time of sentencing.

For the group of convicted defendants as a whole, Du Page imposed far gentler penalties than Erie and especially Kalamazoo. It did not use diversion at all, but gave probation or a fine to more than two-thirds of its defendants. Penitentiary sentences went to fewer than one defendant in ten. Figure 7–7 illustrates nicely the diversity in outcomes that American courts produce.

The leniency accorded defendants convicted in Du Page is clear in Figure 7–7. But in judging the harshness of its dispositions, we need to remember that both defendants' prior records and the crimes they committed invited less harsh punishment. The county jail was at or beyond capacity during our research, also discouraging jail sentences for less serious crimes. The technique we employed in Chapters Five and Six for comparing outcomes by looking at sentences for particular crimes helps explain these differences. Figure 7–8 shows the proportion of convicted defendants who were arrested on four different charges and who went to jail. Though only eight Du Page defendants arrested for armed robbery were convicted, each received incarceration, reflecting the mandatory six-year sentence that this offense carried in Illinois. The number of defendants represented by the bars for the other three crimes depicted in Figure 7–8 all exceed 100, making the results stabler. For two of the crimes, burglary and hard drugs, incarceration rates fell below those of both other counties. The 26 percent incarceration rate for burglary is especially low, supporting evidence for the defense attorney's contention that overcharging was frequent.

Figure 7–9 adds the data from Du Page to the second method of comparing the harshness of sentences used in Chapter Six, the median length of incarceration for four offenses. The short sentences imposed on defendants arrested for burglary provide further support for the possibility that their crimes were not considered as very se-

---

[2]The figures for Du Page, Kalamazoo, and Erie are respectively: for any type of reduction, 52.8 percent, 15.8 percent, 59.1 percent; for reduction in primary charge, 12.2 percent, 12.8 percent, 8.6 percent, and drops in the number of counts, 46.2 percent, 12.2 percent, and 59.0 percent. Peter F. Nardulli, Roy B. Flemming, and James Eisenstein, *The Tenor of Justice* (Champaign-Urbana, Ill.: University of Illinois Press, 1987), Chapter 8.

Figure 7–7

Comparison of Distribution of Sentences Imposed on Erie, Kalamazoo, and Du Page Defendants, 1980

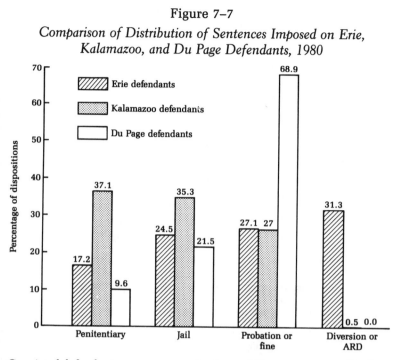

Convicted defendants as a group received very different sentences. Du Page relied heavily on probation and fines, Kalamazoo on a prison or jail sentence, and Erie on ARD.

Source: Case samples

rious. Indeed, the sentences for burglary, larceny, and hard drugs are all dramatically below those in Erie and Kalamazoo. The eight armed-robbery defendants sentenced to prison had a mean effective sentence higher than those in Erie but about half as great as those in Kalamazoo.[3]

Comparing the time elapsed from arrest to disposition presented in Chapter Six (Figure 6–5) showed Du Page to be very similar to

[3]Because Illinois defendants in 1980 routinely received a one-day credit for good time for every day served, sentences effectively were half those which were officially imposed as the minimum. The arrangement differed in Michigan and Pennsylvania; to avoid misleading comparisons, we halved minimum sentences in Illinois before comparing them to sentences in the other two states.

Figure 7–8

Comparison of Percentages of Convicted Defendants Incarcerated for Four Selected Arrest Charges in Erie, Kalamazoo, and Du Page, 1980

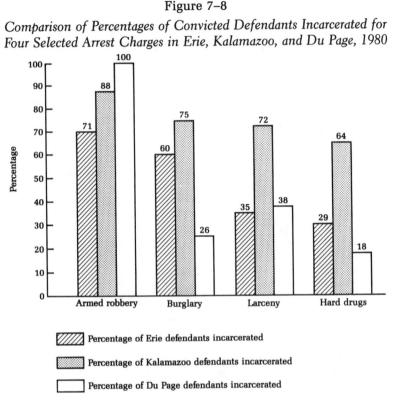

Percentage of Erie defendants incarcerated

Percentage of Kalamazoo defendants incarcerated

Percentage of Du Page defendants incarcerated

The proportion of convicted defendants sentenced to prison or jail varied according to the offense. Armed robbers consistently received incarceration more often than burglars within the same county. Holding constant the offense, differences by county were clear, with Kalamazoo generally harshest and Du Page, excepting its treatment of the few armed robbers, most lenient.

Source: Case samples

Erie. It took only nine days longer to dispose of the median case in Du Page than in Erie. As in Erie, the spread between the 25th-percentile case and the 75th-percentile case was narrower than for Kalamazoo. In Erie, this figure was 129 days, in Du Page 143 days, but in Kalamazoo 244 days.

Figure 7–9

Comparison of Median Months of Minimum Sentence for Erie, Kalamazoo, and Du Page Defendants Incarcerated for Selected Arrest Charges, 1980

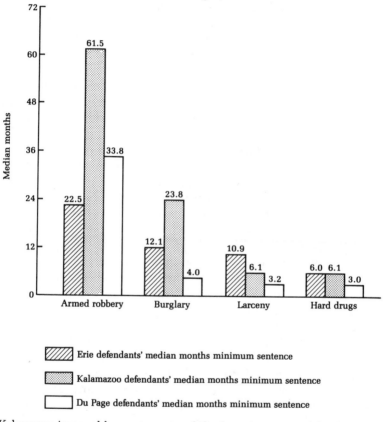

Erie defendants' median months minimum sentence

Kalamazoo defendants' median months minimum sentence

Du Page defendants' median months minimum sentence

Kalamazoo imposed longer terms on defendants incarcerated for the more serious crimes of armed robbery and burglary. Differences in sentence length among the counties for larceny and hard drugs were small, with Du Page somewhat more lenient, and Erie a little severer. Remember that the *rates* of incarceration, however, were much higher in Kalamazoo, as Figure 7–8 clearly shows.

Source: Case samples

ILLINOIS EFFECTS

We have mentioned several features of the Illinois judicial system impinging upon its court communities. In particular, the provision for circuit judges' electing associate judges who staff the lower courts resulted in much tighter control. Illinois associate judges displayed much less independence than their counterparts in either Pennsylvania or Michigan. Head public defenders in Michigan and Pennsylvania owed their position to elected county officials. Other members of the court community could influence them only insofar as they had access to these elected officials. Thus, Erie's President Judge could do little when the PD's case-assignment policies clogged the docket because the County Executive was a political ally of the PD. But in Illinois, the judges themselves elected the public defender, guaranteeing his responsiveness to their interests. Finally, defense attorneys could, as a matter of right, move a case out of the courtroom of the judge originally assigned by requesting a substitute judge.

Because our purpose is to show how Du Page, Kalamazoo, and Erie differed, we need not describe completely court structure and procedure in Illinois. Differences in the speedy-trial rules and sentencing provisions, however, warrant brief summary.

The Illinois speedy-trial provisions fell somewhere between the strict rules in Pennsylvania and Michigan's nearly toothless ones. Cases not commenced within the statutory deadlines were to be dismissed. For incarcerated defendants, the prosecution faced a 120-day deadline. Various circumstances, though, could extend this deadline. Delays caused by the defense stopped the 120-day countdown; the prosecution automatically received a twenty-one-day extension if requested during the last twenty-one days. Defendants freed before disposition had to demand a speedy trial in writing. If they did so, the prosecution had 160 days, but similar rules on extensions applied.

Major revisions in the sentencing code came into force in 1977. Previously, judges had sentenced defendants to indeterminate prison terms, with the actual release date decided by a parole board. The new system established six classes of offenses, with a statutorily defined minimum and maximum. Judges sentenced defendants to a specific term within this range, and defendants had to serve that term. For each day of "good behavior" in prison, though, this term was reduced by one day, which meant in practice that most defendants served half the minimum prison term imposed. Defendants convicted of the two most serious classes of crime could not receive probation. Habitual offenders or those committing especially brutal crimes could be sentenced with "enhanced" penalties, double the maximum for the class. Defendants convicted of attempts were subject to penalties for the next lowest class of crimes, giving prosecutors the opportunity to plea bargain similar to that of Michigan prosecutors.

The details in a state's sentencing code like those just presented rapidly fade from memory. After all, what difference does it make what the Illinois criminal code provided in 1980? Though such details are not in themselves particularly significant, we must understand that whatever their specific content, such provisions influence how court communities dispose of cases. In addition, variation in sentencing patterns between states depends in part on differences in their sentencing codes. In Chapter Eight, we will compare the harshness of the criminal codes of the three states.

SUMMARY

Chapter Seven expands our view from two to three court communities, introducing a third state's system and a county with many different characteristics. What does the description of Du Page's criminal court community add to our map of the contours of justice?

Knowing how Du Page's social and economic characteristics affect the caseload sharpens our understanding of the links between them. The rate of serious crimes reported by the police is lower; the mixture of cases brought to court contains fewer crimes of violence; defendants are predominantly white, less often have a prior record, usually win release from jail before disposition, and more often can afford to hire an attorney. The county's wealthy, white, suburban nature helps account for these characteristics.

The patterns of case outcomes that we found reinforce our belief that few strong ties connect the attitudes of the larger community and the criminal court members on the one hand, and decisions on the other. Despite the conservative orientation of Du Page and the hard-line views of the head prosecutor and his staff, which ranked first among the nine counties studied in "belief in punishment," defendants did not receive harsh sentences. Though most defendants were convicted, sentences less often called for prison or jail terms, and when they did, the terms were generally shorter than those in Erie and Kalamazoo.

This chapter also helps refine our understanding of how court communities are molded by the political context in which they operate. The decline in the cohesiveness and political prowess of the Du Page Republican party organization, itself the result of changing demographics, permitted an insurgent from outside the county to capture the district attorney's office. The public defender's office provided patronage opportunities for individuals connected to various party factions. The ability of the office to discipline its members and to forge a cohesive, spirited organization suffered as a result. Its head's ability to act vigorously was constrained also by his dependence on the judges for his appointment and continuation in office. Finally, the fissures in Du Page's Republican party surfaced on the bench, preventing the judges from taking concerted action or exercising strong leadership. These factors, coupled with the dispersion of private defense attorneys throughout the county, produced a stunted grapevine.

Du Page demonstrates that a county may be wealthy and socially and politically conservative, but these qualities do not guarantee that its criminal court community will exhibit cohesiveness or cooperation. In this county, just the opposite was true. Indeed, even the link between community orientations and the attitudes of key community members is not always straightforward. Despite Du Page County's conservatism, its judges ranked high in "regard for due process" and low in "belief in punishment" among the judges in our study, contrasting sharply with the prosecutor's office.

In Erie, the chief judge's influence exceeded that of his counterparts in the other two communities. In Kalamazoo, the district attorney exercised leadership. Du Page lacked a comparable concentration of leadership and influence, and it was too fractured to permit collective governance. Of course, the actions of the state's attorney's office produced significant effects, not by leadership and persuasion, but rather in an atmosphere of conflict through unilateral policies such as those pertaining to guilty pleas. The private defense bar, though unhappy with this state of affairs, was too diffuse and unorganized to mount an effective challenge. The PD's office, lacking strong leadership and cohesion, and staffed with politically well-connected veterans devoted to their private practices, also offered little effective opposition. The trial judges, split internally, played a role like that of Kalamazoo's bench, failing to match the influence wielded by Erie's judges.

Our examination of one county from each set of triplets drawn from each of three states provides a good initial view of how middle-sized courts differ, but does not reveal the full range of diversity among all nine of our courts. Chapters Eight and Nine complete our presentation of the results of our research in the full complement of counties examined.

CHAPTER EIGHT

Court Communities in Nine Counties

The descriptions of Erie, Kalamazoo, and Du Page illustrate in detail a major proposition in this book: Criminal court communities display significant differences in their composition and structure, in the procedures they employ, and in the outcomes they produce. Applying the metaphor of courts as communities is a useful approach to understanding the complex reality of their functioning, and avoids the misleading and overly simple conclusions that flow from applying the legal metaphor.

Although our focus on these three counties reveals some features in the terrain formed by criminal court communities, our research took us to six other counties. Equally detailed descriptions of these six courts would be tedious to present and even harder to remember: the details of nine court communities would merge into a confusing jumble. Fortunately, comprehensive and detailed descriptions are not necessary. We can draw upon research from the other six counties to enhance our demonstration of how the metaphor of courts as communities helps in understanding courts and to identify general patterns. Specifically, we will selectively draw from those research findings which clarify how the elements of the metaphor presented in Chapter Two can help highlight the contours of justice.

COUNTY LEGAL CULTURE

Our research shows that the content of county legal culture significantly shapes the behavior of court communities, both in members' ways of dealing with each other and the ends that defendants' cases come to. We did not embark on our research intending to study county legal culture. Consequently, what we can say is limited to the most prominent features in the counties' legal cultures.

"Going rates" are a crucial part of legal culture. The core members of the community usually develop a common understanding of what penalties ought to be attached to which crimes and defendants. The shared belief is that defendants with particular prior records committing specific crimes should, if convicted, receive a standard penalty. Going rates provide only a starting point in determining a sentence, as we will see in Chapter Nine. They help, however, to explain differences in sentences among counties, especially those in the same state. Peoria's court community displayed a high level of genuine harmony. Its members respected one another. They shared a sense of identification and pride in the city of Peoria. Its defense bar scored higher on the "belief in punishment" scale than prosecutors in St. Clair, and higher than public defenders in any of our counties. One defense attorney said: "Sometimes I feel awkward because I subscribe to the ideas that [the prosecutors] do. You know, I live here. I don't want any bums on the street." These factors in combination help explain why Peoria's going rates generally exceeded those in the other two Illinois counties.

The initial discussion of county legal culture in Chapter Two introduced the notion of differences in the degree of identification with the community, in beliefs about what practices were acceptable in disposing of cases, and in how members treated one another. The detailed studies of each county provided richer descriptions of these differences, but did not fundamentally alter their character. We found many people in Montgomery who repeated the slogan, "We are one family" in describing the courthouse, including non-court-related offices. Most plea bargains there included agreement on what sentence should be imposed, which was communicated to the judge and almost always accepted. In Erie, all the judges absolutely refused to take recommendations as part of pleas offered in open court; several would discuss sentences in chambers, but only rarely. People interviewed in Peoria and Montgomery claimed that the degree of trust one could place in the word of another attorney was high. Defense attorneys did not trust Du Page's prosecutors much. Similarly, most people in Montgomery tried to "work things out"; in other counties, including St. Clair, conflict was tolerated as part of the game.

We found other significant aspects of county legal culture. It ap-

peared that the willingness to accept partisan considerations in hiring assistant prosecutors and public defenders varied widely. In
Montgomery, partisan considerations had long ruled and drew little
criticism. Most assistants in both offices could demonstrate ties to
the county Republican organization. In Oakland and Peoria, the
prosecutor's office did not hire on a partisan basis. In fact, when
Peoria's prosecutor declined to seek reelection in 1980, two of his
assistants sought the Republican nomination and three the Democratic. There may also be community-wide feelings about how the
work of the court should be organized and accomplished, with some
courts stressing "efficiency," some preferring "formalistic" arrangements to infuse professionalism and planning into the work of the
court, and some adopting a "pragmatic" approach, haphazardly
working through problems ad hoc as they arise.

INHABITANTS OF COURT COMMUNITIES

The permanent residents of the nine court communities, not unexpectedly, mixed similar and different characteristics. The specific
structure of these similarities and differences warrant brief summary.

Size and Familiarity

Perhaps the most striking characteristic these inhabitants display is
that "strangers," people of unknown name, characteristics, and past
behavior, rarely appear except as defendants. Even "nonregular" defense attorneys; that is, local attorneys who handle only one or two
criminal cases a year, usually are not strangers in middle-sized jurisdictions. Judges, court personnel, and experienced prosecutors will
recognize nonregulars' names and faces. They may have gone to
school with them or their parents or children, attended the same
church, or seen them in court on a civil matter. Brand new attorneys,
of course, may be strangers, but not for long. Unless the local bar is
very large, only a lawyer from another county will be a stranger.

Among members of a court community, however, regulars and
nonregulars vary in how well known they are. The number of judges
and prosecutors who regularly handled criminal cases in our counties
ranged from about a dozen to three dozen. Though a three-to-one
ratio in absolute terms, the number of people involved was small
enough that all could know one another very well indeed. Their lo-

cation in the same building and participation in a common grapevine ensured that even a prosecutor fresh from law school would soon come to know and to be known to the others.

The size of the defense bar varied much more. In the six counties with public defenders and the one with contract attorneys (Kalamazoo), we measured concentration in the defense bar by adding the proportion of defendants handled by publicly paid lawyers and by the fifteen most frequently retained private attorneys. In Du Page, together they handled about 60 percent of the defendants; at the other extreme, Kalamazoo's ten contract attorneys and busiest private attorneys, a total of twenty-five, accounted for almost 90 percent of the caseload. Two counties that relied exclusively on attorneys in private practice, however, appointed them case by case to represent the poor. In Saginaw, ninety-three lawyers handled the same proportion of defendants as the core of twenty-five in Kalamazoo. In Oakland, ninety-one appointed attorneys accounted for only 75 percent of defendants. The number of attorneys representing defendants in Montgomery, Du Page, Oakland, and Saginaw was large. Therefore, the proportion of defendants handled by nonregulars was high. In the other five counties, about twenty-five attorneys handled about 80 percent of defendants, leaving fewer cases to nonregulars. Where the defense bar was larger, the court community tended to be more diffuse and the grapevine's reach and strength less pronounced.

Demographics and Social Interaction

Noteworthy similarities in the career lines and experience of community inhabitants came out in the survey of the nine counties. Prosecutors and public defenders hired immediately upon graduation were usually at least twenty-six years old. The low starting salaries paid beginners in both offices, limits on salary increases that soon caused office members to make less than they could in private practice, and the desire of most hirees to obtain experience before entering private practice produced high turnover. Experienced attorneys in private practice found the salary they could get even if hired at a relatively senior level too low to be attractive. The absence of career positions with some job security further discouraged experienced private attorneys from abandoning their practice and encouraged current office members to leave. Consequently, most assistant prosecutors and public defenders came and left while still young.

The average age of prosecutors handling felony cases, for example, fell between thirty in Peoria and thirty-four in Du Page and Kalamazoo.

Another noteworthy similarity in community members' characteristics can be summarized briefly. The predominance of white male attorneys in Erie, Kalamazoo, and Du Page's court community typified the other six communities. A scattering of young assistant DAs or PDs or judges who were female or black could be found, but the proportion was very small. Hardly any women were career prosecutors or established private defense attorneys.

The age structure of an office sometimes shifted suddenly when the office head changed. Experienced people resigned or were asked to leave in both Erie and Du Page. Montgomery, however, seemed destined to experience high turnover continuously so long as it adhered to its tradition of paying new assistants very low salaries with the expectation that they would leave within two years. Several of the larger offices, including Oakland, sought to retain an experienced core of trial assistants. Even Montgomery employed several older assistants who aspired to be career prosecutors.

Some important differences appeared within the general similarities just described. Though 5.7 years of experience as a prosecutor in Oakland may seem like a narrow margin over 2.3 years in St. Clair, in practice this difference is significant. Rookie prosecutors change as dramatically and mature as quickly as most college students. The 3.4-year range between St. Clair and Oakland is equivalent to the difference between a high school junior and a college sophomore. In that time, young lawyers change from novices to experienced trial attorneys. Most young prosecutors accept the relatively low salary because they can acquire valuable trial experience unavailable to beginners in private practice. Once they gain this experience, which may take from one and a half to three years, young prosecutors seek to cash in on it by launching a career in private practice. When they leave, a slot is open for another newcomer seeking a crash course in how to try cases. The high turnover in most offices means assistants handle important cases within two years.

Other differences congruent with characteristics of the larger community also turned up in prosecutors' offices. Some recruited "home-county" people affiliated with the dominant political party. In Montgomery, six of ten felony prosecutors were Republicans, and two were independents. They lived an average of 78 percent of their lives in Montgomery County. St. Clair showed a similar preference for home-town Democrats. But Kalamazoo's ten prosecutors were split almost evenly between Republicans and Independents, and they had spent just 22 percent of their lives on average in the county.

We found similar patterns in the characteristics of public defenders and judges. Because the differences among PDs generally resembled those just discussed for prosecutors, we can ignore most of the details. Several features of judges' characteristics deserve mention, though. The difference in average age ranged from a high in Kalamazoo of 63.7 to a low of 49.5 in Oakland. Years of experience showed a similar range. Saginaw's judges averaged 12.8 years, just above Erie's 12.0. St. Clair's three judges averaged just five years on the bench, about the same as in Du Page. The close relationship between age and experience exhibited by prosecutors weakened for judges. Kalamazoo's judges exceeded Erie's in average age, but had much less experience on the bench. Judges in each county were considerably older than prosecutors or public defenders, and had spent most of their lives there. In no county did the judges average less than four-fifths of their lives in the county; in six, the average exceeded 90 percent. As in Du Page, Montgomery's judges reflected the county's strongly Republican cast. None of the five judges there who filled out our questionnaire indicated any affinity with the Democratic party. In fact, among the thirty-nine judges for whom we have data, only four said they were Democrats. Seven considered themselves independents, leaving the strong majority in the Republican column.

Differences in distribution of age and experience among each county's judges, prosecutors, and defense bar appeared to affect the court community in consequential, subtle, and as yet not entirely clear ways. Large generation gaps separating judges from prosecutors and defense attorneys probably inhibited communication and impeded casual, frequent interaction. Certainly, if the head public defender or prosecutor matched some of the judges in age and experience, their interactions would reflect this equality. Where experienced private defense attorneys took a significant share of the cases, differences in how cases were handled depended on the attorney. Experienced private attorneys, for example, felt comfortable appearing before and talking to Dauphin judges, whereas young public defenders did not.

Attitudes of Community Members

We have shown that the attitudes expressed toward punishment and due process differed from person to person and position to position. Is any pattern to be found in the attitudes of judges, prosecutors, and public defenders across all nine counties?

A number of reasonable possibilities exist. Attitudes could be a function of role. One could argue that the act of prosecuting criminals and dealing with police and crime victims will nudge prosecutors everywhere toward common punishment-oriented attitudes, but defense attorneys become attuned to the importance of due process and limitation of punishment. Alternatively, the political culture of a state and the effects of state-mandated procedures and appellate court decisions might produce similarity in the attitudes of judges, prosecutors, and defense attorneys in that state. Or perhaps the effects of the local community will result in convergent attitudes in all three positions within each county, but with differences among counties in the state. Combinations of these patterns are also possible. Prosecutors in each state may have similar views, but differ from judges and defense attorneys in their state, and from prosecutors in other states.

What patterns resulted from our analysis? Figure 8–1 partially summarizes them by depicting the average scores of people in the position for each county. Notice that these data conceal disparity within each office. Because Saginaw and Oakland had no public defender's office, no data appear for them in these two counties.

One broad and fairly obvious generalization about the effects of position can be drawn. Prosecutors score higher on "belief in punishment" than both judges and public defenders, except for Dauphin alone, where the judges barely topped the prosecutors. Similarly, public defenders score lower on punishment than judges and prosecutors. Public defenders display higher regard for due process than prosecutors in every county, and higher than judges everywhere but in Peoria and St. Clair. Prosecutors scored lower on due process than judges everywhere but Dauphin and Erie.

The effects of county legal culture and other factors do, however, significantly shape attitudes of those occupying the same position, producing some large differences from county to county. As a group, Dauphin's judges expressed much stronger "belief in punishment" than Kalamazoo's. Peoria's public defenders actually scored on the positive side of the "belief in punishment" scale; Dauphin's were

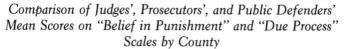

Figure 8–1

*Comparison of Judges', Prosecutors', and Public Defenders'
Mean Scores on "Belief in Punishment" and "Due Process"
Scales by County*

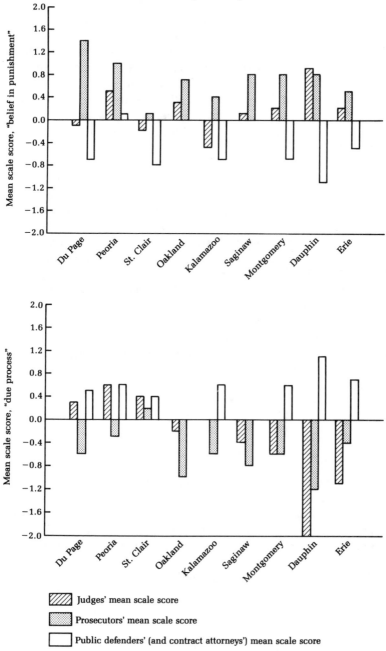

strongly negative. The gap between prosecutors in Du Page and St. Clair was about as great.

If such state-level factors as the legal culture and methods of recruitment strongly influenced attitudes, occupants of the same position in each state would display similar views, but they did not. Du Page's prosecutors expressed much higher belief in punishment than their downstate counterparts in St. Clair. The same reasoning applies to county-level factors. If county legal culture, the grapevine, and other county-based factors affected attitudes, the differences found within each county's community would be small, as indeed they seemed to be in St. Clair. In Dauphin, however, attitudes differed substantially, as shown by the varying position of the bars for that county in Figure 8–1.

The variety we saw in the patterns of attitudes toward punishment and due process defies easy summary or explanation. With the partial exception of role's apparent effect, no configuration appears consistent with any of the alternative explanations.

What is the significance of attitudes? No simple, direct links can be found between any position's attitudes and case outcomes. Kalamazoo judges believed less in punishment than did Erie judges, but they imposed harsher sentences for the same offense. But then, a careful observer of a court community cannot help becoming aware of differences in attitudes. Moreover, the residents of court communities themselves pay careful attention to and frequently discuss the content of the attitudes of fellow inhabitants. Finally, as our analysis of sentencing shows, in some circumstances case outcomes do reflect the influence of attitudes.

STRUCTURE OF STATUS AND POWER

Status and power are scarce resources whose value depends on individuals' desire to compete for them. Success in acquiring them brings dominance and attention, which are valuable in satisfying present needs and ambitions for the future. The participants' relative status and power in the life of a court consequently affect the community's operation.

Erie, Kalamazoo, and Du Page displayed three patterns in the distribution of power and prestige among the principal decision makers. In Erie, the chief judge wielded most influence, and was backed by most of his colleagues. In Kalamazoo, the head prosecutor enjoyed high prestige and exerted leadership through his prominence in the media and policy initiatives. Du Page lacked a center of power or prestige, which resulted from a divided bench, an unaggressive public defender, and a highly controversial and disliked prosecutor. A number of counties played out variations on these themes as officials or individuals exploited opportunities to gain political visibility or advantage. Peoria's popular, management-oriented prosecutor enjoyed a status similar to Kalamazoo's, though Peoria's bench avoided the divisive conflict found in Kalamazoo. Oakland's prosecutor, like Du Page's, aggressively pursued a policy of innovation. He too aroused some opposition, but enjoyed somewhat more success in carrying out his initiatives. Politically ambitious, he ran unsuccessfully for the GOP nomination for governor and senator. Several of the Oakland judges aspired to an appellate court post. Such ambitions produced an outward-looking perspective rather than a court–community-centered view. The judges rarely acted cohesively, and the weak structure of Oakland's Republican party provided no outside unifying force, leaving the bench as a whole somewhat at the mercy of the prosecutor's policies and political prominence.

Two other patterns can be identified. Saginaw and especially St. Clair undertook relatively few efforts to bring about changes. Rather, everyone seemed content to continue current practices, pragmatically making minor adjustments only as the need arose. No individual or office sought to take leadership, so that events spotlighted first one official and then another rather than having any one seek out change for self-promotion. In Montgomery and Dauphin, power and status were shared, not competed over. Montgomery's judges prided themselves on their innovative and professional approach to court management, strongly supporting the office of court administrator. At the time our research began, they had started to implement a reform in juror service, requiring those called to spend one day at the courthouse or if selected, to serve on one jury. The prosecutor stiffened office policy on sentences for burglaries and retail thefts. Thus, several sources of change and innovation operated simultaneously. Looming over the whole enterprise and dampening any potentially divisive conflict was the local Republican party organization. Dauphin lacked as strong a Republican organization, but exhibited a similar pattern of shared influence and avoidance of sharp conflict.

EMOTIONAL UNDERCURRENTS AND GRAPEVINES

Descriptions of Erie, Kalamazoo, and Du Page enlarged upon our initial discussion of personal friendships and animosities in court communities. If the notion that communities abound with friendship, warm relations, and harmony need to be dispelled, our analysis should do it. Du Page's prosecutors aroused intense ire in its established private defense bar; conflict festered among some judges in Montgomery over who was pulling their weight and doing their fair share of the work under the master calendar; as we saw in Kalamazoo, judicial tensions sometimes became sharp; Erie's DA and PD were rivals, and tensions spilled over to their staffs. The picture drawn from all nine counties has more detail, but the principal conclusion remains. Emotional currents of every description swirl about in every court community, and they structure interactions, job satisfaction, and atmosphere in the workplace.

Grapevines helped communicate the substance of these emotional undercurrents. Because explicit research on courthouse grapevines has never been undertaken, we can draw only tentative conclusions about them. What can we say about the crucial question: What difference do grapevines make? Where grapevines flourish: (1) everyone knows more about other community members' values, personalities, strengths, and weaknesses; (2) policies of judges, prosecutors, and public defenders are better known; (3) work schedules are better known, permitting more sophisticated strategies to "route" cases to judges; (4) consensus is more likely to develop on how cases should be handled, other members treated, and defendants sentenced; (5) everyone encounters less uncertainty in performing the job; and (6) those who deviate from accepted behavior patterns can be more effectively punished by critical gossip or lack of cooperation.

Our research found some form of grapevine in every community, but its structure, reach, and effectiveness varied. Certainly, they did not always flourish. In larger communities, other things being equal, the grapevine will reach a smaller proportion of the court community and carry less information. Most private criminal attorneys spend less time in the courthouse than public defenders, and so are less likely to be as well connected to the grapevine. Counties with diffuse, privately oriented defense bars, then, will face more obstacles in establishing going rates and achieving consensus on other important aspects of county legal culture. Furthermore, as the likelihood of encountering nonregular defense attorneys increases, so too does judges' and prosecutors' uncertainty about how they will handle their cases.

Of course, other things are not always equal. The geographic distribution of attorneys in the county and the physical layout of the courthouse also shape the grapevine. So do local tradition and personalities. Montgomery's grapevine owed some of its vigor and reach to the cohesion its centralized political structure brought to the courthouse. Oakland lacked an analogous centralizing force. Furthermore, its case-assignment techniques produced concentrations of prosecutors and attorneys within individual judges' courtrooms. Its grapevine resembled a vineyard, with separate vines rooted in these courtrooms, but with some connections.

In most counties, components of the grapevine flourished among the prosecutors, judges, and public defenders, facilitating the flow of information within offices. If an individual in an office learned a juicy tidbit from a contact elsewhere in the courthouse, often the whole office learned of it. The diffuse structure of public defenders' offices in Erie and Peoria, however, rendered their internal grapevine less vigorous.

In many respects, internal grapevines reflected the structure of the sponsoring organization itself. By the same token, the characteristics of a court community helped determine its grapevine.

SPONSORING ORGANIZATIONS

Differences in the structure, the policies, and the dynamics of sponsoring organizations in the nine counties abounded. The descriptions of sponsoring organizations in Erie, Kalamazoo, and Du Page clearly demonstrate this fundamental fact. Little would be accomplished by a comprehensive inventory of the varied organizational peculiarities, internal policies, and characteristic forms of interaction found. There is some value, however, to indicating the general ways in which they differ and to describing the most unusual attributes we encountered.

The Judges

The principal difference among judges lay in their decisions on the technology used in scheduling cases for trial and assigning them to courtrooms. Variation in the judges' relations with one another in Erie, Kalamazoo, and Du Page convey such differences across all nine counties. The closeness of Dauphin County's judges, however, was extraordinary, and contrasted sharply with the situation in Kalamazoo. The former held an informal monthly dinner meeting to conduct business. Two drove to work together each day. Two had practiced law together. All considered themselves friends of the others. One captured the flavor of their relations when he observed:

> The thing about our court is that we're all pretty good friends. Actually, most of us are of the same vintage. We were practicing lawyers together and we were post-World War II veterans who came back about the same time and we've known each other for twenty-five to thirty years on a very close basis. . . . And we respect each other, I would say, and we feel perfectly free to go to someone if we have something that we want to talk to them about.

Saginaw's judges enjoyed similarly close and cordial relations. If anything, they were able to coordinate their policies as a group even more effectively than the judges in Dauphin.

Prosecutor Offices and Bureaucratic Controls

Prosecutors' offices differed in case-assignment procedures employed, degree of centralized control over assistants' handling of cases sought, and scope and content of general policies they tried to implement. The decisions they made on these matters shaped both the offices themselves and their performance, as well as the structure and dynamics of the court community as a whole.

Most offices assigned different assistants to handle different stages in a case. Especially in the larger offices, a screening unit, a grand jury unit, a preliminary hearing unit, and a trial unit would each have a chief and group of attorneys assigned to it. This can be thought of as a "horizontal" assignment scheme. Prosecutors used two methods of deciding which assistants would prosecute which defendants. One, relied on by most of the offices, employed some procedure to assign assistants case by case, often matching the case to the assistant's experience and skill. This was the technique used in Erie. Oakland and Kalamazoo relied on the other method — assigning assistants to one courtroom, where they prosecuted all defendants assigned it by the court.

Only Saginaw did not utilize some version of horizontal prosecution. Instead, it assigned assistants to cases at the start, and had them follow the defendant from stage to stage until final disposition. Its assistants did not specialize in preliminary hearings or trials, but rather did everything in a case. This "vertical-prosecution" scheme made assistants very familiar with cases by the time they were ready for disposition. It also spread their appearances before the various judges evenly.

The Erie DA's office represented one end of the range of central control sought by administrators among the nine jurisdictions. It promulgated few formal written policies, gave most of its assistants fairly wide latitude to dispose of cases in ways consistent with the general aim of the office, and relied on informal supervision. Du Page defined the other end. It was highly centralized, rigidly enforcing the "bottom-line" pleas established by the indictment committee. The DA's office relied on a formally structured hierarchy to administer its policies. The other counties fell between Erie and Du Page, but the other two large, suburban ring counties, Oakland and Montgomery, approached Du Page's highly centralized structure. All three had a more bureaucratic, formal, detailed, and rigid system of policies and enforcement mechanisms. Oakland centralized plea bargaining. The DA established written policies prohibiting his assistants from making any agreements involving sentences. He also forbade any charge reductions whatsoever for some defendants (habitual offenders) and for serious charges such as armed robbery, burglary, weapons, and hard drugs. Smaller offices could effectively utilize the informal techniques prevalent in Erie to establish and enforce policies.

Differences in the content of office policy, case-assignment procedures, and supervision shaped the quality of assistant prosecutors' work lives and determined how much and when their personal characteristics and attitudes could shape outcomes. Where offices reviewed all case files to ensure that policies had been followed, some assistants felt uncomfortable, as if they were not completely trusted and had to be watched. In offices where every plea agreement had to be reviewed and approved by a supervisor, individual discretion was reduced. This treatment also bothered some, but not all, assistants. The stringency with which the office administration enforced policies affected the general level of tension. Oakland trial assistants related how one of their colleagues was summarily fired on the same day he violated an office policy on plea bargaining. They resented and feared the administrator who did so. They also adhered closely to policies. In most offices, being fired for violating office policy did not even occur to assistants.

The DA's office in each of the three counties described earlier established its own specific policies on plea bargaining, screening, the sentences it sought in particular crimes, and so on. Each of the other six offices had its unique combination of policies, not easily summarized or categorized. Their specific content, though, is not especially important. Rather, we need only point out that policies on screening, arrests, charging, and plea bargaining shape the behavior and work lives of assistants, and affect the extent of variation and discretion. Furthermore, such policies change, and the changes produce a "ripple effect" of changes that spread throughout the court community.

Judicial Policies, the Defense Bar, and Public Defenders' Practices

Compared to the other counties, Oakland and Saginaw relied upon very different procedures for providing defense counsel to poor defendants. These procedures shaped the structure of the court community, and warrant brief summary.

In Oakland, the trial judge to whom an indigent defendant's case was randomly assigned after initial arraignment appointed a private attorney to represent that defendant in all proceedings, including the preliminary hearing. During a three-month period in 1980 about half the judges spread out their appointments among some fifty lawyers, averaging only 1.7 cases each. Another group concentrated appointments among only about twenty-six lawyers, each averaging 3.7 cases. A third group gave an average of 2.2 cases to thirty-nine attorneys. Saginaw also relied exclusively on private attorneys, who were paid by the county. The Office of Assigned Counsel, however, run by a part-time administrator and a full-time administrative assistant, appointed attorneys in rotation from a list of some ninety approved attorneys.

Both techniques affected the structure of the defense bar and court community, but in somewhat different ways. In Saginaw, more cases involved defense attorneys who were not "regulars," who were not well connected to the grapevine, and who did not feel they needed to be well informed. But in Oakland, the judges who concentrated appointments among a small group of attorneys created a stable of "regulars" who appeared frequently before them and become familiar with the judge and prosecutors assigned to that courtroom. In a sense, each of these stable clusters of judge, prosecutor, and handful of privately appointed attorneys formed their own subcommunity. They exhibited the same characteristics, such as familiarity, consensus on procedures, and mutual influence, that characterized the entire court community in smaller jurisdictions. Other Oakland judges drew upon a larger pool of attorneys for representing indigents. In their courtrooms, the patterns of relationships resembled those found in Saginaw generally. Thus diversity within Oakland's courtroom work groups was considerable because of the judges' varying practices in appointing attorneys to defend the indigent.

Of the six public defender systems in the Pennsylvania and Illinois counties, only Erie's had a head who sought to establish and enforce office-wide policies. This similarity reflects a basic tenet in the ideology of the legal profession; that a public defender should enjoy the same professional autonomy to which any lawyer representing a client is entitled. The six PD offices differed, however, in employing only full-time assistants, part-time assistants, or a mixture of the two; some permitted part-timers to take private criminal clients, others forbade it.

TECHNOLOGIES OF CRIMINAL COURT COMMUNITIES

Figure 8–2 locates the nine counties among the combinations of docket assignments and trial terms available to judges, introduced in Chapter Two. Erie and Kalamazoo both used periodic trial terms with dockets that alternated between civil and criminal cases. Du Page judges also heard criminal and civil cases, but scheduled trials

Figure 8–2

Docket Assignments and Trial Terms in the Nine Courts

	Type of Docket Assignments	
	Mixed (Civil and criminal)	Specialized (Criminal only)
Type of trial term		
Continuous	Du Page (7 of 12)[a]	Peoria (2 of 7) Montgomery (5 of 14)
Periodic (Rotating systems)	Oakland (7 of 7) Kalamazoo (4 of 4) Saginaw (5 of 5) Dauphin (5 of 6) Erie (5 of 5)	St. Clair (3 of 7)

[a]Number of judges hearing criminal cases, among total number of judges

continuously rather than during designated weeks. In the brief description here of the procedures used in Peoria, Montgomery, and St. Clair, we clarify the characteristics of the combinations presented in Figure 8–2 and examine their effects.

Two of Peoria's seven judges, five of Montgomery's fourteen, and three of St. Clair's seven devoted themselves exclusively to criminal cases for periods of six months or more. Thus, some of their judges specialized in criminal work at any one time. In Montgomery, judges served a six-month term on criminal cases; some received several consecutive criminal assignments. At the time of our field research in spring and summer 1980, Peoria's two criminal judges heard only criminal cases. The three counties differed, however, in the scheduling of trials. In Montgomery and Peoria, they interspersed trials with guilty pleas and hearings continuously. In St. Clair, the judges specializing in criminal work heard trials for two weeks, and then spent two weeks on other criminal matters.

Criminal courts also employ several techniques for organizing calendars and assigning cases to specific judges. As we saw in Chapter Two, individual calendar systems assign cases to a specific judge early in the life of a case. That judge normally bears full responsibility for the case until final disposition. Master calendar systems dispatch cases ready for a hearing, plea, or trial from a central pool to a judge using one of three techniques: random draw, sequential (the next case in an established queue), and personalized (at the discretion of some official designated to make the decision). Figure 8–3 summarizes the combinations of calendars and assignment methods used by the courts we studied. Two of the combinations possible in theory did not appear.

The technologies employed by the other six counties included features important to understanding how case assignment and calendaring affected their court communities' work. In Peoria, the prosecutor's office decided which of its assistants would handle each case, and the case was then sent to the judge to whose courtroom the assistant was permanently assigned. In effect, this system permitted the prosecutor to pick which judge heard each case. An experienced assistant prosecutor in Dauphin also assigned cases to courtrooms.

In Peoria in 1980 we found relatively little difference in the two judges hearing criminal cases. Nearly everyone, however, singled out one judge in Dauphin as a tough sentencer who loved to preside over trials. Many defense attorneys felt that since everyone knew a case that went to trial might end up in his courtroom, that awareness shaped plea bargaining to the prosecutor's benefit. Others argued that this judge spent a lot of time hearing trials that would have resulted in stiff sentences anyway, thereby pushing other defendants

Figure 8–3

Types of Calendars and Case-Assignment Methods

| | Type of Calendar | |
Assignment method	Individual	Master
Random	Du Page Oakland Kalamazoo Saginaw	
Personalized	Peoria	Erie[a] St. Clair[a] Dauphin[a]
Sequential		Montgomery[a]

[a] Plea routing is possible.

before less harsh judges. Everyone agreed, however, that who the judge would be was an important topic in discussions leading to guilty pleas.

Montgomery County employed a unique technology that also shaped the content of pleas and the strategies attorneys used. For each case, a card with the name of the defendant, prosecutor, and defense attorney was made. The cards were placed in a queue determined by an employee of the court administrator, who established a sequence of cases weeks before scheduled disposition based on what other cases the prosecutor and defense attorney had coming up. As cases went to courtrooms, cards for those remaining in the queue ascended a pegged standby board. When cases scheduled for trial got to the top of the board, the card was placed on the peg representing the courtroom that had just cleared, and the attorneys were sent to that judge. Cases headed for a guilty-plea disposition, however, could usually be routed in a particular judge's courtroom upon agreement by the attorneys, and before they had reached the top of the standby board.

The assignment room containing the pegged board and cards was the hub of the entire procedure. Every defense attorney and prosecutor appeared there personally several times before a case actually went to a courtroom for disposition. It was a natural place to hang out and gossip while waiting for a case to be assigned. More of the tangled branches of Montgomery's elaborate grapevine met in the assignment room than anywhere else. The procedure depended on the competence, fairness, and toughness of the woman who established the queue and routed pleas and trials to open courtrooms. Nearly everyone echoed these observations by a private defense attorney: .

> I'll tell you, one of the biggest problems this county would ever have is if _____ got up one day and quit. The criminal courts would come into some real problems, because she handles attorneys very well. When I say attorneys, I mean DAs and defense attorneys. And she knows who does what and who does it best. She does an excellent job, I'll tell you.

Guilty pleas in Montgomery often included agreement on which judge would take the plea. Defense attorneys' decisions to plea sometimes depended on their ability to avoid a specific judge. Consequently, the guilty-plea process revolved around decisions made in the assignment room. A private defense attorney told us he didn't like to plead clients before Judge A. We asked if he ever said to the assignment clerk, "Don't send me to Judge A." His response provided a glimpse at the intricate and subtle interactions that took place:

> Yeah. I've often done that. I'll go to _____ and say, "Look _____ . I got this case. If you send it to Judge B or Judge C or Judge D or somebody like that, it's a guilty plea. If you send it to Judge A, it's a jury trial." Her function, of course, is to move cases. . . . the judges don't know they're next in line for a case and she doesn't send it.

The operation of Montgomery's assignment room provides support for our assertion in Chapter Two that assignment procedures subtly but profoundly influence case outcomes and the work lives of court community members. The implications of scheduling in courts, however, extend beyond convenience and preference for participants to the very way in which they go about their work. The effect of different technologies in Peoria and Dauphin counties illustrates this influence especially well. Both had about the same number of judges and prosecutors, but used different technologies, as Figure 8–2 shows. In Peoria, two judges handled criminal cases continuously. The prosecutor assigned two attorneys to each, with a fifth shuffling between the courtrooms as needed. While one assistant prosecutor handled a case, the other assigned to that courtroom could prepare the next. Dauphin, however, scheduled periodic criminal trial terms during which five judges simultaneously presided over trials or took pleas in cases scheduled for trial. Every assistant prosecutor worked almost full time during criminal trial weeks, handling a sequence of cases without a break. This schedule left little or no time to prepare the next case. The sequence of preparing a number of cases during non-trial weeks followed by hectic trial terms in Dauphin resembled the system in Erie.

How well cases could be prepared and how competently they could be presented was affected substantially by this arrangement. Dauphin's criminal trial weeks reminded its assistant prosecutors of those times in their college career when they had five final exams scheduled in two days.

Figure 8–4 summarizes the distribution of assignment patterns

Figure 8–4

Assignment Practices of Indigent Defense Systems

| | Assignment Practices | |
	By Judge	Case-by-Case
Representation practices Continuous	Oakland	Dauphin Erie Kalamazoo Saginaw
Discontinuous	Du Page Peoria	Montgomery St. Clair

used by the nine counties' indigent defense systems. In three counties, the judge to whom a defendant's case was sent dictated which publicly paid attorney represented him or her. Du Page and Peoria assigned their public defenders to one judge's courtroom, and they handled the cases of defendants who arrived there; in Oakland, the judges chose poor defendants' attorneys after the case appeared on their docket. The other six counties used a variety of procedures, depending on the case, to choose the attorney who would represent each poor defendant. Who the judge might be had little effect in assigning a defender in these six counties.

As Figure 8–4 indicates, five counties provided "continuous" representation by the same attorney throughout the life of a case. Contract attorneys in Kalamazoo and public defenders in Dauphin appeared at their clients' preliminary hearings and stuck with them to the end of the case. In Montgomery, however, representation was "discontinuous" in that preliminary hearings took place in twenty-nine geographically dispersed lower courts, where a private attorney was paid $40 by the county for the privilege of representing indigents. When they got to the trial court, a regular full- or part-time member of the PD's staff took over.

The differences reflected in Figure 8–4 affected the criminal process in several vital ways. The quality of the relationship between attorney and client obviously suffered when different attorneys took over the case. Some information about the case evaporated when representation was not continuous. Finally, attorneys in Oakland, Du

Page, and Peoria who stayed in one courtroom could develop close working relationships with the judge.

SPATIAL RELATIONS AND GEOGRAPHY

The arrangement of various offices within a courthouse subtly influences the structure of courthouse communities and their grapevines. A number of examples have already been presented. The proximity of Erie's judges to one another facilitated informal communication among them, and made it easy for prosecutors and defense attorneys to drop in. The two Kalamazoo judges with strained relations shared adjoining quarters separate from the other two judges. Montgomery's case-assignment room served as a center of gossip and neutral gathering place for prosecutors and defense attorneys.

The other counties provided additional examples of the effects of physical location, but did not provide additional insights into them. The city of Peoria had most of the county's population, and nearly all its attorneys worked within a few blocks of the courthouse. Members of the bar ran into each other not only in the courthouse, but on the street and in the eating establishments downtown that they frequented. Saginaw's courthouse, located downtown, also sat within a few blocks of the offices of Saginaw's lawyers. It housed the courtrooms of the county's district judges, further concentrating the criminal court community. A neighboring restaurant provided a regular table at lunch for courthouse regulars that was a place not only for trading gossip, but also for discussing and resolving problems. Oakland's multibuilding governmental campus physically separated the courts from other county offices, and the entire campus sat in splendid isolation from both private offices and restaurants.

LINKS TO OTHER COMMUNITIES

To what extent do court communities reflect external influences emanating from the communities, regions, and states they serve? The differences found among counties within a state suggest that local characteristics shape court communities. Looking at all nine courts also, however, indicates that "state-related" factors have an important part in shaping the work of court communities. We will look at these factors first.

Characteristics Associated with States

Prison capacity, which depends on the legislature's willingness to spend the large sums new prisons require, varied substantially.[1] Michigan's legislature apparently had been willing to do so. Since 1970, it had funded six new prison facilities, whereas Illinois had built two, and Pennsylvania none. Michigan had more than 127 prison spaces available for adults per 100,000 of population in 1979, Illinois almost 101, and Pennsylvania just under 69. Michigan's higher capacity did not result solely from a higher arrest rate. Looking at the number of spaces per adult arrest for violent personal crimes plus burglary shows Michigan had almost twice as much prison space as Pennsylvania (.64 versus .34); the Illinois rate at .43 came closer to Pennsylvania's. We also examined incarceration rates after controlling statistically for differences both in the rate of reported violent crimes and in actual arrests for the nine counties. Michigan again ranked most punitive by a big margin, with Illinois slightly more so than Pennsylvania. At the beginning of 1980, Michigan had filled its greater capacity and then some. Its prison population soared to 115 percent of rated capacity. Illinois and Pennsylvania came in at 99 percent and 91 percent of capacity, respectively.[2]

The content of state statutes pertaining to criminal justice also differs. Laws on speedy trials appear to shape case length directly. The relatively toothless speedy-trial law in Michigan described in Chapter Six probably accounts for the longer disposition times found there. The symbolic severity of punishment as reflected in the criminal code also varied. Examination of statutory maximums for eleven common and easily compared offenses found Michigan's clearly higher than those of either Pennsylvania or Illinois.[3] Two analyses

[1]For a discussion of the three states' correctional facilities and capacity, see Peter F. Nardulli, Roy B. Flemming, and James Eisenstein, *The Tenor of Justice* (Champaign-Urbana, Ill.: University of Illinois Press, 1987), Chapter 4. See also United States Department of Justice, *Sourcebook of Criminal Justice Statistics* (Washington, D.C.: 1981), Tables 1.67–1.70.

[2]United States Department of Justice, *Sourcebook of Criminal Justice Statistics* (Washington, D.C.: 1981), Tables 1.67–1.70.

[3]For a discussion of how these measures were obtained, see Nardulli et al., *Tenor,* ibid., Chapter 4.

of these maximums led to the same conclusion: Michigan's sentencing code was severest; the Illinois and Pennsylvania codes differed little.

These characteristics may help to explain why all three Michigan counties sentenced defendants more harshly than the six counties in the other two states. Our research was not designed to test the contribution of prison capacity or the severity of the criminal code to case outcomes, and so we cannot empirically demonstrate such links. The inference that the increased prison capacity in Michigan contributed to harsher sentences seems to make sense, however. Maximum sentences are mainly symbolic because they are rarely imposed. They suggest, though, that the state political culture supports strict punishment, encouraging higher incarceration rates and longer terms. Michigan's higher prison capacity provided the opportunity to translate the desire to punish into reality.

Other evidence that Michigan's political culture contributed to the greater harshness its three counties displayed can be cited. Though difficult to measure and describe precisely, differences can be seen in the expectations people have about what government should do, the characteristics of the political elite, and the practices used in governing. Using data on religious affiliation in the population, students of state political culture have placed Michigan among the "moralistic" states, and Illinois and Pennsylvania among the "individualistic" ones.[4]

The moralistic culture sees government and politics as a means for making judgments and improving society. The individualistic culture sees politics as conflict, a means for seeking one's self-interest. The moralistic culture supports reliance on punishment and the individualistic one promotes accommodation of demands by individuals and groups for lighter sentences. These inferences are plausible but not especially clear or convincing. Historical data on incarceration rates do, however, provide some support for the role of moralistic culture in sentencing. They show that Michigan imprisoned a much higher proportion of its residents than Pennsylvania did between 1926 and 1980, and a somewhat higher proportion than Illinois for all but a brief period in the 1930s.[5]

[4] Charles A. Johnson, "Political Culture in American States: Elazar's Formulation Examined," 20 *American Journal of Political Science* (1976), pp. 491–509; Daniel Elazar, *American Federalism; A View from the States* (Thomas Crowell: New York, 1966).

[5] Nardulli et al., *Tenor*, op. cit., Chapter 4.

A mixed bag of other state-related factors seems to shape court community characteristics. Michigan law gave prosecutors control over charging by requiring their approval of proposed police charges before initial arraignment. Its state Supreme Court exercised tighter supervision over the lower courts than did that of Pennsylvania or Illinois. Differences among the three states in the control that trial judges had over the hiring, supervision, and removal of lower court judges ranged from almost nonexistent in Pennsylvania to substantial in Illinois. Finally, jurisdictions in a state may adopt similar technologies partially as a result of communication at statewide conferences or through magazines published by statewide associations.

State-related factors exert a significant but not overwhelming influence in shaping the operation of court communities. No analysis of courts can be complete without taking them into account.

County Legal Cultures

So many intricate connections appear between the characteristics of the counties and the criminal court communities that it is impossible to describe court communities without referring to them. For each of the aspects of court communities we have discussed, a link can easily be found. A few brief examples of each will recall and highlight such links.

The court community culture of Peoria fit naturally into the local pride and civic boosterism that characterized the city and county. The political culture and structure of Montgomery and St. Clair injected partisan considerations into the hiring of court personnel and the selection of judges. The interdependence of St. Clair and Erie court community members stemming from out-of-court friendships, and ties based on family, religion, school, and common business enterprises obviously reflected the small-town, stable feeling in the larger community. The distribution of power in the court community and the level of conflict among its principals varied in Montgomery and Du Page partly because the local Republican organizations differed in effectiveness. The grapevines in these two counties also mirrored these differences. Montgomery's public defender's office responded to the needs of the private bar by carefully scrutinizing defendants' eligibility for public defense in order to avoid taking business away from private attorneys. The PD's office in Dauphin walked a fine line between providing vigorous defense on the one hand and not offending the judges or the local political establishment on the other. It avoided "rocking the boat" in some instances to maintain operating freedom in other areas, always aware that going too far would result in political trouble. The technique used to assign attorneys to poor defendants in Saginaw came about in response to newspaper stories criticizing the previous practice, which resulted in a few attorneys representing many defendants. The change this criticism induced expanded the court community substantially by bringing many nonregular attorneys to court handling only a few cases each year. The effects of the physical arrangement of the courthouse and the distribution of attorneys' offices on social relations and the grapevine have been repeatedly referred to.

SUMMARY

The separate characteristics of court communities discussed in each of this chapter's sections are analytically distinct. It was useful to discuss each in turn. This method of presentation should not, however, obscure the fundamental reality of these court communities. They are organic wholes, with numerous interconnections. County legal culture, the physical layout of the courthouse, the grapevine, the structure and strength of the political parties, and so on, interact in ways too numerous and subtle to describe completely. This fundamental connectedness provides an appropriate concluding observation to our argument that understanding criminal courts improves by looking at nine counties. It is that one can usefully inquire into the nature of a court community by examining each of the elements of the metaphor presented in Chapter Two. It is also necessary, however, to then integrate them in order to understand fully the intricate structure and dynamics of the court community.

CHAPTER NINE

Case Outcomes in
Nine Middle-Sized Courts

INTRODUCTION

Society charges criminal courts with disposing of the defendants' cases sent to them. Understandably, then, many of the questions typically asked about criminal courts are focused on case outcomes: How many defendants are convicted? Do they enter a plea of guilty or demand a trial? If they plead guilty, what causes them to do so? Do they get anything in return? What sentences do court communities impose on convicted defendants? Is justice swift or slow?

We begin this chapter with a summary description of the answers to these questions that we found in the patterns of case disposition among our nine counties. First we sketch the variations found in the raw material with which they work—the characteristics of the charges and defendants who come to court. Then we look at the patterns of disposition, giving close attention to guilty pleas. This discussion sets the stage for a summary of the sentences imposed. Finally, we present information on how long it took to finish cases from arrest to disposition in all nine counties. During this initial description we will not attempt to explain why these outcomes were reached.

Merely presenting the end results of cases ignores the dynamics that produced them. Though we cannot describe the guilty-plea process in our other six counties in as much detail as we provided for Erie, Kalamazoo, and Du Page, we can identify several general features in the dynamics of the guilty-plea process.

What accounts for the patterns we found? To ask the question in its most elemental form, Why? To what extent do the "case-specific" characteristics of the crime and defendant, independent of the context, determine outcomes, and to what extent do the many factors suggested by the metaphor of courts as communities come into play? This question is pivotal for this book, for its answer will help assess how much the metaphor helps in understanding courts. This inquiry cannot be undertaken, however, without discussing what we can expect to be able to explain and predict. That is, we need to lay out the limits to explanation and prediction that courts present. We conclude this chapter by discussing such explanation and its limits.

CASES AND DEFENDANTS IN THE NINE COUNTIES

The mixture of cases brought to the nine court communities for disposition varied substantially. These differences stemmed only in part from the patterns of crime found in each. The attrition that took place in Erie in crimes reported by the police to actual arrests to charges heard in the trial court occurred everywhere. Court communities usually do not affect patterns of crime and police enforcement practices, and when they do, their influence is indirect and quite small. Only where the prosecutor effectively screens the cases the police propose to bring to court or where lower judges can be induced to dismiss or screen weak and minor cases can components of the court community shape the caseload. Some prosecutor screening took place everywhere but in the three Pennsylvania counties, though the degree to which it molded the caseload varied. Illinois lower court judges responded to initiatives from the trial judges who hired them, but Pennsylvania's lower judges, generally immune to such pressure, typically screened very few cases with weak evidence.

The combined effects of differences in number and types of crimes reported to the police, arrest rate, and screening practices produced wide disparity in the charges defendants faced, as Figure 9–1 shows. It confirms our previous assertion that property crimes constitute a much greater proportion of caseloads than crimes of violence. It also reveals, however, major differences in the mixture of crimes in the caseloads among the counties within this general pattern. Some of these differences seem to result from state-related factors, most notably with drunk-driving cases. With just three counties in each state, however, we cannot be entirely certain. In fact, we found wide differences *within* the three Illinois and Pennsylvania counties in the proportion of cases involving crimes against the person. Counties in the same state thus dealt with different profiles of

Figure 9–1

Proportion of Caseload for Three Broad Crime Categories,
by County

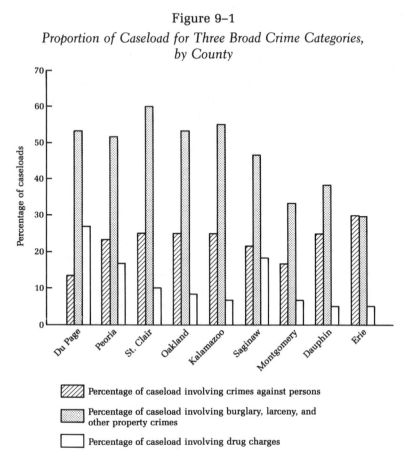

☑ Percentage of caseload involving crimes against persons

▨ Percentage of caseload involving burglary, larceny, and
  other property crimes

☐ Percentage of caseload involving drug charges

Du Page, with 12.5 percent, and Erie at 30 percent, sit at the poles of the range for the proportion of defendants facing charges involving crimes against persons. Their positions were reversed for drug charges. The Pennsylvania counties handled large numbers of drunk-driving cases, which did not fit into any of the three broad categories used for this graph, reducing the proportion of property crimes in the Pennsylvania counties' caseload.

Differences *within* states are large. St. Clair has almost double Du Page's proportion of crimes against persons—24.6 versus 12.5 percent; for Erie and Montgomery, the gap was equivalent, 30.0 and 17.2 percent.

Differences within each *type* of county were also found. The ring counties of Du Page and Montgomery heard fewest crimes against persons, though Oakland ranked in the middle. Drugs made up more than one-fourth of Du Page's cases, less than 10 percent of Oakland's and Montgomery's.

Source: Case samples

charges. Our data also suggest equivalent differences within each group of triplet counties.

The substantial differences in the crimes represented in the caseload cannot be fully accounted for by either the type of county or the state in which it is located. The contours of caseload composition exhibit some big bumps. The relative infrequency of personal crimes compared to property crimes like burglary and theft did, however, characterize all nine counties. Other research has uncovered the same pattern.[1] Despite media attention to crimes and cases involving interpersonal violence, in practice criminal courts deal mostly with defendants charged with crimes against property.[2]

The composition of the caseload varies in other ways. The proportion of defendants with no prior criminal record ranged from about one-fourth in Kalamazoo to more than half in Du Page. St. Clair, with the highest percentage of blacks in its population, found that 64 percent of its defendants were black, but in four other counties more than two-thirds of the defendants were white. The details of these differences evaporate quickly but the principal fact stands out: Caseloads vary. The content of this variation is a critical piece of the puzzle that we seek to assemble for each county because the shape and size of other pieces depend directly on it. The level of bail, the proportion of defendants released, the seriousness of defendants' prior criminal record, and the harshness of sentences imposed are all influenced by the variation in caseload.

CONTOURS OF CASE OUTCOMES

Data on how cases from all nine counties ended confirm what the patterns in Erie, Kalamazoo, and Du Page implied. Hardly any cases ended in the manner that the legal metaphor would suggest — a conviction or acquittal after a full jury trial. In fact, fewer than 8 percent of the pool of cases from all nine counties were decided by a trial, including both traditional jury trials and trials conducted before a

[1] Even in jurisdictions notorious for high rates of violent crimes, the proportion of property offenses is high. See the study of New York City's courts by the Vera Institute of Justice. *Felony Arrests: Their Prosecution and Disposition in New York City's Courts* (New York: Vera Institute of Justice), p. 5.

[2] Of course, property crimes are often quite disturbing to victims, especially when a home or apartment is invaded by a stranger and burglarized. A property crime can be serious.

judge alone. Of the 7,051 defendants for whom we have disposition data, only 553 went to trial. Just 151 won acquittal; more than 2.5 times as many were convicted.

What happened to the rest? The overwhelming proportion pled guilty or accepted the close equivalent of a plea, diversion into a program like Pennsylvania's Accelerated Rehabilitative Disposition (ARD) or Michigan's Youth Training Act (YTA). Just over 11 percent, one in nine, had their cases dismissed.

The similarity in the pattern of distribution of outcomes across all nine jurisdictions is striking. Figure 9–2 shows in a bar graph the proportion of cases ended by plea or diversion, trial conviction or acquittal, or dismissal in each county. The dominant bar representing guilty pleas and diversions indicates that the other counties basically conformed to the pattern in Erie, Kalamazoo, and Du Page.

Of course, we saw some differences in the distribution of outcomes. Pleas and diversion ranged from Peoria's 74 percent to Montgomery's almost 90 percent rate. And though dismissals everywhere made up less than 20 percent of dispositions, Montgomery's 4.8 percent rate was almost one-fourth the high of 17.7 percent in Peoria. These differences do not, however, alter the basic similarity in outcomes pictured in Figure 9–2, a similarity all the more striking because the composition of the caseload and defendants' characteristics vary.

DIFFERENCES IN GUILTY-PLEA PROCESSES

If all the counties obtained a conviction or its equivalent through a guilty plea or diversion for most defendants, they nonetheless used different routes to arrive at this common outcome. For one thing, four counties relied heavily on diversion—the three Pennsylvania jurisdictions and Oakland. The details of just how guilty pleas came about, described in all their subtlety and complexity for Erie, Kalamazoo, and Du Page, showed just as much variety and intricacy in each of the other counties. We cannot hope to provide equally elaborate and sophisticated descriptions of their guilty-plea processes, but we will identify general patterns in the guilty process that stand out as we look at them across the nine counties.

Figure 9–2
Method of Disposition of County Caseload

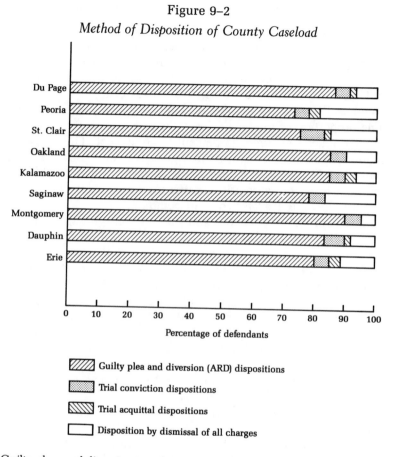

Percentage of defendants

▨ Guilty plea and diversion (ARD) dispositions

▦ Trial conviction dispositions

▧ Trial acquittal dispositions

☐ Disposition by dismissal of all charges

Guilty pleas and diversion together, represented by the left-hand portion of each bar, account for most dispositions in every county. Though the differences in disposition patterns among counties were small, they were not meaningless. Nearly 12 percentage points separate the highest guilty-plea rate in Montgomery from the lowest in Saginaw. One defendant in six won dismissal of all charges in Saginaw and Peoria; in Montgomery, it was one in twenty. Trial acquittals were too infrequent in Oakland (1.3 percent), Saginaw (1.3 percent), and Montgomery (.7 percent) to display in the bar chart.

Source: Case samples

Reductions in Charges and Count Drops

Each county's guilty-plea procedure evolved its own practice on changes in counts and charges. As we explained in Chapter Five, guilty pleas often involve reductions in the number of charges against a defendant, or reduction in the most serious offense charged.

Unless more than one offense was initially charged, no reduction could be offered in the number of counts to which a defendant pled. The proportion of multicount cases in Erie exceeded Kalamazoo's rate by a factor of three, 48 percent to 16 percent. The equivalent figure for each county appears in Figure 9–3. Montgomery County topped all others by a wide margin; St. Clair came close to Kalamazoo. Clearly, these significant differences affected the latitude for count reductions available to court communities.

The contrast between the guilty-plea system in Erie and Kalamazoo shown in Table 6–1 reveals meaningful differences in count bargaining. Kalamazoo prosecutors sought "on-the-nose" pleas, reducing neither the number of counts nor the seriousness of the first charge. One other county, Dauphin, followed a very similar practice. We refer to it as a "minimalist" count and charge-bargaining pattern to indicate that few guilty pleas dealt with changes in either. Nearly 90 percent of defendants who pled guilty in Dauphin and 85 percent in Kalamazoo did so to the same set of charges on which they were initially arraigned. The equivalent figure for the next closest county, Oakland, is only 63 percent. Figure 9–4 summarizes the pattern of count drops for the nine counties.

Erie and Du Page, along with Montgomery, formed a second pattern of count bargaining. They readily dropped the number of counts, but preserved the most serious charge. Because sentences for additional counts usually add little or nothing to a defendant's sentence, we call this the "symbolic" pattern. As Figure 9–4 shows, defendants in these three counties rarely won reduction in the primary charge. A drop in the primary charge, from armed robbery to assault or from burglary to unlawful entry, is the sort of reduction most likely to lead to a less severe sentence.

Peoria, St. Clair, and Oakland offered reductions in both the number of counts and the seriousness of the first charge, but at moderate rates. This practice earned them the accurate if undramatic label of "middling" counties. Finally, Saginaw stands alone as a "maximalist" county, frequently giving reductions in both the number of charges and, more important, the seriousness of the first one. A noticeable

Figure 9–3

*Proportion of Trial Court Defendants Initially Charged
with More Than One Offense*

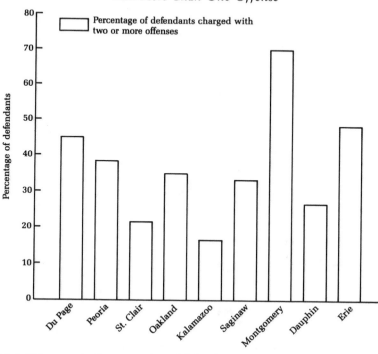

Vast differences in the proportion of defendants facing more than one charge
are displayed. Montgomery and Kalamazoo present extreme contrasts, but
even the discrepancy between the other counties, where the range extends
from 21 percent to 48 percent, is substantial.

Source: Case samples

peak for Saginaw shows up in Figure 9–4 in the bar representing
frequency of reductions in the primary charge.

Because lowering the most serious charge is the most meaningful
change in counts, differences in their frequency are an especially
significant characteristic of the guilty-plea process. The unusually
high rate in Saginaw, double that of the next highest county, should
not overshadow the significant differences among the other counties. Only one guilty plea in twenty in Dauphin included a drop in
the primary charge; in Peoria and St. Clair, the ratio was one in five.

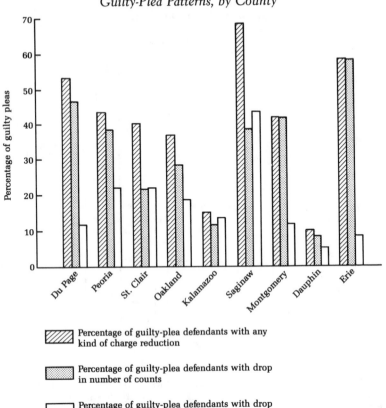

Figure 9–4

Guilty-Plea Patterns, by County

Percentage of guilty pleas

- ▨ Percentage of guilty-plea defendants with any kind of charge reduction
- ▦ Percentage of guilty-plea defendants with drop in number of counts
- ☐ Percentage of guilty-plea defendants with drop in level of the primary charge

The first bar for each county, which indicates the percentage of cases with any type of count change, shows that court communities employ very different disposition techniques. Six counties range between 40 percent and 60 percent; Saginaw at the upper end, and Kalamazoo and Dauphin at the lower, fall outside this midrange. The third bar, indicating the frequency of drops in primary charges, also confirms the wide variation.

Source: Case samples

Sentence Agreements and Plea Routing

Guilty-plea systems differ in several ways other than changes in the number or level of counts. Most significant is whether agreements on sentences were on the guilty-plea agenda. As we explain in Chapter Six, such pleas involve a stated agreement between prosecutor and defense attorney on the sentence that will be recommended, followed by the judge's acceptance. Their presence usually cannot be detected by examining court records, but they profoundly shape guilty-plea systems. Indeed, counties with similar patterns of changes in the number and level of counts may differ in whether or not sentences enter into plea agreements. Whereas in Erie the judges were reluctant even to hear recommendations about sentences, such recommendations were routinely made and accepted in Montgomery. Though Erie and Montgomery fell into the symbolic pattern on *count and charge* reductions, the explicit understandings about sentences added in Montgomery meant that in practice plea agreements there were not merely symbolic, but instead were often very substantive. Similar differences appeared between the minimalist counties. Kalamazoo prosecutors readily included sentence recommendations with their on-the-nose pleas; Dauphin prosecutors offered neither reductions in the number or seriousness of charges nor sentence recommendations.

Another difference in guilty-plea systems—availability of routing—emerges when we compare Kalamazoo and Dauphin. At the time of our field research, the random assignment of cases to judges in Kalamazoo allowed no shopping. But the prosecutors in Dauphin, the other minimalist county, routinely used their power to assign cases to judges as an integral part of their plea offers. As in Erie, the judge to whom the plea would be taken became a vital part of many plea agreements. Most prosecutors and defense attorneys in both counties told us they felt that in some cases who the judge was made a difference in the sentence imposed. Table 9–1 summarizes the combinations we found in availability of routing cases to judges and presence of sentence agreements.

DISTRIBUTION OF SENTENCES

When we pooled convicted defendants from all nine counties and examined the sentences imposed, we found that a majority walked out of court with some combination of probation, fine, and diversion.

Table 9–1

Guilty-Plea Systems: Sentence Bargaining and "Routing" of Cases

Do guilty pleas include sentence recommendations usually followed by judges?			Is "Routing" of cases to judges possible?		
Yes	Occasionally	No	Yes	Occasionally	No
Montgomery Du Page Peoria Kalamazoo	St. Clair	Dauphin Erie Oakland Saginaw	Montgomery Dauphin	St. Clair Erie	Du Page Peoria Kalamazoo Oakland Saginaw

They did not spend additional time incarcerated after sentencing. Of those who did serve time, more than half did so in the county jail rather than a state penitentiary. The predominance of property crimes over more notorious and threatening crimes of violence and the high proportion of first offenders in large part account for these outcomes.

The overall rates of incarceration, of course, conceal substantial variation among the counties, though most conformed roughly to the general pattern. In Chapter Seven we show that Kalamazoo sent defendants to the penitentiary at four times the rate Du Page did. Figure 9–5 presents the distribution of sentence types for all nine counties. The bottom two sections of each county's bar represent the incarceration rate—the proportion sent to the penitentiary or county jail, respectively. The incarceration rate varied dramatically, from a low of less than 24 percent in Montgomery to Kalamazoo's 72.4 percent. In most of the counties, less than half of convicted defendants spend additional time in custody.

The prevalence of ARD dispositions in Pennsylvania reinforces the point that differences in a county's caseload can produce misleading conclusions about sentencing if we look only at the rough measures of severity used in Figure 9–5. Comparing sentences for convicted defendants arrested for the *same* offense is a more sophisticated way of measuring harshness. Figure 9–6 presents such a comparison. It provides additional evidence for the general conclusion that sentences differed significantly among the nine counties.

Figure 9–5

Type of Sentence Imposed on Convicted Defendants

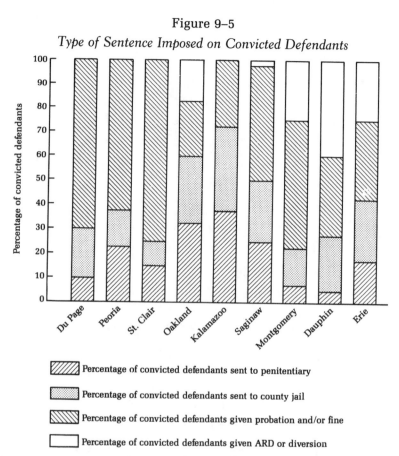

Percentage of convicted defendants sent to penitentiary

Percentage of convicted defendants sent to county jail

Percentage of convicted defendants given probation and/or fine

Percentage of convicted defendants given ARD or diversion

Counties sentenced convicted defendants very differently. All three Pennsylvania counties relied heavily on diversion; only Oakland among the others did so. The rates for all four types of sentences represented, in fact, differed significantly.

Source: Case samples

Information on the median length of sentence imposed for these same offenses produces similar conclusions. Figure 9–7 displays the same information as Figure 7–9; comparing them will help in understanding both.

The foregoing analysis of severity required looking at several graphs, each with much information on a limited aspect of sentenc-

Figure 9–6

Incarceration Rate for Three Offenses, by County

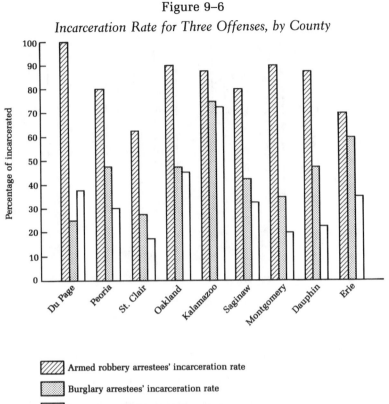

◪ Armed robbery arrestees' incarceration rate

▩ Burglary arrestees' incarceration rate

▢ Larceny arrestees' incarceration rate

In all but two counties, 80 percent or more convicted defendants arrested for armed robbery went to prison or jail. Erie at 72 percent and Saginaw at 62 percent are the two exceptions. The 38 percent spread between Erie and Montgomery, however, is less than the spread for burglary or larceny. Kalamazoo's severity, which surpassed Erie's and Du Page's, as shown in Figure 7–9, ranks high on burglary and larceny among all nine counties. Oakland also appears harsh, St. Clair lenient.

ing. The convoluted discussion this method of presentation produced raises the question of whether there might be a simple way to summarize these data. The answer is no, there is no *simple* way. We do, however, have a *complicated* way of producing one measure comparing median sentence length. By merging all 5,578 sentenced defendants and applying a statistical procedure called analysis of co-

Figure 9–7

Median Months Incarcerated for Three Offenses, by County

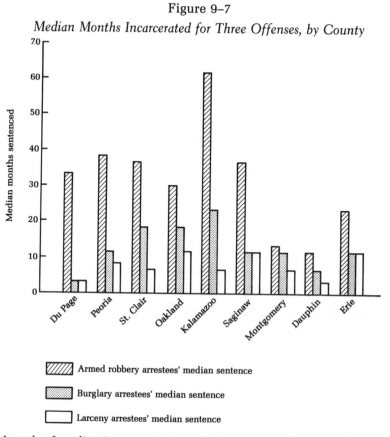

Length of median incarceration varied dramatically, with Kalamazoo appearing most severe, the three Pennsylvania counties most lenient. Variation in sentence length for armed robbers exceeded that for the other two offenses, particularly larceny.

variance with stepwise regression, we can compare minimum sentences for each county. This procedure takes into account (statistically controls for) differences in the offenses charged and the prior records of defendants.[3] Figure 9–8 presents the results of this anal-

[3]For a complete discussion of this analysis, see Peter F. Nardulli, Roy B. Flemming, and James Eisenstein, *The Tenor of Justice* (Champaign-Urbana, Ill: University of Illinois Press, 1987), Chapter 10.

Figure 9–8

Analysis of Covariance for Minimum Months of Confinement

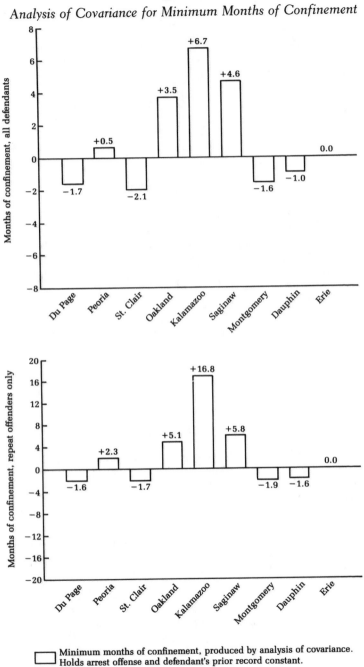

Minimum months of confinement, produced by analysis of covariance. Holds arrest offense and defendant's prior record constant.

ysis. It confirms the impression of Kalamazoo's relative harshness from the earlier analysis when all nine counties are compared in this manner. Kalamazoo sentenced more severely than the other eight counties, and by a substantial margin.

THE PACE OF JUSTICE

Comparing how long it took to dispose of cases poses far fewer problems than analyzing sentencing patterns. Figure 9–9 presents a box-and-whiskers diagram on case length or the number of days from arrest to final disposition for all nine counties. It provides another variation on the continuing theme of intercounty differences through the obvious differences in shape of box and length of whisker. It also clearly shows the relative slowness of the three Michigan counties when it comes to disposing of defendants' cases. Peoria was especially swift, in part reflecting the personalities and work habits of the two judges assigned to criminal cases during our field research.

CONCESSIONS AND CONSENSUS IN THE GUILTY-PLEA SYSTEM

In Chapter Five we introduce two competing explanations of how a guilty plea can come about. The concessions model emphasizes explicit bargaining over the terms of the agreement, haggling in the style of a middle-eastern bazaar. The consensus model likens agreements to a shopper's acceptance of a supermarket's posted prices. Once the nature of the item is known, the posted price, the "going rate," prevails. In Chapter Five we also promise later discussion of

---

These figures compare relative severity in length of all sentences, using Erie, which ranked in the middle, as the benchmark. The top figure shows that defendants with the same criminal record charged with the same offense received on average a minimum sentence 6.7 months longer in Kalamazoo than in Erie. The Michigan counties' severity stands out.

Differences in sentence length among counties increase when just repeat offenders are examined. As the bottom figure shows, both Kalamazoo and Peoria appear to sentence repeat offenders much more harshly. The other counties, however, did not handle repeat offenders much differently from all defendants.

Figure 9–9
Days from Arrest to Disposition for All Cases by County

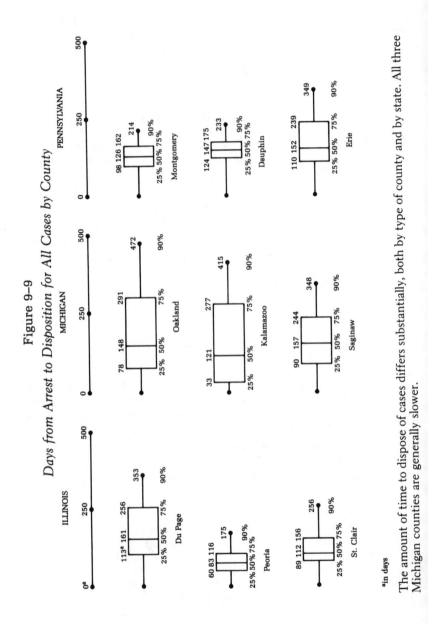

[a]in days

The amount of time to dispose of cases differs substantially, both by type of county and by state. All three Michigan counties are generally slower.

the relative frequency with which pleas result from consensus or concessions. We are now able to present this discussion.[4]

We believe both methods will occur in every jurisdiction. The crucial question is: What is the *relative frequency* of each? Our study can provide a useful start toward an answer, which rests on analysis of actual case outcomes for thousands of defendants in our nine counties. Of course, the conclusions reached for our group of nine middle-sized counties will not indicate what happens elsewhere. Keeping these qualifications in mind, we can draw several important conclusions about the frequency of each type of plea.

The principal conclusion states that in most of our nine counties a very high proportion of pleas results from consensus rather than concessions. An analysis of all cases ending in a guilty plea provides the main source of evidence for this conclusion. We looked at the changes that occurred in the number and level of counts between arrest and conviction. Sixty percent of the 5,600 defendants pled to the identical charges they faced at arrest. If no reduction in the number or level of charges occurred, no successful bargaining over counts produced the plea. Of course, the concession type of bargaining could have involved the type and length of sentence. We know, in fact, that this bargaining sometimes occurred in counties like Kalamazoo and Montgomery. As we will see, however, 65 percent of sentences in guilty-plea dispositions for common offenses involved no jail or prison time, and 15 percent fell into one of two narrow ranges. This result suggests that, overall, the 60 percent of the pleas that were on the nose did not involve haggling over the length of sentence. Instead, defendants usually got no time or the standard incarceration time. The rarity of sentence bargaining was reinforced by the policy of some judges in several counties who simply refused to hear pleas that included an agreement on sentence.

Nevertheless, in 40 percent of the pleas, some change in counts occurred. Might this figure not be strong evidence for the granting of concessions? We think not, and our reasons provide a second piece of evidence for the predominance of pleas based on consensus. Our interviews revealed standard count drops in many counties. Furthermore, most changes consisted of dropping the number of counts without changing the most serious one. In fact, of the 2,025 cases

[4]A detailed presentation of material that we can only summarize here appears in Nardulli et al., *Tenor*, ibid., Chapters 7, 8, and 9.

involving reduction of charges, 1,289, or 64 percent, did not see a change in the primary charge. Furthermore, not all changes in counts charged can be attributed to plea bargaining. The charging policies of the police, the screening practices of the prosecutor, and the problems with evidence that arise in many cases may require or justify a charge regardless of haggling. Of this fact we have striking evidence from looking at what happens to charges in cases where there is no possibility of concessions bargaining; that is, in cases that went to trial. For defendants convicted at trial, almost as many received a reduction in counts or primary charge as did defendants who pled guilty. Thus, though 29.9 percent of defendants pleading guilty got a reduction in the number of counts, 23.1 percent of those convicted at trial did also. For reductions in the primary charge, the figures are 15.1 percent and 10.9 percent, respectively. Thus, in many instances, changes in counts and charge levels resulting from a plea would have occurred at trial anyway, reducing the extent to which such reductions represent true concessions.

Analysis of the ninety most frequently appearing charges, accounting for two-thirds of guilty pleas, is a third source of evidence pointing to the dominance of consensus pleas. We examined the distribution of sentences for each charge category separately because the type of offense determines more than anything else the general range of the sentence. Armed robbers receive harsher sentences than pickpockets.

What can the distributions of these sentences tell us? If going rates reflecting a consensus rather than individually negotiated deals involving exchange of concessions lead to pleas, then sentences for individual crimes should fall into just a few categories. In other words, a standard formula for determining sentences will produce two or three clusters of sentences. On the other hand, if concessions shaped by such factors as strength of evidence, skill of the attorneys, condition of the docket, and characteristics of the defendant result in pleas, the sentences should be more scattered. The distribution of sentences would then reflect the trading of concessions that individually calibrate penalties to the specifics of the case.

Examining the distribution of sentences revealed striking evidence that consensus pleas predominate. A huge number of sentences fell into the same cluster. Specifically, as mentioned earlier, probation or diversion stands out as the going rate for many defendants in each jurisdiction. In fact, among the 4,000 guilty-plea defendants arrested for the ninety most common charges, nearly two thirds (65.8 percent) received probation or diversion.

This figure is significant. Defendants care *far* more about whether they will be sentenced to any time in jail or prison than about the amount of fines and costs or the terms of probation.[5] Though we did not analyze in detail the amount of fines imposed, our conclusion is that they too are calculated using going rates. Set amounts for court costs and program fees for diversion programs add to the predictability of monetary penalties. Even if some haggling occurred over the amount of a fine, it would not involve concessions on matters regarded as very important compared to length of incarceration.

In every county, then, many cases ended routinely in probation. After all, many crimes involved garden-variety property offenses and defendants with no prior criminal record. That the court community did not get excited about them, and that it relied on routine dispositions for routine cases, is no surprise. Nor is it surprising that the defendants under such circumstances were willing to enter a plea without haggling over the details. The question most on their minds, "Will I have to go to jail, or will I be able to stay on the street," had been answered. The combination of their offense and prior record meant that probation would be the outcome. Going to trial would prolong uncertainty and carry the risk of some jail time. Analyzing strength of evidence in guilty-plea cases, though necessarily crude due to the difficulty of assessing it from information in court records, suggested that conviction was likely. We assumed that the evidence against the defendant was strong when there were either two eyewitnesses or a positive identification of the defendant, *and* where either a confession or physical evidence linked the defendant to the crime. Almost two-thirds of the guilty-plea cases met both conditions. On the other hand, the best possible outcome, acquittal at trial, differed little from a guilty plea in the most essential outcome—the ability to walk out of the courtroom instead of going into a jail cell.

Our analysis also found that another 15 percent of these guilty pleas resulted in incarceration for a period of months that fell into one of two narrow clusters. Thus, 80 percent of the guilty pleas we

---

[5]This is a consistent conclusion of research that is based on interviews with defendants. See one of the first and best such studies, by Jonathan Casper, *American Criminal Justice* (Englewood Cliffs, N.J.: Prentice-Hall, 1972).

examined in the pool of cases from all the counties resulted either in no incarceration or fell into one of two other clusters. This finding is strong evidence that pleas based on consensus prevailed.

Although this analysis clearly suggests that most pleas result from consensus, it also provides evidence that some do not. Twenty percent of the 4,000 guilty-plea defendants examined received sentences that fell outside the cluster. Going rates do not completely dictate sentences. Though the guilty-plea process does not resemble a huge bazaar, in places trading of concessions does take place for a small but significant minority of defendants.

Our data suggest a second vital conclusion about the guilty-plea process. The proportion of pleas based on concessions versus consensus varies from one jurisdiction to another, as most clearly illustrated by the pattern in Saginaw, which often reduced the primary charge, the most meaningful type of concession we could readily measure.

This analysis of the frequency with which consensus versus concessions produce guilty pleas is by no means the last word on the subject. We do not know the full extent of the contours of variation in their proportions for all jurisdictions in the United States. Nor does it answer all objections to plea bargaining based on the assumption that most pleas are individually bargained. Some people believe that even infrequent concessions bargaining, especially when a defendant feels coerced to give up the constitutional right to a trial in return for some sort of break, is unacceptable. Our analysis suggests, however, that in many jurisdictions most pleas result from routine application of a going rate accepted as appropriate by judge, prosecutor, and defense attorney.

EXPLANATIONS OF THE GUILTY-PLEA PROCESS
AND THEIR LIMITS

How can we account for the patterns of guilty-plea processes and sentences just described? How do the many specific characteristics of court communities, their inhabitants, and their sponsoring organizations discussed in this book produce differences in sentences?

Such questions stem from a healthy impulse, the desire to answer the query, "So what?" This impulse leads directly to a crucial consideration. It is, simply, what kinds of questions can be answered?

Formulating interesting questions that cannot be addressed accomplishes little. Indeed, it can be harmful if it crowds out consideration of important ones that can be dealt with.

A common view of the world as composed of a set of clear "if-then" causal chains leads to questions that cannot be answered. What, for example, is the effect on sentences of the low "belief in punishment" attitudes expressed by Dauphin public defenders? How much does a mixed docket, where judges hear criminal and civil cases during alternating trial terms, affect the proportion of concession-based guilty pleas? These and other questions meant to find simple and direct links between characteristics of court communities on the one hand and defendant outcomes on the other assume that the social world behaves like proofs in geometry, with linear causal chains that can be discovered.

If causal links are not so clear-cut, and if the obstacles to understanding social reality are formidable, then such questions cannot be answered. There is, in fact, an alternative view of the social world that better represents the reality of criminal court communities and their work. Holders of this view recognize that the elements of the social world are complexly interacting, and that lines of causation are multiple, contingent upon other factors, and shifting. Rather than conceiving of the world as a series of linear causal chains, they see it as holistic and complex.[6] It also implies, therefore, that no precise statements linking attitudes to sentences or docket technologies to guilty-plea systems can be made.

The two views of the world compete vigorously. The first generates many questions. Reality intervenes and produces answers more in conformity with the second. Everyone encounters this notion repeatedly. What effect does a windy day have on the outcome of a football game? How does a two-career marriage affect the relationship? Answers to such questions rapidly become convoluted, full of references to contingencies.

Thus, the inability to draw a tight connection between court community characteristics on the one hand and case outcomes on the other reflects not lack of understanding or reluctance to ask significant questions. Rather, it results from the complexity and intercon-

[6]For a fascinating explanation of this viewpoint, written by a physicist, see Fritjof Capra, *The Turning Point: Science, Society, and the Rising Culture* (New York: Simon & Schuster, 1982).

nectedness of the world, the difficulty of studying it, and the limits to human time, energy, and mental capacity available to contemplate it.

This argument does not mean, however, that we can say nothing useful about how the characteristics of court communities affect outcomes. It only suggests limits on their specificity. With these thoughts in mind, we consider several explanations derived from our research. What determines sentences? Why do going rates differ? What shapes the patterns of guilty pleas in a county? What accounts for variation in the proportion of those involving concessions? Why do some courts dispose of cases faster than others?

Going Rates and Guilty Pleas

The role of going rates in determining sentences appears repeatedly in our descriptions of case outcomes. Two factors, the seriousness of the offense and the defendant's prior criminal record, determine the going rate. Our sample of cases permits quantitative assessment of the role these two characteristics play. The results merely confirm that which much prior research reports.[7] Excluding murder and rape cases, whose long sentences distort the statistical analysis, we can account for a third or more of the variance in sentence length using offense and record in five counties; in only two does the proportion fall below 25 percent. Nature of offense counts most heavily, but for a given level of seriousness, prior record also matters. Combining all guilty pleas for frequently appearing offenses and looking at the effect of prior record on sentence demonstrates its importance. More than 90 percent of those with no prior record received probation or diversion; fewer than 60 percent with a serious prior record got an equivalent sentence.[8]

Why do going rates differ? The question indeed is crucial, the answer elusive. We have some partial answers. Important differences can be associated with state-level factors. Certainly a crucial one accounting for the more severe sentences in the three Michigan counties was its harsher criminal code. Another was the capacity of the penitentiary system relative to population. Michigan had the largest

---

[7]See, for example, James Eisenstein and Herbert Jacob, *Felony Justice: An Organizational Analysis of Criminal Courts* (Boston: Little, Brown, 1977), Chapters 7 and 9.

[8]The details of this analysis can be found in Nardulli et al., *Tenor*, op. cit., Chapter 10.

prison capacity. Of course, capacity in turn depends on other things, including political culture, and so clear lines of causation cannot always be identified. We also found a modest relationship between the rate of reported crimes against the person and sentence. The relationship, however, varied by defendant's prior record. Where the personal crime rate was high, repeat offenders who committed less serious crimes received lighter sentences than those which similar defendants received in counties with lower personal crime rates. But repeat offenders convicted of more serious crimes got longer sentences in high-crime counties. We also found evidence that courts' political environments, including degree of conservatism and nature of the local news media, had a real though modest part in shaping these decisions.

The large part that offense and record play in shaping sentences suggests that the many other case-specific factors — strength of evidence, identity of the judge and attorneys, social characteristics of the defendant and victim, and so on — which might shape sentences do so only *after* offense and record have been taken into account. Thus, these factors produce modifications of sentence above or below the going rate. The starting point, however, remains offense and record.

Because going rates do not account for all variation in sentences, what can we say about the role of these factors? In particular, *under what conditions* are they likely to shape sentences?

Our analysis identifies one overriding factor — seriousness of the offense. In most cases, neither the type of crime nor the defendant's prior criminal record stand out. Such cases provide the daily routine of criminal court communities. They bring forth no special effort, attract no particular interest. Standard pleas and going rates, often consisting of probation or diversion, are used to dispose of them without anyone's having to bother much.[9]

Serious crimes are something else. More people, including the news media, watch how they are handled. Experienced attorneys prosecute and defend, and they pay more attention to the task. Our analysis showed that the more serious the crime, the less likely a convicted defendant's sentence is to fall into a cluster. Either the

[9]For a fine description of how those handling misdemeanor cases arrive at consensual dispositions, see Douglas M. Maynard, "The Structure of Discourse in Misdemeanor Plea Bargaining," 18 *Law and Society Review* (1984), pp. 75–104.

case goes to trial, or explicit discussions and the concessions type of bargaining precede a plea. Furthermore, such cases provide the courtroom participants with a broader range of possible sentences within which to maneuver.

The number of serious cases in each county's sample was not large enough to uncover by statistical analysis the complex interaction of factors shaping their sentences. A study of a pool of cases from counties in which the triad of judge, prosecutor, and defense attorney had handled at least five defendants, however, showed that in serious cases, sentences were somewhat shaped by other factors.[10] These included participants' belief in punishment, their personality, their operating style, and the characteristics of other members of the triad. Analysis of the set of cases found that offense and record exerted the primary influence on a county's going rate, and that other factors came into play primarily in more serious cases.

What else can we explain about the guilty-plea process? One analysis looked for a relationship between changes in the number or level of counts and such defendant characteristics as race, sex, pretrial confinement, type of attorney, and case characteristics such as presence of a confession, physical evidence, and motions.[11] In general, few relationships were found. Blacks and women, for example, were treated no differently than whites and men. Furthermore, the few instances in which differences were found proved to be the exception, and the differences were small. Where physical evidence was strong, defendants were slightly less likely to obtain such a change. Private attorneys were only 5 percent more likely to get a drop in the level of the primary charges than publicly paid attorneys. Defendants in jail awaiting disposition got changes worth about 2.5 months less than those not confined.

We also discovered something of a "trial penalty" by comparing sentences given to defendants who pled guilty compared to those convicted at trial, statistically controlling for differences in offense seriousness, criminal record, and pretrial detention.[12] First offenders who went to trial were somewhat more likely to be sentenced to jail.

---

[10] This analysis is described in Peter F. Nardulli, Roy B. Flemming, and James Eisenstein, "Unraveling the Complexities of Decision Making in Face-to-Face Groups: A Contextual Analysis of Plea-Bargained Sentences," 78 *American Political Science Review* (1984), pp. 912–928.

[11] See Nardulli et al., *Tenor,* op. cit., Chapter 8.

[12] Ibid., Chapter 10.

Repeat offenders more often received longer sentences. These findings help explain why defendants plead guilty, and suggest that the belief prevalent in jail grapevines and county legal cultures about such a trial penalty has some basis in fact.

Why Guilty-Plea Systems Differ

What accounts for the differences in the guilty-plea systems found among the nine counties? We have pointed to county legal culture in general and, at least for some counties, the shared beliefs of judges as determining whether or not sentence recommendations accompany pleas. This variation does not stem from state-level factors, for such differences are found among counties in the same state.

What about the different patterns of changes in counts and charges that we found? Here too, state-level factors appear unimportant. Michigan is home both to Saginaw, the lone maximalist county, and to Kalamazoo, which sits at the opposite (minimalist) pole. Rather, several characteristics of court communities interact in intricate ways to produce these patterns. Sponsoring-organization policies are especially important. Prosecutors' practices on the early screening of cases and the charging of defendants facilitated Kalamazoo's on-the-nose policy. Saginaw's prosecutors applied lax screening policies, and even tolerated police "shopping" for an assistant who would authorize prosecution. Assistants controlled charging, and often added charges to facilitate their subsequent dismissal as part of a plea agreement. The two offices also differed in the content of the head prosecutor's policies and the rigor of their enforcement: The Kalamazoo DA sought on-the-nose pleas and tough sentences. The Saginaw DA did not care if pleas were on the nose, and he established few policies on the sentences he wanted to see imposed. He also invoked few procedures to oversee the work of his assistants.

Technologies also shaped guilty-plea systems. The procedure used to provide attorneys for poor defendants in Kalamazoo produced a concentrated defense bar. Its ten contract attorneys, eager to avoid the financial and other difficulties their predecessors had encountered, could easily join in a consensus on going rates that also accommodated the DA's desire for on-the-nose pleas by agreeing on sentence recommendations. Saginaw's very diffuse bar had many attorneys who handled only a few cases, too few to develop a feel for going rates. To them, a criminal case was not routine. Further, spending more time on it had fewer clear-cut negative consequences for their work life and income. These factors encouraged their active involvement in a process that included concessions on both the number of counts and the level of the most serious charge.

Docketing and case-assignment technologies also had direct and obvious effects on the ability to route cases to particular judges. Where routing was impossible, a plea agreement could not include understandings on which judge would accept it.

We could continue to spin out descriptions of the intricate connections among characteristics of the court community and the guilty-plea process in a county. Our basic point, though, should be clear. Guilty-plea processes result from the rich mixture of elements in the metaphor of the criminal court as a community.

Pace of Justice and Contextual Influences

Finally, what explains differences in case length? Here the analysis is complicated because total time reflected in the box-and-whiskers diagram in Figure 9–9 results from the combined time the case spent in the lower court and in the trial court. Our detailed analysis of trial court disposition times found that characteristics of the individual cases and their method of disposition did not have a uniform effect across all counties, with the sole exception of whether or not defense motions were filed.[13] The filing of such motions increased case disposition time in all nine trial courts. But whether the case was tried or pled, the seriousness of the crime, whether the defense attorney was privately retained or provided by the state, the judge's identity, the defendant's race, and so on did not always affect case length. Further, the shifting combinations of these factors that were found to affect disposition time in a county sometimes explained little of the variance.

Contextual factors such as whether there was a court administrator, whether individual dockets or master calendars were employed, and the stringency of state speedy-trial laws, also affected case length, but not consistently. Michigan's three trial courts were slower, partly because they used individual calendars, and because of the less stringent speedy-trial law in Michigan.

We found that both contextual variables — attributes of the court

[13]See Roy B. Flemming, Peter F. Nardulli, and James Eisenstein, "The Timing of Justice in Felony Trial Courts," *Law and Policy* (forthcoming, 1987).

community and its environment — and case-specific factors shape disposition time in trial courts. Though some common relationships may affect case length in many courts, discovering them will require looking at more than nine courts.

SUMMARY

Chapter Nine completes our survey of criminal court communities in nine middle-sized jurisdictions. The patterns of case outcomes exhibit mixed similarities and differences resembling those covered in earlier chapters. The conviction rate and heavy reliance on guilty pleas and diversion to produce these convictions varied only moderately, despite some significant differences in the composition of crimes and defendants' characteristics. Furthermore, the criminal court communities we studied relied on consensus to produce most pleas, rather than hammering out concessions in give-and-take bargaining. The proportion of pleas of the concessions type, however, was somewhat higher in several counties. When plea agreements involved concessions, they usually did so in nonroutine cases involving serious charges.

The dynamics of the guilty-plea systems that produced the similar patterns of outcomes just described, however, displayed visible differences. The patterns of count drops and charge reductions, the role of sentence recommendations in plea agreements, and the prevalence of understandings about whether the case would be routed to a particular judge all varied. So too did the severity of sentences and the elapsed time from arrest to disposition.

What can we make of these findings? Certainly, they offer compelling evidence against the explanatory power of the legal metaphor. These nine criminal courts did not mechanically apply laws and procedures dictated by precedent, higher courts, or statutes. Differences among counties in the same set of triplets or in the same state suggest instead that attributes of the local criminal court community produce differences in going rates, guilty-plea systems, and many other characteristics.

The causal links between attributes of court communities and case outcomes rarely are direct and linear. Rather, the many elements encompassed by the metaphor of courts as communities interact to

produce a complex web of interconnections. The local political structure, the county legal culture, the state sentencing code, the technologies men and women employ to get the work done, the policies
that elected prosecutors and appointed public defenders seek to
implement — these and similar attributes of court communities together determine how local criminal courts dispose of the cases
brought to them.

PART THREE
Contours of Justice

In the chapters in Part Two we illustrated how the metaphor of courts as communities could be applied to understand how criminal courts operated. We began by exploring one court from each set of "triplets," each in a different state. In Chapters Eight and Nine we summarized the contours of justice for all nine middle-sized courts.

In the two concluding chapters we take a large step back, expanding our focus to all state trial courts in the United States. How can the metaphor of courts as communities most usefully be applied everywhere? Our answer draws heavily on a simple but powerful characteristic — the size of the jurisdiction. We argue in Chapter Ten that major differences in court communities are associated with size. In fact, size is probably the most important feature shaping court communities.

We conclude *The Contours of Justice* by exploring how useful the metaphor of courts as communities is for evaluating proposals for reforming criminal courts. Citizens encounter a continuous stream of proposals for reform. In Chapter Eleven we argue that by drawing upon the perspective presented in this book, intelligent judgments can be made about the likely success of many such proposals.

CHAPTER TEN

Contours of Justice: Criminal Courts in the United States

INTRODUCTION

The metaphor of courts as communities offers useful insights into the nature and dynamics of criminal courts in middle-sized communities. But the focus on middle-sized jurisdictions leads naturally to questions about the metaphor's utility in larger and smaller courts. If, as we assume in this book, one cannot understand American society and politics without a working knowledge of how state criminal courts operate, it is essential to broaden the inquiry to include all courts.

In this chapter we describe how the size of court communities shapes crucial aspects of their operation. In the discussion we cover mainly unexplored territory, because students of criminal courts rarely consider the effects of size. Previous efforts to develop theories about courts naturally drew upon empirical research, nearly all of which focused on large urban courts in the country's major cities.[1]

---

[1]Here is a significant sampling of research on felony courts that is focused primarily on large jurisdictions: Isaac D. Balbus, *The Dialectics of Legal Repression: Black Rebels Before the American Criminal Courts* (New York: Russell Sage, 1973); Abraham Blumberg, *Criminal Justice* (Chicago: Quadrangle Books, 1967); Barbara Boland et al., *The Prosecution of Felony Arrests, 1979* (Washington, D.C.: National Institute of Justice, 1983); Kathleen B. Brosi, *A Cross-City Comparison of Felony Case Processing* (Washington, D.C.: Law Enforcement Assistance Administration, 1979); Suzanne R. Buckle and Leonard G. Buckle, *Bargaining for Justice: Case Disposition and Reform in the Criminal Courts* (New York: Praeger, 1977); James Eisenstein and Herbert Jacob, *Felony Justice: An Organizational Analysis of Criminal Courts* (Boston: Little, Brown, 1977); Roy B. Flemming, *Punishment Before Trial: An Organizational Perspective of Felony Bail Processes* (New York: Longman, 1982); Peter W. Greenwood et al., *Prosecution of Adult Felony Defendants in Los Angeles Court: A Policy Perspective* (Santa

We argue that casting our net more widely to encompass courts of all sizes strengthens the case for looking at courts as communities. Knowing a jurisdiction's size allows one to draw inferences about important features of the court community and its operations. Jurisdictional size, however, also powerfully affects how the community metaphor is applied. Combining the community metaphor with the notion of size produces a relatively simple, easily remembered, yet extremely powerful framework to employ in trying to understand criminal courts.

CONCEPT OF SIZE IN SOCIAL AND POLITICAL LIFE

Everyday experience suggests that the number of people participating in social interaction matters greatly. Compare the dynamics of a committee composed of twenty-five people to one with a membership of five. Or observe what happens to social interaction in families as additional children arrive. The size of a group obviously makes a difference. In fact, size often serves as an evaluative criterion. College students generally like small classes and dislike very large ones. Proponents of big business argue that large enterprises produce economies of scale that benefit everyone. Americans may disagree as to whether "small is beautiful," but most recognize that size significantly affects how things work.

It seems obvious that size affects politics too, including criminal courts. Surprisingly, much of that which appears obvious from personal experience has escaped students of politics. Political scientists do not frequently employ size as an analytical concept, a neglect that is all the more puzzling because the powerful effects of size were identified long ago. One of the most frequently quoted passages in discussions of the American system of government, drawn from

Monica, Calif.: Rand, 1973); Robert Hermann et al., *Counsel for the Poor* (Lexington, Mass.: Lexington Books, 1977); Martin A. Levin, *Urban Politics and the Criminal Courts* (Chicago: University of Chicago Press, 1977); Lynn M. Mather, "Some Determinants of the Method of Case Disposition: Decision-making by Public Defenders in Los Angeles," 8 *Law and Society Review* (1974), p. 187; Pamela J. Utz, *Settling the Facts* (Lexington, Mass.: Lexington Books, 1978); The Vera Institute of Justice, *Felony Arrests: Their Prosecution and Disposition in New York City's Courts* (New York: Vera Institute of Justice, 1977).

James Madison's *Federalist* No. 10, utilizes size as a crucial component in the justification for adopting the Constitution. It is for Madison a means to control the harmful effects of "faction"; that is, interests:

> The smaller the society, the fewer probably will be the distinct parties and interests composing it; the fewer the distinct parties and interests, the more frequently will a majority be found of the same party, and the smaller the compass within which they are placed, the more easily will they concert and execute their plans of oppression. Extend the sphere, and you take in a greater variety of parties and interests; you make it less probable that a majority of the whole will have a common motive to invade the rights of other citizens; or if such a common motive exists, it will be more difficult for all who feel it to discover their own strength, and to act in unison with each other.[2]

Madison's observation that increasing size leads to greater diversity and greater obstacles to forging a narrow consensus still ranks as one of the most direct and insightful statements on the effect of size.

Since Madison's analysis, scholars have occasionally employed the concept of size to produce perceptive analyses of politics.[3] It is rarely, however, their primary focus.[4]

We begin our discussion by defining the core concept. Size of a court can be defined in several ways—the number of people living within its jurisdiction, the number of judges, or the number of people at the core of the court community—to name the most obvious ones. These measures, of course, correlate with one another. The larger the population, the more judges are needed to serve it. Numbers alone do not, however, determine the size of the judiciary. For instance, a metropolitan area with significant manufacturing and financial activity and large numbers of impoverished people will face greater caseloads in both the civil and criminal dockets, and consequently show a higher ratio of judges to population. Research on the

[2]Cited in Grant McConnell, *Private Power and American Democracy* (New York: Random House, 1966), p. 103.

[3]See especially McConnell, ibid., passim.

[4]For a notable exception, see Robert A. Dahl and Edward R. Tufte, *Size and Democracy* (Stanford, Calif.: Stanford University Press, 1973). One study of courts employs the concept of size extensively. See John Paul Ryan et al., *American Trial Judges: Their Work Styles and Performance* (New York: Free Press, 1980), especially Chapter 3.

responses to crime of ten large cities between 1948 and 1978 found that the judge-to-arrest ratio varied widely, and that the rate of change in the ratio also differed.[5] The existence of such differences suggests that political considerations govern the size of court communities.

Regardless of our definition, size will range widely. For our purpose, it is convenient to employ general words like "small," "middle-sized," and "large." The analysis does not, however, stand or fall on where we draw the line between such categories. A four-judge court is smaller than an eight-judge court, regardless of the category of size we place each in, and it will exhibit more of the characteristics of smaller courts.

All but one of our counties ranged in population from 200,000 to 650,000, and the number of judges from four to more than a dozen. We call these "middle-sized." Courts with just one or two judges are clearly small. Most rural counties, and many counties not classified as rural but with populations of fewer than 75,000, employ the services of just one judge. Similarly, most of the courts that serve the 148,000,000 people who live in counties with populations of more than a million are large, and have at least fifteen judges.[6]

Regardless of the definition used, then, substantial numbers of Americans live under the jurisdiction of small, medium, and large courts. Because major differences are based on size, they are useful in understanding state criminal courts throughout the United States.

CRIMINAL COURTS IN SMALL JURISDICTIONS

For many of the characteristics exhibited by criminal court communities, the middle-sized jurisdictions described in Part II fall between poles defined by larger and smaller courts. The differences between middle-sized and small courts, however, appear to be more substantial. We therefore begin our discussion by considering small courts.

Rural courts and courts serving small but nonrural jurisdictions,

[5]Herbert Jacob, *The Frustration of Policy: Responses to Crime by American Cities* (Boston: Little, Brown, 1984), p. 129.

[6]Ryan et al., *American Trial Judges*, op. cit., who surveyed all trial judges in the United States by mail, found that more than 40 percent of the judges in their study served on courts with four or fewer judges, and only 20 percent on courts with more than twenty-five (p. 48).

indeed all courts with only one or two judges, have rarely been studied.[7] Consequently, the empirical foundation for the following discussion fails to match that available for middle-size and large courts. Much of the material that follows is necessarily speculative and preliminary.

Brief Sketch of a Very Small Criminal Court

We begin our inquiry into small court communities with a summary based on research into the guilty-plea process in four rural counties, conducted by one of our graduate students. He used the same framework and methodology employed in our nine middle-sized jurisdictions.[8] We will sketch the smallest county to illustrate the underlying dynamics of such courts.

Nearly all of this county's small population lived in one town and its vicinity. The town, only six blocks wide, served as the county seat. It had no fast-food restaurants, no movie theater, no hospital. Only one doctor, a dentist, the eight attorneys in the county bar association, and the teachers and administrators in the school district held college degrees. A judge, who spent most of his time in a neighboring county, visited once a month and scheduled additional days if necessary. Four police officers and the state police provided all law enforcement. A lower-court judge, a part-time public defender, and a part-time district attorney handled almost the entire caseload. Fewer than one hundred defendants reached the preliminary hearing stage each year. Crime was minimal. Drunk driving, petty thefts, minor assaults, and welfare fraud accounted for most of it. Both the DA and PD attended nearly all preliminary hearings.

Trials occurred rarely. In fact, the DA and PD resolved most cases either at the preliminary hearing or through a guilty plea. The judge routinely accepted any guilty plea upon which the DA and PD agreed. Everyone was thoroughly familiar with the principals in each case—the arresting officer, the defendant and his or her family, the victim, witnesses, and the attorneys. The DA and PD shared the desire to avoid trials. Cost was one reason. The bill to the county gov-

[7]For a review of literature on rural courts up to 1981, see James Eisenstein, "Research on Rural Criminal Justice: A Summary," in Shanler D. Cronk, ed. *Criminal Justice in Rural America* (Washington, D.C.: National Institute of Justice, 1982).

[8]David A. Klinger, "The Guilty Plea Process in Three Small Pennsylvania Judicial Districts: An Inquiry into the Nature of Rural Criminal Justice," Unpublished Master's Essay, Department of Political Science, Pennsylvania State University, 1986.

ernment for an aggravated assault case that went to trial amounted to $1,000. Both the DA and PD expressed interest in saving money. They also recognized that, given their low salaries, they could ill afford many trials. The DA said:

> I'm going to do everything I can do to avoid trying a case because, with just me, you know, if I try four cases a year, that's gonna ruin me. . . . I can't afford to try four cases on the salary, frankly. Most of the cases, they can be bargained.

Caseload size affected the guilty-plea process. Except for drunk driving and welfare fraud, for which ARD was the going rate, no crime appeared frequently enough to establish a history of previous dispositions. Furthermore, the small number of such cases made each of them unique. Although not enough criminal matters arose to allow them to become routine, knowledge of each case was very high. Prosecution and defense were "vertical." Defendants and victims were familiar to the attorneys. In cases not involving welfare fraud or drunk driving, discussions focusing on the specifics of each case and defendant produced pleas. These cases thus conformed closely to the "concessions" mode of arriving at plea agreements. The PD described the guilty-plea process:

> What we do is we have each case on a case-by-case basis, and we try to tailor a plea bargain to fit the facts and circumstances of each case. So, sure, there's a lot of haggling back and forth. But sometimes things are so cut and dry.

Two other features of the guilty-plea process in this county warrant attention. First, the PD cooperated with the DA when cases had weak evidence by not pushing them to rapid conclusion. Rather, they were allowed to linger until they were dismissed for exceeding the 180-day rule. In the meantime, the defendants were kept under some control due to their anxiety about what would happen. The attorneys recognized the practice as a device to deter, at least for a while, additional criminal activity by defendants. Second, with almost the entire docket controlled by just two men, a different form of haggling arose. The attorneys "logrolled"; that is, they traded concessions in cases involving different defendants. The PD explained: "But just like the district attorney cuts me slack in certain cases, I cut him slack in certain cases. . . . So that's how we juggle back and forth."

Characteristics Directly Attributable to Smallness

Some characteristics of small court communities flow directly from the mere fact that few people participate in the disposition process. These attributes therefore should be found in all small courts, regardless of location or other features. Though the very rural county just described is an extreme example, even somewhat larger jurisdictions served by one or two judges can involve fewer people handling both civil and criminal cases than just the number of prosecutors in the largest courts. When few people judge, prosecute, or defend, they become extremely familiar with one another. Frequent interaction raises mutual interdependence. The proportion of any participant's work life spent dealing with everyone else is high. After all, if only two people staff the prosecutor's office, a defense attorney knows he or she will deal with one or the other in every case.

The concept of sponsoring organizations contributes little to understanding very small courts. A two-person public defender's office displays little hierarchy. Any policies that guide the behavior of prosecutors or public defenders will grow from informal and generally unplanned discussions. There is no structure to the judge's organization where only one judge presides. Instead of looking to characteristics of offices or sponsoring organizations, in small jurisdictions we directly examine the personal views and attributes of the prosecutor, the public defender, their assistants, and the judge.

Characteristics Flowing from Similarities in Small Jurisdictions

The image of rural America as a homogeneous collection of farmers distorts reality. In practice, rural places display considerable diversity.[9] Nonetheless, many rural and small-town locales in the United States share characteristics that shape the nature and dynamics of their court communities.[10]

---

[9]See, for example, the descriptions of two counties that have been studied. "Rural Poverty and the Law in Southern Colorado," 47 *Denver Law Journal* (1970), pp. 82–176. "The Legal Problems of the Rural Poor," *Duke Law Journal* (1969), pp. 495–621.

[10]See Dahl and Tufte, *Size and Democracy*, op. cit., passim, and Donald D. Landon, "Clients, Colleagues, and Community: The Shaping of Zealous Advocacy in Country Law Practice," *American Bar Foundation Research Journal* (1985). Reviewing the literature on urban-rural differences, Landon concludes, "Most research continues to

Table 10–1
Index of Crime by Jurisdiction Size

	All U.S.	SMSAs	Other cities	Rural
Violent	580.8	702.1	353.1	182.4
Property	5319.1	6055.5	5042.7	2108.0

Source: Crime in the United States, Federal Bureau of Investigation, U.S. Department of Justice, 1980.

For one thing, the rate of crime measured both by victimization studies and by crimes reported to the police is lowest in small jurisdictions.[11] Likewise, actual arrest rates for the serious crimes in the FBI's Part I Index are lower in less populous jurisdictions.[12] The composition of the crimes also differs. Violent crimes less often arise; petty offenses are more common.[13] A variety of sources can be called upon to illustrate these points, and Table 10–1 is one. It is based on information from the FBI's Uniform Crime Reports for 1980.

Significant differences also appear in the prior criminal records of defendants. Those arrested in smaller jurisdictions typically are not career criminals; they lack sophistication in planning and executing crimes; they work alone rather than with others; and they less often consider themselves to be criminals.[14]

Again, we are speculating on broad trends. Individual small jurisdictions undoubtedly can stray far from these generalizations about the composition of crimes and defendants that make up the caseload. As a generalization, however, it is probably valid and useful.

The population of such areas, though usually not homogeneous, frequently exhibits less diversity than metropolitan centers. The number of incoming strangers is low, which also holds for the local bar, mostly composed of hometowners who return to their place of

---

find in the rural environment a close sense of community and a pervasive friendliness, a rather fundamentalist religious outlook, a puritanical, prejudiced, and conservative attitude on political issues, sharply distinguishable social attitudes and behavior, but an increasingly pluralistic outlook, with most obvious differences being exhibited between farmers and nonfarmers," p. 85.

[11]Eisenstein, "Research on Rural Criminal Justice," op. cit., p. 112.

[12]Ibid.

[13]Ibid.

[14]Ibid.

birth after law school. They are likely to have common origins in the local social and economic elite, hold similar conservative views toward crime and criminal-justice issues, distrust outsiders, and view with skepticism appellate courts and indeed anyone from outside the immediate vicinity. The attorneys share an explicit sense of community and the outward trappings of friendliness found in small towns and rural areas.[15]

It is only natural that under these circumstances the handful of attorneys who bear full responsibility for the criminal caseload come to know each others' habits, thoughts, and behavior intimately. One rural DA in Pennsylvania described his familiarity with the judge, whom he had once served as a law clerk:

> I mean, it's down to the point where if he starts tapping his pencil on the bench or makes a particular movement with his chair, I think I know what his mood is at the time. You get to know someone like that after you've practiced in front of him many years.[16]

Familiarity extends beyond the bar to jurors, defendants, victims, and civil litigants. In a study of small-town attorneys in Missouri, one of the few empirically grounded, published studies of rural practice, Donald Landon reported one respondent's problems arising from familiarity and multiple social ties.[17] The attorney sued a former schoolmate whose mother was a school chum of his mother. Both women belonged to the same garden club. Both families attended the same church. A majority of the attorneys in this study said they knew at least 75 percent of their clients before they represented them in a legal matter. Thus, unlike larger jurisdictions where people who encounter one another in the courthouse never again have dealings with each other, in small courts a web of formal and informal relationships connects everyone. St. Clair and Erie displayed some of these complex interconnections, but the scope and number of such ties in small jurisdictions far exceeds what we described there.

The familiarity of everyone with each other, coupled with community-wide grapevines, makes the actions of attorneys highly visible to their clients, to opposing attorneys, and to the community

---

[15]Landon, "Clients, Colleagues, and Community," op. cit., p. 85.
[16]Klingler, "The Guilty Plea Process," op. cit., p. 39.
[17]Landon, "Clients, Colleagues, and Community," op. cit., p. 193.

as a whole. An assistant DA in a rural Pennsylvania jurisdiction explained how this closeness led to problems:

> Probably the biggest source of dissatisfaction that I see in a small community like this is that you know everybody. . . . Awkwardness results from knowing the people you're dealing with. . . . You usually know something about the individual that you're prosecuting. You still do what you have to do, but it makes it very difficult.[18]

Reputations made and lost within the court community in places like Montgomery extend further into the general community in rural areas. Landon's study quotes one lawyer:

> I discovered quick and in a hurry that arguing a case before a jury of twelve ends up being talked about all over the county. Those twelve people talk to their friends, relatives, and acquaintances, and your ability is soon known by everybody.[19]

Use of the grapevine to sanction an attorney's misbehavior, a technique described to us in Saginaw, probably is routine in most small jurisdictions. One of Landon's attorneys expressed it: "If an attorney messes me up, I'll sing like a canary at coffee the next morning."[20]

In small jurisdictions, the grapevine's greater reach increases the significance of the consequences that flow from such gossip. The number of people constituting the criminal process is simply too small to support formation of a distinctive community with its own grapevine, its own secrets, its own ways of doing things. Rather, the goings-on in criminal cases become common knowledge to the newspaper publisher, the local farm-implement dealer, the banker, the county commissioners, and anyone else who can be counted among the local elite. Every case considered important, every squabble between the prosecutor and the judge, every accusation that someone messed up or lost his or her temper becomes common knowledge and a topic of conversation. Visibility is further enhanced by the policy of some rural newspapers to print all case outcomes on the front page.[21]

These features combine to make the court community members more visible to one another, to clients, and to the community at large,

[18]Klingler, "The Guilty Plea Process," op. cit., p. 22.
[19]Landon, "Clients, Colleagues, and Community," op. cit., p. 89.
[20]Ibid., p. 108.
[21]Klingler, "The Guilty Plea Process," op. cit., p. 115.

increasing accountability to the community and reducing discretion. Coupled with the very small number of people directly involved in the disposition of criminal cases, these attributes suggest it makes little sense even to talk about a *criminal court* community. Instead, the relevant metaphor is the "local elite community," some of whose members specialize in handling criminal cases.

It is also true that the larger environment faced by criminal justice personnel is usually less diverse and complex than in larger jurisdictions. The factors cited by James Madison about the greater diversity of interests in larger political units and the likelihood that in more restricted ones narrow interests will dominate, produce precisely that result in many places. In small towns and rural counties, the diversity of organized interests is narrower.

Diminished diversity reduces the probability that dissenters and mavericks will find enough people to employ them in legal matters to allow them to survive economically. Similarly, dissenters are too few for them to provide one another with the social support and mutual referral of clients to sustain a pattern of nonconformity to local traditions.

Two other characteristics of small jurisdictions are consistent with what we have just described. First, the pace of change in these places is slow. Population shifts generally are gradual. Changes in who controls political offices or exercises control over wealth come about even more gradually. Patterns of crime and technologies used in the courts remain fairly stable. The same group of people staffs the legal system, changing primarily as a function of gradual entry and exit because time passes. Second, governments in small and rural counties often must try to meet substantial demands with insubstantial sources of revenue. Though not all rural areas are poor, few enjoy a tax base comparable to that found in many larger counties. Consequently, funding levels for the court community are low. Judges less often have clerks. The PD and DA receive only a small salary for part-time work. Their staffs, if any, are also small and poorly paid. Jail capacity is low, and its condition poor. Even money for witness and juror fees is tight. Judges, prosecutors, and public defenders, sharing local wariness about the expense of trials, find themselves the object of subtle but effective pressures to keep jury trial costs down, whereas their counterparts in larger jurisdictions rarely face such intense pressures.

These common tendencies of small jurisdictions affect the nature of conflict among participants in the criminal process. When conflict arises, it often extends beyond the workplace to other spheres of life. When a handful of attorneys in small communities permeates local government and the leadership of voluntary organizations, the likelihood of encounters after work increases.[22] An argument in court or a hallway can spill over to strain social interaction at church, a school board meeting, or a conference on a civil matter between different clients. Such conflict can be explosive, intense, and lasting. It can easily spread as others with ties to the principals in the dispute inevitably are sucked into the melee. An attorney in Landon's study described what happened to a community when its lawyers did not get along:

> Relations between attorneys here are pretty bad. There are too many of us for what business there is. We're on opposite sides of the political fence, too. . . . I guess it's kind of polarized the county.[23]

Attorneys recognize the high costs of conflict. This recognition, combined with local traditions of working things out informally, promotes cooperation and discourages conflict. Attorneys therefore are likely to treat one another with respect and to avoid combative tactics. An assistant DA in a rural Pennsylvania county contrasted conduct in criminal cases there with what he had seen in Allegheny county, home to the city of Pittsburgh:

> You do not go into the courtroom like you do in Allegheny County and tear apart the opponent. I think counsel here don't pull underhanded things. We're pretty open in our discovery. . . . you're not guaranteed anything like that in Pittsburgh because most attorneys don't know each other and they go for the throat in court.[24]

The characteristics of small jurisdictions that discourage conflict, of course, do not eliminate it altogether. The study of rural Pennsylvania counties referred to earlier included one in which the public defender narrowly lost a bitter election to the district attorney who

---

[22]Landon, "Clients, Colleagues, and Community," op. cit., pp. 101–102. In Landon's sample of rural lawyers, 68 percent were active in church, 64 percent belonged to civic organizations, 57 percent had held political office, and 66 percent were serving on some sort of local board.

[23]Ibid., p. 106.

[24]Klingler, "The Guilty Plea Process," op. cit., p. 21.

was seeking another term. "Quite frankly," the DA observed, "there's a personality problem between him and myself." Matters were not helped by their offices being on the same floor of the county courthouse.

The similarities in small jurisdictions summarized here do not appear everywhere. In counties where most lawyers and other community elites live in the county seat, such patterns will be stronger than in counties with several population centers. Social homogeneity among the elite varies; even more likely, standing rivalries among factions in the local elite may inhibit informal negotiation and avoidance of overt conflict. Just because a community is small does not automatically ensure that everyone who exercises influence in it comes from the same social circle and shares the same values and preferences for handling conflict. Nonetheless, the likelihood remains fairly high that small jurisdictions will have such a pattern, much higher than in the larger communities we studied.

Case Outcomes and the Guilty-Plea Process

The mixture of crimes in small jurisdictions has fewer serious ones, and fewer defendants have long prior records. The serious cases that form part of the daily routine in large cities appear much less frequently. Burglaries committed by thrice-convicted burglars and armed robberies come to court every day in major metropolitan centers. In small jurisdictions, such cases form a smaller proportion of the court's work, and they are infrequent in absolute numbers. Therefore, the crimes are relatively more serious. Bail levels and sentences for such crimes are higher.[25]

Although sentences for serious crimes differ, the method of conviction — the guilty plea — does not. All the factors that produce a high proportion of pleas in middle-sized jurisdictions operate also in small courts. In fact, the latter have additional pressures for using the guilty-plea process. Our sketch of a very small court identified several. Trials cost the county money. The small community simply

[25]A study of sentences in Pennsylvania conducted by that state's Sentencing Commission found that county incarceration rates were inversely related to overall population density. The more urban counties, which also handled a higher proportion of serious crimes and defendants with long criminal records, produced the lowest incarceration rates. See John H. Kramer and Robin L. Lubitz, "Pennsylvania's Sentencing Reform: The Impact of Commission-Established Guidelines," 34 *Crime and Delinquency* (1985), p. 492.

cannot afford too many. Neither can part-time prosecutors and public defenders, who must devote time to their private practice to supplement their small salaries. Finally, the predisposition in small communities for working things out informally and avoiding conflict encourages pleas.

Can any common features of the guilty-plea process in small jurisdictions be identified? Several generalizations can be extracted from the limited information available. First, the guilty-plea process displays as much variation as in middle-sized communities. Differences in the content of the plea agenda do turn up. Sometimes sentence recommendations are made or the most serious charge is reduced. Sometimes neither occurs. Only the ability to route cases to different judges is more restricted. The techniques used to arrive at pleas — when and where the participants reach agreements, the role played by the judge, and so on — also differ.

Second, going rates play a lesser role simply because the cases are fewer. Especially in the smallest jurisdictions, once the most common offenses (drunk driving, simple assaults) are accounted for, only a few dozen cases involving one of a handful of offenses appear. Too few cases to establish precedents for many combinations of offense and prior record come to court.

Third, a low caseload means that too few matters are handled for many to be considered routine. Even in middle-sized jurisdictions, criminal court inhabitants spend most of their time on criminal work, sometimes specializing in some kinds of cases. In small courts, inhabitants divide their time among a variety of tasks, many of which do not involve criminal matters.

Weaker going rates and lower likelihood of seeing any criminal case as routine combine to increase give-and-take, concessions-oriented guilty pleas. Standard pleas may exist for the handful of offenses that appear regularly, but they form a small proportion of the caseload. An assistant prosecutor in a small Pennsylvania county described discussions with defense attorneys for cases not resolved by ARD or a going-rate disposition for a minor offense at the preliminary hearing: "They normally shoot low. I mean, they come in here and ask for the world. And you come back and shoot high and figure you meet somewhere in [the middle]."[26]

Of course, differences appear among small counties. In a small

<hr>

[26]Klingler, "The Guilty Plea Process," op. cit., p. 86.

Pennsylvania county with about 200 cases per year, the DA had served for eight years. He handled or knew about nearly all dispositions. "Consensus" on appropriate outcomes became much easier with this concentration of experience. Further, he consciously sought consistency, observing that he strove to offer the same plea that others had received in the past for the same crimes rather than considering each case individually.

In the smallest jurisdictions, though, we find the possibility of a different type of plea bargaining — "logrolling the docket." In our earlier description of a very small county, we quoted the public defender on how he and the DA juggled back and forth, cutting each other "slack" in some cases. In a slightly larger county, the PD handled 90 percent of the cases. Each month, a pretrial conference was held in which all current cases were discussed. The public defender said, however, "You wouldn't really call it a pretrial conference. It's more like a meeting between the public defender and the district attorney once a month."[27] It is likely that in such situations implicit or even explicit trade-offs among cases will occur. Both attorneys know they cannot try all or even most of the cases. Neither they nor the judge has time to do so. Too many trials will bring financial woe to themselves and the county treasury. They know that what they decide absolutely determines the entire trial rate. In larger jurisdictions, though participants in the guilty-plea process understand that their decisions affect the trial rate somewhat, they know that other pairs of attorneys are making decisions that also affect it. Thus, each pair of attorneys discussing pleas participates in a marketlike encounter in which their individual decisions influence but do not completely determine the trial rate. In the small county described, the public defender and prosecutor occupy a monopoly position.

CRIMINAL COURTS IN LARGE JURISDICTIONS

Compared to their smaller cousins, large courts display more complexity and offer more opportunities for a variety of factors to interact in intricate ways. More things can make a difference, and they do. Consequently, even fewer generalizations that apply to all or even most large jurisdictions can be made confidently. Large courts vary

[27]Ibid., p. 64.

considerably. Simple explanations for any given court community's taking the form it does are elusive. The simple truth is that the best general answer to "Why?" is "It depends."

Moreover, surprisingly few empirical studies of large courts systematically cover many of the aspects of their structure and dynamics that the community metaphor suggests are important.[28] Although large courts served as research sites for many empirical studies, they often looked only at one position or one aspect of the disposition process.[29] For these reasons it would be misleading to sketch a large jurisdiction similar to the one presented for the small Pennsylvania jurisdiction described earlier. Enough is known about these courts, though, to permit extracting some generalizations about their criminal court communities.

Characteristics Directly Attributable to Largeness

In small jurisdictions, extensive familiarity is inevitable. In large jurisdictions, the situation is far more complicated. Even though the number of judges, prosecutors, and defense attorneys regularly handling criminal cases may be ten or even twenty times as great as in middle-sized jurisdictions, these people are far from complete strangers. Even a group of two-hundred persons, if they interact long enough, can come to know each other somewhat, as the high-school experience of many Americans suggests. Furthermore, there will be far fewer judges than prosecutors, and fewer prosecutors than defense attorneys. Attorneys consequently come to know judges fairly well, not only by appearing before them but also by sharing gossip about them flowing through the grapevine. Nevertheless, the familiarity in large courts will not approach the intimate knowledge acquired by the handful of criminal court community inhabitants in very small jurisdictions. Perhaps more significant, even where familiarity is fairly high in a large court, the degree of mutual dependence typically is not. Only a small portion of one's work life will be spent interacting with any other member of the community.

In small jurisdictions, almost everyone knows one another. In large

[28]Exceptions include Levin, *Urban Politics*, op. cit., and Eisenstein and Jacob, *Felony Justice*, op. cit.

[29]For example, Hermann et al., op. cit., focus on public defenders; Thomas Church's *Justice Delayed: The Pace of Litigation in Urban Trial Courts* (Williamsburg, Va.: National Center for State Courts, 1978), examines the elapsed time for initiation to disposition of civil and criminal cases.

courts, familiarity varies considerably depending upon case assignment procedures and other features of the technology employed. In Baltimore during the early 1970s, for example, familiarity was not high.[30] A master calendar with last-minute assignment of cases to the next available courtroom placed defense attorneys and prosecutors before a different judge on almost every case. Assistant prosecutors left after two years, causing a constant influx of new people unfamiliar with the court. Judges rotated on and off criminal duty every year. Chicago, on the other hand, utilized case-assignment techniques that produced pockets of stability, familiarity, and mutual dependence that resembled what we found in some Oakland County courtrooms.[31] Judges spent a number of years hearing criminal cases exclusively. Assistant prosecutors and public defenders were assigned to an individual judge's courtroom, handling all cases assigned there. Some private regular defense attorneys managed to concentrate their cases before a few favorite judges. We do not know how often such segmented pockets of high familiarity and stability develop in large courts, but Chicago was probably atypical. These patterns can easily be disrupted by changes in docketing procedures or case-assignment policies. Thus, it stands to reason that generally in large courts each participant encounters everyone else less frequently. The likelihood of their knowing each other from prior association or nonwork encounters is lower. Familiarity and mutual dependence vary substantially, but practically never match the level reached in small or middle-sized jurisdictions.

Another characteristic of large courts rests in its members' diverse social backgrounds, personalities, and styles of practice. In part, this diversity is a function of the law of averages. The more people, the more likely it is that some oddballs will appear. Greater social diversity in most large metropolitan centers increases the likelihood of finding different types of people in the court community. Eccentric individuals less frequently get weeded out before becoming judges, career prosecutors, or successful private attorneys. Furthermore, less interdependence reduces the effectiveness of sanctions against deviants. Nonconformists are more likely to find kindred spirits who provide the social and psychological support needed to encourage and sustain nonconformity.

[30]Eisenstein and Jacob, *Felony Justice*, op. cit., Chapter 4.
[31]Ibid., Chapter 5.

These characteristics make it possible for combative, thoroughly disliked attorneys to survive in larger jurisdictions. In Detroit, for example, a militant black attorney specialized in taking cases involving possible police misconduct in arresting black defendants.[32] Such attorneys become well known, and encounter little cooperation from most of the court community. But they find some allies in the private bar and even some community regulars. In Detroit, one faction of black and liberal white judges on the bench were more favorably disposed to militant defense attorneys. In a study of a jurisdiction with a population of one million dominated by a major urban center, Jerome Skolnick reported that prosecutors grouped defense attorneys into four categories.[33] The smallest group, the "gamblers," handled few cases but did so in a highly adversarial manner. They encountered hostility from the DA's office, and preferred trials to pleas.

Grapevines in large courts also exhibit distinctive characteristics. Large numbers of people in the community do not keep a grapevine from forming. Every court community has a grapevine of some sort, as do all human institutions. They can be surprisingly effective. A researcher making an initial foray into a Detroit courtroom was approached by the court clerk and asked what he was doing. Learning that no proceedings were scheduled for that morning, the researcher left the room, waited several minutes for an elevator up to the next floor, and walked into another courtroom for the first time, to be greeted by the question, "Are you the fellow doing that study?"[34] The sheer immensity of large court communities does, however, restrict the grapevine's ability to carry news of all significant goings-on to all inhabitants. Where distinct groups or factions divide the judges or defense bar, the grapevine may not bridge the gaps. The physical isolation of the courthouse from other governmental agencies (as in Oakland) also reduces the reach of the grapevine into other parts of the community. Defense attorneys who appear infrequently will seldom be connected to the grapevine at all.

In large courts, diverse social backgrounds and operating styles and less effective communication through grapevines bar development of a widely shared, strong consensus on the content of the local

[32]For a description of Detroit, see ibid., Chapter 6.

[33]"Social Control in the Adversary System," 11 *Journal of Conflict Resolution* (1967), pp. 58–59. They were "inexperienced" people taking few cases, "experienced" high-volume regulars, public defenders, and adversarial "gamblers."

[34]Based on the personal experience of one of the authors.

legal culture. They are likely to have less consensus on the need for cooperation, informality, and mutual trustworthiness in dealings among members. On the other hand, the county legal culture probably better tolerates diversity. The effects of community size on the level of agreement on going rates are unclear. Perhaps they depend on the structure of the court community. Where it is segmented into semiautonomous subgroups centered in individual courtrooms, different going rates may evolve.[35] More cohesive communities may establish elaborate going rates for a number of offenses, thanks to the frequent appearance of those offenses, which rarely appear on smaller courts' dockets, and to specialization within the PD's and DA's offices.

Sponsoring organizations also reflect the effects of size. Judges' organizations and prosecutors' offices in particular display many more characteristically bureaucratic features in larger jurisdictions. The judges typically meet formally and regularly. The bench may separate into several divisions, with one judge designated to handle administrative matters for each. Committees may be formed to report to the full meeting of judges, recommending changes in policy or practices. Formal votes are even taken, on occasion. Prosecutors divide their offices into separate units, each headed by a supervisor and sometimes a deputy. Formal policies are established, communicated in regularly scheduled staff meetings, and incorporated into a formal policy manual. Regular procedures also are set up for checking the behavior of assistant prosecutors, and for formally evaluating their performance. Despite informal communication through the office grapevine, it becomes difficult for everyone to know everyone else. The larger staffs found in big offices permit greater flexibility in meeting the challenges of coping with the caseload. They can usually juggle their personnel so as to spare assistants who will undertake major, time-consuming cases when they come up. A major trial disrupts the work of a small office.

Assistant prosecutors consequently exhibit many of the characteristics associated with life in a bureaucracy. They feel compelled to follow policy, recognize that their behavior is being monitored and evaluated by administrators, clear important decisions with supe-

[35]For a study of the effects of local legal culture on court operations including going rates, see Thomas W. Church, Jr., "Examining Local Legal Culture," *American Bar Foundation Research Journal* (1985), p. 449.

riors, and frequently identify strongly with the organization and its leadership. They are not, however, just like clerks in a Social Security office or a university financial aid office. As professionals representing the state, they enjoy higher status and more discretion than most bureaucrats. Judges exhibit hardly any tendencies to behave as the stereotypical bureaucrat does, even in the largest courts. Each owes his or her office to the electorate or an appointing executive such as the governor. Judges do not usually identify strongly with the interests or policies of the bench. Cohesion among such a group of such independent-minded individualists is difficult to achieve. Indeed, factions probably develop among judges in most large courts.

The characteristics of court communities that derive primarily from the large number of inhabitants engaged in handling criminal cases all point to an overriding pattern. Such communities tend, other things being equal, to be more diffuse in structure. At the same time, they are also more diverse. That is, some will be coherent, with much familiarity, strong consensus, and moderate mutual interdependence. Similarly, in some, distinctive courtroom work groups develop, each with its own pattern of interaction and going rates. Many descriptions of the criminal process, though, employ the notion of courtroom work groups too widely. Such work groups develop distinctive identities only in large courts and under special conditions. The notion of the criminal court community is far more useful, and can encompass courtroom work groups as a special "segmented" configuration that communities sometimes take.

Characteristics Flowing from Similarities in Large Jurisdictions

As with small jurisdictions, we can make some generalizations about characteristics that are frequently found in communities with large populations. The rate of serious crime, and the proportion of the caseload involving serious crimes charged against repeat offenders, is greater in larger jurisdictions. An important consequence is that, unless effective measures are employed to ensure that similar defendants charged with the same crimes receive the same sentence throughout the state, sentences in larger jurisdictions will be less severe.

As James Madison argued, larger jurisdictions are likely to encompass more diversity in population and economic interests. Though small jurisdictions exhibit more diversity than the stereotypical view of rural America suggests, some do have a fairly homogeneous population engaged in a dominant economic endeavor like farming or mining. Larger communities more often encompass varied economic enterprises, income groups, and racial, religious, and ethnic backgrounds. Consequently, the range of organized groups in larger jurisdictions will be broader. Enough people having common interests are around to form an organization based on that interest. Mothers Against Drunk Driving (MADD), the American Civil Liberties Union (ACLU), women's groups watching over prosecution of rape and spousal assaults, groups representing the interests of minorities who frequently appear as defendants, business associations concerned about the threat of burglary and retail theft, homeowners' organizations worried about street crime in the neighborhood — these and similar groups sometimes pay attention to case dispositions, raising the visibility of routine decisions normally known to very few.

Nevertheless, the court's routine operations are usually much less visible in large jurisdictions than in small courts. Small-town newspapers often publish all dispositions, and these reports are eagerly and widely read. The grapevine supplements the printed record. In middle-sized jurisdictions, neither the newspaper nor the grapevine informs the citizenry of routine dispositions. Elites, especially those who share space in the courthouse, keep apprised of developments through the grapevine. In large courts, neither elites nor the citizenry is usually aware of what is going on.

The same is not true of *nonroutine* matters in large jurisdictions and in middle-sized courts whose communities have their own newspapers and television stations. In the largest jurisdictions, court communities face one or more daily newspapers that can afford to hire reporters to cover the courts full time. Television stations hunger for crime and court stories to air on the nightly news. Thus, both focus on sensational trials when they cover the courts, but analyses of the court's operation as a whole or the policies pursued by the prosecuting attorney rarely appear. Only when a crisis arises — a huge case backlog, a riot in an overcrowded jail, a public squabble between the DA and PD — will the emphasis shift temporarily from big cases.

If change comes slowly to small jurisdictions, it often arrives swiftly in major metropolitan centers. A fiscal crisis results in a sudden reduction in budgets. A riot or rapid increase in crimes and arrests quickly overloads the jail and clogs criminal dockets. A politician running a media-based campaign for office demands that "something be done" about crime. The police institute major changes in enforcement or arrest policies that alter the composition of the caseload. These and other changes present large courts with a constantly shifting environment.[36]

How free are court communities in large jurisdictions from external controls? In general, they appear to enjoy a good deal of autonomy, more than those in smaller places. Though media pay attention to the courts, they rarely stray far from juicy jury trials. A few groups care about the court's work, but their influence is not great. Other elites know little about routine activities. In large jurisdictions, attorneys worry less about word-of-mouth gossip among the community's elite.

In the competition for status and power, prosecutors in large jurisdictions enjoy advantages that their counterparts in smaller communities usually do not. The prosecutor becomes a natural focus for media attention. He alone heads a large staff of people. The bench, however, consists of many individuals, each selected independently and retaining some independence. Also, the office of district attorney attracts politically ambitious individuals with the drive and flair for acquiring power. Therefore, prosecutors probably more often dominate large court communities.

How does conflict in large courts compare to that found elsewhere? It is probably more frequent. The disincentives arising from threats to nonwork lives and career prospects that dampen conflict in small jurisdictions less often operate in large courts. Because disagreement arises often, it is also less disruptive. Formal mechanisms such as coordinating committees and regular meetings of sponsoring-organization heads render conflicts and their resolution more routine.

Contours of Justice in Large Jurisdictions

Because more research has been done on the operation of courts serving major cities than rural places, we can depict their diversity more thoroughly. In the following paragraphs we will sample briefly some of these differences in order to convey the extent of this di-

[36]Jacob, *The Frustration of Policy*, op. cit., Chapter 2 summarizes such changes in ten large American cities. For a general discussion of the characteristics of large courts and the contribution that size of jurisdiction makes to these attributes, see Ryan et al., *American Trial Judges*, op. cit., Chapter 3, especially p. 68.

versity and to show how components of the community metaphor can be used to describe them.

Though the activities of large court communities attract less attention from outside, leading to greater autonomy for sponsoring organizations in setting policy and for its members in implementing it, the environment nonetheless shapes large criminal court communities in much the same way as described for middle-sized jurisdictions. The diversity in Detroit's population, coupled with the mobilization of its black community and labor union members was reflected in the competing ideologies and diverse social characteristics of its bench. The environment also supported a few zealous defense attorneys, some of them working for the privately organized Legal Aid and Defenders Association. This organization received a number of appointments from favorably inclined judges to represent indigents, sharing this task with private attorneys, who often had close ties to a judge. Baltimore's black community displayed much less political mobilization, and the city's generally more conservative political climate produced a more conservative, less diverse bench, and few if any zealous defense attorneys.[37] A study of ten major cities from 1948 to 1978 found that only Boston failed to increase court resources in comparison to the increase in arrests, reflecting the Boston court system's unusual isolation from the city's politics.[38] Judges were appointed by the governor. Its prosecutor, in office more than sixteen years, was practically invisible.

Chicago's criminal court system, during the era in which the Cook County Democratic party led by Mayor Richard Daley ruled the city, was an exception to the generalization that large-city court communities are usually autonomous. Its principal administrative judges held major posts in the Cook County Democratic organization. Prosecutors, defense attorneys, and judges shared many ties running through the Democratic party. As in Montgomery County during our research, the cohesion of the dominant political party produced a similar structure within the court community, reducing conflict and providing an effective external mechanism for achieving an unusual degree of coordination.[39]

[37]For a more extensive discussion, see Eisenstein and Jacob, *Felony Justice*, op. cit., Chapter 4.

[38]Jacob, *The Frustration of Policy*, op. cit., Chapter 6.

[39]See Eisenstein and Jacob, *Felony Justice*, op. cit., Chapter 5.

Research on large courts also confirms how much technology shapes the structure and dynamics of the court community. Thus, it was the case-assignment policies used in Chicago that produced stable, familiar courtroom work groups. Also, the structures of indigent defense vary widely. Detroit's Legal Aid and Defenders Association managed to survive through the payments it received when its zealous employees represented individual defendants. At the same time, less aggressive private attorneys engaged in general practice supplemented their income by receiving a share of these appointments from the judges. Baltimore's part-time public defenders handled a portion of the caseload themselves and assigned any they could not handle to one of the private attorneys on a roster kept by the office. The public defender's relatively high salary for part-time work made the position attractive. And political ties helped some people obtain appointments. For the most part, they were well established and experienced, not the fire-breathing young advocates found in Detroit's Legal Aid and Defender's Association.

The internal policies of sponsoring organizations in large courts affect both the operation of the organization itself and the disposition process generally. Prosecutors' offices can and do adopt a variety of techniques to screen cases early, and choose from several criteria.[40] Thus, the variation found in prosecutor screening policies in our middle-sized courts — from none in Pennsylvania to stringent "trial sufficiency" in Kalamazoo — is duplicated in larger courts.

The role of both local political culture and county legal culture in shaping large court communities has also been documented. Martin Levin traced the links among political culture, the methods of recruiting judges, the treatment attorneys and defendants received in courtroom interactions, and the sentences imposed in Pittsburgh and Minneapolis.[41] Pittsburgh, with a tradition of machine politics and face-to-face interaction, selected judges in partisan elections; the courtrooms were informal and warm, and sentences were consistently lower than in the more formal, cold, and correct Minneapolis courtrooms presided over by appointed judges. Thomas Church's study of the sources of court delay, after examining a number of

[40]See Joan Jacoby, *The American Prosecutor: A Search for Identity* (Lexington, Mass.: Lexington Books, 1980).

[41]Martin A. Levin, "Urban Politics and Judicial Behavior," 1 *Journal of Legal Studies* (1972), p. 193.

alternative explanations, concluded that the chief determinant of the pace of litigation was local legal culture — that is, attorneys' and judges' expectations of how long cases should take.[42]

The contours found in patterns of case disposition in large courts resemble those produced by our nine middle-sized courts. Research provides ample documentation of these similarities and differences. Because the differences lie only in the details on the extent of variation in trial rates, incarceration rates, sentence lengths, patterns of changes in the number and level of charges, and other aspects of case outcomes, it is not necessary to present them here.[43]

SIZE AND COURT COMMUNITIES: A SUMMARY

The most revealing question to ask about a court community is simply "How big is it?" The boundaries and character of the court community vary in predictable ways depending on size. In small courts, the relevant community extends beyond those involved directly in the courtrooms to encompass other members of the local elite. In middle-sized courts, the criminal court community is the primary concept. It consists at its core of judges, prosecutors, public defenders, and regular defense attorneys, and at its fringes of defense attorneys who appear occasionally and various other individuals such as newspaper reporters and bail bondsmen. In large jurisdictions, the criminal court community can still be considered the core concept,

---

[42]Church, *Justice Delayed*, op. cit., p. 83.

[43]Some brief examples indicate what such a rendition of these details would look like. A study of fourteen jurisdictions, most of them large, found that most cases ended in pleas, with trials accounting for about 15 percent or less in all but two courts, and dismissals falling between. This same study listed differences in dismissal rates, with some jurisdictions reaching 33 percent. See Kathleen B. Brosi, *A Cross-City Comparison of Felony Case Processing* (Washington, D.C.: Enforcement Assistance Administration, 1979), p. 9. This study also found no reduction in the most serious charge for robbery, burglary, assault, and larceny in Washington, D.C., for between 36 percent and 46 percent of the cases; in New Orleans, the proportion of cases with no such reduction ranged from 78 percent to 92 percent (at p. 39). In another study that looked at eighteen jurisdictions, most of them urban, incarceration rates ranged from 42 percent of convicted defendants (Denver) to 88 percent (Los Angeles), and average sentence length for robbery from 3.8 years in Los Angeles to 9.8 in New Orleans. See Bureau of Justice Statistics, U.S. Department of Justice, *Sentencing Outcomes in 18 Felony Courts* (Washington, D.C.: Bureau of Justice Statistics, 1985).

but it is likely to be much more diffuse. In some large courts, it may be segmented into a number of semi-independent courtroom work groups that develop their own going rates and understandings about case processing and disposition. In other large courts, however, sponsoring-organization technologies may inhibit formation of stable work groups so that their triads will not develop distinctive characteristics. Instead, judge, prosecutor, and defense attorney will rely on the local court community's definitions of going rates and proper disposition modes. Thus, in some large courts, courtroom workgroups will be created by the court community's technology, and can provide a useful focus for understanding courts. In others, the general court community, which will be less well defined and will exhibit less consensus than in small jurisdictions, will provide the most useful core concept. Table 10–2 summarizes the differences in court community characteristics associated with size of court.

OTHER FEATURES OF CRIMINAL COURT COMMUNITIES

In this chapter we argue that many significant differences in court communities derive from their size. What other general statements can be made about these communities? In this section, we will speculate on several that we think warrant brief consideration.

Correlates of Conflict

We have presented some significant conclusions about conflict in court communities. Most important of these is that conflict is not at all uncommon. Though some jurisdictions boast that they are "one family," divisive conflict is hardly unknown in extended and even immediate family groups. Of course, general cultural norms and national legal culture both structure and moderate conflict. In theory, everyone subscribes to the adversary notion of justice. Justifications for going to trial, cross-examining witnesses, objecting to questions, and the like are commonly accepted. Community members hardly ever resort to fisticuffs or blackjacks.[44] Ironically, however, the sort

---

[44]For an interesting discussion of the national legal culture's role in forging consensus on procedures and limiting conflict, see Stuart Scheingold, *The Politics of Law and Order* (New York: Longman, 1984), p. 229.

Table 10–2

Summary of Court Community Characteristics by Size of Court

Characteristic	Small courts	Middle-sized courts	Large courts
Central concept	Local elite community	Criminal court community	Diffuse, possibly segmented court community
Degree of autonomy	Low	Moderate	High
Role of mobilized interest groups	Very low, almost none	Low, few exist	Moderate, more exist, but activity episodic
Scrutiny of mass media	Very low, protective	Moderate, criticism rare	High, sensationalistic, sometimes critical
Influence of external elites	High, continuous	Moderate, continuous	Low, episodic
Organization of sponsoring organizations	Very low, informal	Moderate, some hierarchy and formality	Hierarchical very formal, and bureaucratic
Influence of sponsoring organization	Very low	Moderate	Moderately high
Grapevine	Highly developed, community wide	Developed, courthouse wide	Developed, but mainly confined to criminal court building
Nature of sanctions	Effective, broad, career and social, life-long	Moderately effective, career only, mid-range	Limited effectiveness, career only, short-term
Visibility of performance	Very high to local elites, moderately high to public	Moderately high to elites and public	Low to political and other elites, episodic and selective to public
Severity of sentence	Relatively high	Moderate	Relatively low

of conflict suggested by the legal metaphor — vigorous battle in the courtroom during full jury trials — is relatively infrequent. Instead, we find in many court communities antagonism developing among members of the same sponsoring organization or between the people who head them. We also identified some differences in the frequency, nature, and consequences of conflict by size of jurisdiction. It arises less often in small courts, but when it does appear, it is more intense, expands to include out-of-the-workplace settings, and can impair the process of disposing of defendants and even polarize the larger community. Conflict in large courts is probably the rule rather than the exception, but it is usually accepted and kept within manageable bounds.

It is clear, however, that the level of conflict found among jurisdictions of similar size varies considerably, and with great consequences. What factors, beyond size, shape the level of conflict? Our study suggests several likely candidates. First, where the local political structure is cohesive and strong, the control mechanisms it uses can be applied to limit and resolve conflict in the court community. The Montgomery County Republican party in 1980 and Mayor Daley's Cook County Democratic machine in Chicago in the early 1970s appeared to do so effectively. Where local politics consists of a diverse set of mobilized groups in conflict with one another, external mechanisms for imposing order in the courts do not exist. In fact, conflict within the court community sometimes reflects the patterns displayed in the local political system.[45]

Second, the attributes of the major sponsoring organizations' leadership shape conflict. Where they entertain dreams of moving on to an appellate judgeship or statewide political office, prosecutors and judges seek publicity and try to cultivate an image of aggressiveness and competence. Personality also seems to play a part in shaping the level of conflict. Combative leaders provoke and seek out conflict. Third, a sudden crisis, especially when resources to deal with it are unavailable, also encourages conflict. Finally, the content and strength of county legal culture can induce cooperation and pride or teach that struggle and conflict are normal.

These factors undoubtedly shape the level of conflict, but they do not determine it. Consequently, predictions cannot be made with

[45]See the description of Detroit in Eisenstein and Jacob, *Felony Justice*, op. cit., Chapter 3.

much confidence. Many characteristics of both Peoria and Kalamazoo point to low conflict. Peoria, in fact, saw little divisiveness. But a personality clash between two Kalamazoo judges and a continuing case backlog injected conflict into its community.

Structural Impediments to Vigorous Defense of Poor Defendants

Features common to nearly all court communities discourage vigorous defense of poor clients. The model of a zealous advocate, one who obeys the imperatives established by the legal metaphor to fight tooth and nail so that the prosecution is forced to prove guilt while adhering to due process, rarely conforms to what defense attorneys actually do.[46]

Several characteristics of court communities impede vigorous defense. First, the structure of indigent defense establishes financial disincentives. Traditional public defenders' offices with full-time employees work for low fixed salaries, often accepting the position to gain trial experience. When they acquire enough of it to become effective advocates, they use it to get a higher-paying position in private practice. Where part-time public defenders staff the office, the need to build a private practice discourages time-consuming, labor-intensive defense work. Especially if part-time salaries are low, the position will attract relatively inexperienced attorneys who will relinquish the post when their private practice income permits it. A different pattern appears where part-time salaries are higher, as in Du Page. There, the position attracted politically well-connected, more experienced, "establishment" people who had learned not to rock the boat and who were not strongly committed to zealous advocacy. Attorneys in private practice who receive periodic appointments (as in Saginaw or Oakland) typically face a payment schedule that also discourages the most active and time-consuming forms of defense. The incentive for attorneys who handle a number of cases for a fixed fee, as Kalamazoo's contract attorneys did, clearly is to avoid financial ruin by disposing of cases expeditiously.

Second, public defender offices rarely are well insulated from

---

[46]This statement is true regardless of whether or not the attitudes expressed by attorneys exhibit a strong commitment to due process and a low belief in punishment. Such attitudes facilitate zealous advocacy, but are not sufficient in themselves to produce it.

pressures that discourage vigorous advocacy. They usually receive funds from the county government, and are headed by someone appointed (and capable of being removed) by the judges or county officials.[47] Private attorneys appointed to represent poor defendants worry whether their conduct will lead to more or fewer subsequent appointments. These considerations result in few gung-ho advocates for defendants who represent large numbers of indigents.

The very fact that these attorneys receive their compensation from the government colors their clients' perceptions and creates problems. Defendants have virtually no say in who will represent them, exacerbating these problems.[48] Thus, defendants mistrust their attorneys and place little confidence in them,[49] complicating client and attorney interactions. The lawyer must worry about impressing the defendant, reducing mistrust and raising confidence. For the attorney, failure to gain "client control" can lead to a bad reputation in the courthouse and jeopardize his or her position. In turn, these pressures raise the value to the attorney of successfully manipulating the defendant's impressions. In a sense, the lawyer must convince the defendant that a vigorous defense effort is being made without actually providing such a defense. Attorneys faced with clients who mistrust them and express little confidence will, of course, respond in kind by finding it difficult to go all out in their defense.

Another factor discouraging vigorous defense arises from shared attitudes toward going rates. Confronted with a defendant who is

[47]A national survey of public defender systems found that 38 percent of PDs were chosen by county governments, and 23 percent by the local judiciary. Thirty-five percent, however, were affiliated with a state agency, opening up some possibility for greater insulation from local political pressures. This study also found that although only 34 percent of counties in the United States relied on public defender offices to provide indigents with counsel, they tended to be in larger jurisdictions. Thus, forty-three of the fifty largest counties, which have 68 percent of the population, used public defenders. Smaller jurisdictions are more likely to use an assigned-counsel system. Bureau of Justice Statistics, *Criminal Defense Systems* (Washington, D.C.: Bureau of Justice Statistics, 1984).

[48]For a classic study of defendants' attitudes toward public defenders and the reasons for them, see Jonathan Casper, *American Criminal Justice: The Defendant's Perspective* (Englewood Cliffs, N.J.: Prentice-Hall, 1972), especially Chapter 4.

[49]For an analysis of relations between defendants and public defenders from the attorney's viewpoint, based on the interviews from our study, see Roy B. Flemming, "The Client Game: Defense Attorney Perspectives of Their Relations with Criminal Clients," *American Bar Foundation Research Journal* (forthcoming, 1987). The discussion here draws from this article.

factually guilty, defense attorneys routinely think of what the client is likely to get. It is a thin line between predicting what the outcome will be and deciding what the defendant deserves. Acquiescence to a going-rate sentence naturally follows. An attorney may fight vigorously to ensure that clients get the going rate, but this is a limited objective. Attitudes toward punishment and due process, and toward defendants as a group, also discourage all-out efforts by some defense attorneys. We have seen that indeed some attorneys for the indigent express little regard for due process and have no problem with seeing defendants punished. Such individuals are likely to be less easily outraged by imposition of harsh punishment or violations of due process. They may still argue on behalf of their clients, but without the passion and conviction of a zealous advocate.

Research substantiates the validity of the factors just discussed as significant shapers of the quality of indigent defenses.[50] However, this research by and large does not conclude that publicly paid attorneys serve their clients less well than privately retained attorneys. In fact, they usually do at least as effective a job, and sometimes even better.[51] Privately retained attorneys, most of whose clients are not very wealthy, also rarely provide a zealous defense. Some of the same financial disincentives to doing so operate for them. Furthermore, most attorneys for the indigent participate in the life of the court community. They are subject to many forces that encourage them to behave in ways that facilitate their continued survival and participation in it.

The argument that indigent defense rarely is zealous needs a strong qualification. We are describing a general tendency. However, within its boundaries, substantial differences appear among jurisdictions. Particularly in larger courts, a small group of attorneys may provide zealous advocacy. Recruitment policies that seek out committed advocates, structural arrangements that insulate the organization from external pressures, a permissive local legal culture, the presence of favorably disposed interest groups, and skilled organizational leadership that nurtures internal morale all increase the likelihood that such a group will gather: we have referred to the presence

---

[50]See especially Blumberg, *Criminal Justice*, op. cit., Casper, *American Criminal Justice*, op. cit., and Hermann et al., *Counsel for the Poor*, op. cit.

[51]See especially Hermann et al., *Counsel for the Poor*, op. cit., and Flemming, "The Client Game," op. cit.

of such attorneys in Detroit. We found occasional flashes of zeal-
ousness in the descriptions that interviewees in Dauphin gave of
some of its public defenders. Thus, the structure of indigent defense
and the attitudes of public defenders in court communities vary. Such
differences sometimes translate into vigorous advocacy.

CONCLUSION

The topography of American criminal justice does not resemble the
uniform plane that the legal metaphor suggests. Rather, justice is
contoured. To be sure, national legal culture, itself closely tied to the
legal metaphor, limits the extent of variation. Nonetheless, significant differences abound. The size of court communities and other
attributes typically associated with small, medium, and large courts
consistently and powerfully influence their structure and dynamics.
Size alone, however, does not determine the contours of justice, for
technologies, conflict, and outcomes vary extensively among jurisdictions of the same size.

What are the consequences of this diversity? The most obvious
one is that the legal metaphor offers a poor guide to comprehension;
it cannot explain variation. Because courts differ, understanding
them requires that we ask and answer several questions.

What questions should be asked? In this book we argue for two:
What is the size of the court? What are the attributes of the court
community? Answers to these questions will go far in unraveling the
complex reality of a criminal court's day-to-day operations. There are
no invariant links between the attributes of a court community and
the patterns of case outcomes. There is more to understanding courts
though, than predicting how long a defendant's sentence will be or
the proportion of dismissals.

The diversity in criminal courts that emanates from the interaction between size and the elements of the community metaphor has
another significant consequence. It can tell us much about what kinds
of reforms can produce change and what kinds will not, and how
attempts at change will produce different results in different jurisdictions. In Chapter Eleven, we explore the implications of our approach for understanding efforts to reform courts.

Reform and the Contours of Justice

INTRODUCTION

In this book we deal with the task of understanding criminal courts, not reforming them. The question of reform can, however, serve as a good test of our principal thesis — that the metaphor of criminal courts as communities is useful. After all, usefulness is the best measure of any metaphor employed to understand human institutions. What good is an explanation that does not explain? As citizens, we most often will have occasion to employ the metaphor as we constantly encounter information about proposed reforms in criminal courts.

Why do such proposals arise so frequently in private conversation and the mass media? Our answer rests on the conception of courts presented in Chapter One. Criminal courts are political institutions: they make important decisions that affect both symbolic and material outcomes, decisions that people seek to shape.

Discontent with the performance of criminal courts fuels calls for reform. In part, dissatisfaction stems from the great expectations about dealing with crime that are attached to courts. This is the argument: People fear and abhor crime. Crime is therefore a public policy problem. Problems can be solved. Courts, along with the police, should solve the crime problem. But crime continues. Something therefore must be wrong with the criminal courts.

A different set of expectations also contributes to dissatisfaction. Courts serve as a repository for basic values to which most Americans subscribe. Among them is commitment to limited government, equal justice, and due process. The legal metaphor instructs criminal courts to adhere strictly to the requirements of due process. Defendants are to receive vigorous representation, equal treatment, respect for their dignity and rights, and a fair trial before an impartial judge and jury. When the substantial gaps between the reality of courts' operations and these ideals become visible, as they periodically do, symbolic commitment to the ideals impels calls for reform. Thus, the notion of Law generates a significant portion of the impetus for change. Together, these two sources of discontent with criminal courts guarantee that efforts to reform them will continue to be made frequently and will attract controversy and attention.

In the pages that follow, we will present a few of the principal lessons that can be drawn, based on the metaphor of courts as communities. This discussion cannot cover fully the topic of reform, but it does illustrate how the metaphor can generate intelligent conclusions about the prospects for reform. We will first look at reforms that higher authorities such as appellate courts and legislators seek to impose "from above." We will then look at reform "from within" the court community. We conclude the chapter with brief observations about the competing values that underlie debate over criminal court reform.

Before beginning this inquiry, however, we need to address a general question about the specificity of the statements we can make about reform. We start by observing that even when one finds agreement on the results that change should produce, one often does not have knowledge about how to achieve them.

Our research demonstrates that court technologies and the dynamics of interaction in court communities influence one another. To some extent, of course, the technologies reflect the values and experiences of the larger community. The patterns of case outcomes produced, however, as when a growing case backlog prompts a shift in calendaring procedures, induce changes in technologies. In turn, such changes affect both the dynamics of interaction and subsequent case outcomes.

What direct links are there between the attributes of the larger community and the technologies that court communities adopt? What effects flow from changes in technology? For example, what changes in sentences in spousal assault cases will flow from a shift to individual calendars from a master calendar? Such questions are easily asked, but the answers are little more than stabs in the dark. The paths of causation in even a small court community are varied and difficult to understand.

Even if one could devise rules that in the abstract linked specific changes in technology, attitudes, or other features of court communities to case outcomes, predicting what would happen would be very difficult. "Linking" statements assume "other things being equal." In the real world, other things are not equal. A court community consists of specific judges with distinctive attitudes toward spousal assault, and usually it will have established going rates for such crimes. Predicting the effect of a switch in calendaring techniques involves too many "ifs." The effect of a shift in case-assignment procedures depends in part on the specific details of a county's calendaring system. Under a master calendar, were such cases informally routed to one or two judges, or were they distributed randomly? Under an individual calendar system, did the initial assignment take into account the judge's reaction to such cases? Is the judge's organization strong enough to impose a court-wide going rate regardless of its members' personal attitudes or case-assignment techniques? Whether such a shift will make any difference, and if it does, what the direction of change will be, depends on these and other factors specific to the jurisdiction.

The inability to tie specified changes to particular shifts in case outcomes does not mean that our knowledge of how court communities work is worthless. Simply being aware that the factors discussed above are relevant can help avoid the common error of assuming that changes in sentences can be achieved merely by passing a new law. It also can help trace the events that transpire when making a reasonable prediction about what such a change might do to sentences *in a particular jurisdiction*. In that case, we can find out just what the configuration of the "ifs" is.

Finally, knowledge about the workings of court communities sensitizes us to the possible effects of changes in the work lives of their inhabitants. Even if we cannot predict how a change from a master calendar to individual calendars will change sentences, we know it will significantly affect the daily experiences of many people. Lazy or methodical judges whose low volume of dispositions remain hidden in a master calendar system may suddenly find their growing backlog receiving substantial unfavorable publicity under an individual calendar technology. Changing the procedure used to assign counsel for indigents or the compensation formula for appointed defense attorneys can alter who represents defendants and how they go about doing it. Tracing the effects of such changes, then, involves more than simply searching for new patterns in case outcomes.

When one examines the question of prediction, our inability to provide hard and fast general rules about the relationship between court community characteristics and outcomes is no surprise. The same is true of other things about which people seem to know a good deal. What is the general rule about the value of baseball teams having speedy players with little power versus those with slow power hitters? None. "Other things" have to be taken into account. How big is the ballpark? Does it have natural grass or artificial turf? After these and other questions are answered, judgments can be made about speed versus power.

This discussion makes, in a different way, a point that has repeatedly surfaced. Courts are complex social institutions.

LESSONS FOR REFORM

Lesson 1. Do Not Expect Too Much

Proponents of reform can be excused for promising more than will be delivered. They must do so as part of the political process that produces attempts to make changes. Citizens should not, however, accept overdrawn claims at face value. Lesson 1 suggests two simple rules to apply in assessing the likely effect of reform efforts: Be skeptical. Be cautious. Two conclusions flow naturally from these rules.

The More Radical a Proposed Change the Less Likely Is Its Adoption

Current patterns of organization and behavior did not develop by accident. Rather, they reflect accommodations among competing values and interests that support these values, accommodations that are superimposed on a common basic structure supported by broad consensus. This consensus accounts for our use of jury trials, the right to counsel, the right to challenge the admissibility of evidence, and other aspects of due process. The content of criminal statutes, procedures used to select judges, and numerous other operating details have grown from long political conflict and compromise. The same forces that helped bring about today's arrangements usually remain powerful supporters of the status quo.

The low likelihood of radical shifts in the structure of criminal courts can be illustrated by a hypothetical example. Imagine these changes: All state criminal statutes are replaced by a comprehensive federal criminal code; state courts are abolished and federal courts vastly expanded; federal judges are recruited from the ranks of young lawyers, trained in Washington, and sent for a limited period to staff courts throughout the country; prosecutors come from a national prosecutor's service that recruits and trains them centrally and dispatches them for one-year rotations throughout the country; and a national public defender's service follows the same formula.

Under this scheme, the prosecutors in all nine of our counties would work for the same Washington-based organization. They would appear in a "local federal court" briefly to join with unfamiliar judges and public defenders similarly dispatched from Washington to enforce a uniform criminal code. Obviously, these provisions would radically transform the current system. The present contours of justice would flatten dramatically, approaching uniformity. The ties of courts to the local community would be shattered. Centralized sponsoring organizations' ability to shape behavior through incentive structures based on promotions, salary increases, and future assignments would become formidable. Though some familiarity among judges, prosecutors, and public defenders temporarily assigned to a jurisdiction would begin to develop, the "communities" would be diffuse, the grapevines ineffective, and the disruptive effects of constant turnover severe. Lacking a local alternative, the operative culture would be national in origin and scope. The characteristics of the guilty-plea system and the structure of going rates would everywhere converge.

If this scheme seems preposterous, it is only because it clashes so directly with the structure of the current criminal justice system. Nothing is inherently unworkable or even extraordinary about it. Nevertheless, a centralized and uniform criminal justice system strikes Americans as an unthinkable vision, almost un-American. If it seems unrealistic, that is because it *is* unrealistic. We are not likely to witness any serious movement to alter the status quo, which gives to states the principal responsibility for establishing and operating their own criminal justice systems. Nor is it likely that substantial changes in the content of national legal culture will occur, such as commitment to due process or willingness to allow the Supreme Court to set nationwide standards controlling some crucial aspects of criminal procedure discussed in Chapter One.

More Modest Changes from Above
Face Obstacles to Implementation

Would-be reformers of criminal justice systems, whether they are appellate courts, governors and legislatures, ideological commentators, or scholars, frequently appear to cling to the traditional notion of

Law. Their proposals and decisions assume that we have a hierarchic, centralized, obedient system of courts that will automatically and faithfully adhere to new rules. Thus, the Pennsylvania Supreme Court can decree that judges may not participate in discussions leading to guilty pleas and that trials must begin within 180 days of arrest. The legislature can create a Sentencing Commission issuing sentencing guidelines that are supposed to eliminate disparities across the state in punishment for the same crimes.

Reform from above does not operate in the vacuum of Law. If changes occur, they must take place in the real world of criminal court communities, where the decisions have to be implemented. This simple fact, which we have emphasized strongly in this book, provides a powerful tool for critically assessing reform. As we have seen, implementation of reform from above is imperfect. In practice, some Erie judges did participate in discussions of pleas. The Pennsylvania Supreme Court's speedy-trial provisions were weakened by informal but effective pressures to enforce county legal cultural norms requiring defense attorneys to agree to some prosecution requests that postponements be mutually requested. And though Pennsylvania's efforts to reduce disparity in sentencing throughout the state beginning in 1982 by means of sentencing guidelines indeed had some effect, they did not entirely eliminate differences in sentences imposed for similar offenses.[1]

We could list many examples of the remarkable capacity of criminal courts to adjust to and effectively thwart reforms. Other scholars have reached the same conclusion.[2] Part of the explanation for this

---

[1]See John H. Kramer and Robin L. Lubitz, "Pennsylvania's Sentencing Reform: The Impact of Commission-Established Guidelines," 31 *Crime & Delinquency* (1985), pp. 481–500. They report that 88 percent of sentences fell within the recommended guidelines, a substantial increase in consistency in sentences found before imposition of the guidelines. For some offenses, though, the pre-guideline consistency already was fairly high. Because the guideline ranges are fairly wide, compliance with their *length* of sentence is easier than in some other states. The analysis was intended to reduce the possibility that changes in the level of charges from arrest to guilty plea was used to maintain going rates not in compliance with the guidelines, but some such manipulations probably continue. The actual rate of noncompliance, therefore, may be somewhat higher than reported by Kramer and Lubitz.

[2]For more discussions of reforms influence in criminal courts, see Raymond T. Nimmer, *The Nature of System Change: Reform Impact in the Criminal Courts* (Chicago: American Bar Foundation, 1978); Malcolm M. Feeley, *Court Reform on Trial: Why Simple Solutions Fail* (New York: Basic Books, 1983); Jonathan D. Casper and

resiliency rests in the complexity of the criminal disposition process. As we demonstrate in earlier chapters, this procedure consists of a series of stages, each with low-visibility, discretionary decisions made by joint interaction among several formally independent but practically interdependent participants. Recognizing that criminal courts exhibit attributes of community, however, enriches the explanation; we can focus on shared beliefs, the county legal culture, which may produce similar reactions to changes imposed from above. This approach also identifies mechanisms for communicating reactions and enforcing participation in efforts to thwart such changes.

The community metaphor helps explain the predisposition that courts display to resist change. Take attempts to increase or decrease the penalties meted out for particular combinations of offenses and defendants' prior records — that is, going rates. The content of a county's going rates comes not from an automatic, invariant mixture of Supreme Court doctrine and the provisions of state sentencing codes. Rather, going rates gradually evolve, shaped by environmental factors and day-to-day decisions by community inhabitants doing their jobs. The result is a routine that cuts the costs of calculation, reduces uncertainty, and helps produce similar outcomes in equivalent cases. Reluctance to overthrow such deeply entrenched and familiar formulas is natural. Communities become comfortable with and attached to established procedures. Changes seen as coming at the behest of outsiders bring forth the response, "What's wrong with the way we have been doing things for years?"

We do not argue that reforms from above never change criminal court communities' operations; the world of criminal justice displays too much diversity and complexity for such a sweeping statement to be true. Sometimes a community may even welcome proposed reforms. More often, some members will support a change and work to implement it but others will stand opposed or apathetic. This conflict may set off a sequence of adjustments. Prosecutors may wel-

---

David Brereton, "Evaluating Criminal Justice Reforms," 18 *Law and Society Review* (1984), p. 121; Roy B. Flemming, C. W. Kohfeld, and Thomas M. Uhlman, "The Limits of Bail Reform: A Quasi-Experimental Analysis," 14 *Law and Society Review* (1980), p. 947; Roy B. Flemming, *Punishment Before Trial: An Organizational Perspective of Felony Bail Processes* (New York: Longman, 1982), especially Chapter 6; and A. Blumstein, J. Cohen, S. E. Martin, and M. H. Tonry, editors, *Research on Sentencing: The Search for Reform* (Washington, D.C.: National Academy Press, 1983).

come mandatory sentences as a way of strengthening their ability to control sentences. To maintain prior going rates, judges and defense attorneys may be forced to adjust the patterns of count drops achieved. Furthermore, going rates do change; one factor in such change is the legislative effort to increase or decrease penalties.

Lesson 2. Reforms from Above Have Widely Varying Results from Jurisdiction to Jurisdiction

The problems faced by the largest jurisdictions in a state often drive the direction and pace of statewide reform efforts. The cost of running such courts is so large, the proportion of defendants handled there and sent to state prison so high, that the troubles of these courts become the troubles of the state's entire court system. State administrators feel compelled to attend to the crises that emanate from their largest courts. Many top officials in the state court administrators' offices we saw had worked in their state's largest jurisdiction. The influence exerted by Chicago, Detroit, and Philadelphia in their respective states' political systems frequently results in the selection of top appellate judges from these areas. Naturally, such people know more about and care about the travails of the criminal courts in their home county.

Efforts to grapple with problems in the largest court thus become the standard applied statewide. Michigan sought to enhance the power of Detroit's chief trial judge to help him deal with his court's case backlog. One change was increasing the term of office from one to two years. But the change applied to all courts in the state.

Because attempts to implement such reforms take place statewide, differences in the criminal court communities and the larger communities they serve guarantee significant differences in the degree of implementation and its effects.

Smaller court communities in particular, if they are united, can successfully resist unwanted changes. The effectiveness of the grapevine, personal intimacy, and the varied sanctions available for punishing potential dissenters in small court communities provide them with strong resources for defying directives for change made from above. Middle-sized courts can also evade changes imposed from above. Oakland County ignored the expansion of the chief judge's term to two years by continuing its tradition of rotating the post annually; the incumbent simply resigned after one year. Likewise, Saginaw continued to choose the man who had long been its chief judge by reelecting him to consecutive terms. When a crisis in Detroit's Recorder's Court led the State Supreme Court to reduce drastically the bail bondsmen's role, Saginaw failed to change its practice of relying heavily on one bondsman. Very large jurisdictions, often having diffuse structure and some isolation from other community elites, also find it possible to resist change imposed from above.

This resistance implies that efforts to implement identical changes throughout a state will fail to gain uniform results. The differences in jurisdictions of varying size, to say nothing of those found among courts of similar size described by our study, guarantee that grand schemes to achieve statewide conformity will not succeed.

Lesson 3. Many Means of Reforming from Above Lie Unused

Most reforms stemming from the impulse to get tough require redefining which acts are criminal and altering the punishment administered. Many states have resorted to sentencing guidelines, mandatory sentences, and determinate sentencing provisions.[3] Efforts to shorten the pace of litigation with speedy-trial rules are a second reform that is frequently adopted.

Our metaphor, however, suggests that other kinds of reforms to shape the ways in which courts work are quite feasible. Specifically, changes can be made in methods for *recruiting* key decision makers, in the *resources* made available to their sponsoring organizations, and in the *technology* used to handle the caseload. Of course, such reforms fail to address directly the causes that motivate many proponents of change, such as severity of sentences. Nevertheless, they can significantly shape court communities' ways of working and therefore can indirectly mold case outcomes.

We will illustrate with one example each how these changes from above can shape the operations of court communities. This discussion is illustrative, not comprehensive.

In Illinois, trial judges recruit judges for lower courts. These judges serve four-year terms and must be reappointed by the trial bench.

---

[3]For example, Illinois adopted provisions for enhancing the sentences of defendants convicted of especially serious offenses (called "X" crimes). Several years after our research ended, Pennsylvania adopted the sentencing guidelines referred to in note 1. An extensive bibliography on reform in sentencing appears in Blumstein et al., op. cit.

Similar procedures could, through the cumbersome procedure for amending the state constitution, be adopted in Pennsylvania, Michigan, or anywhere else.

The mechanisms for funding prosecutors could be changed by apportioning state funding by population. In fact, salary levels could be state mandated. If salaries were high enough, the rate of turnover among prosecutors would drop, especially where salaries had been as low as in Montgomery. Consequently, the level of experience among prosecutors would increase in many courts, and discrepancies between counties would decrease. If such changes were accompanied by provisions giving prosecutors civil service status, the sudden plunges in experience following the election of an insurgent candidate for district attorney would cease.

Michigan law requires the police to obtain approval from a prosecutor before formally lodging charges against a defendant. This procedure forces the prosecutor to institute a screening mechanism. State statutes or higher-court decrees could control other aspects of technology, such as requiring or prohibiting individual calendars.

These changes in recruitment, organizational resources, and technology would all increase a court community's ability to screen cases effectively. Prosecutors would be able to control whether defendants were formally charged with anything, and if so, the charges on which they were initially arraigned. They would have more experienced assistants to assign to the task. The trial judges would be able to influence the lower judges' bail policies and willingness to dismiss weak cases for lack of probable cause, or to encourage guilty pleas for minor offenses. As our descriptions of the Pennsylvania counties showed, inability to screen effectively confronted them with a higher proportion of less serious offenses. In contrast, Kalamazoo's prosecutor screened out weak cases vigorously, and chose carefully when deciding which offenses to charge. Enhanced ability to screen cases is one of the most promising ways to give court communities more control over their work, an especially appealing prospect for courts that find it difficult to devote adequate attention to serious cases. It also is likely to produce or at least facilitate changes in the guilty-plea system.

Lesson 4. Not All Change Is "Reform"

Court communities experience constant change. Our descriptions of nine courts, though covering only a brief period, convey the image of systems in constant flux. A longer time perspective would bring out this image even more clearly. The Du Page prosecutor lost his bid for reelection in 1984. The St. Clair prosecutor, whose stricter screening policies angered the local private bar because fewer defendants able to provide fees came to court, did not even bother to run again, knowing that he faced defeat. In Erie, the President Judge and the judge who had long been his colleague retired, and the number of judges increased, producing rapid turnover in a bench that had been very stable. Other research has documented equally substantial changes. Jacob's study of ten major cities between 1948 and 1978 found constant changes in criminal courts' ways of managing their dockets, organizing administrative functions, keeping track of cases, handling career criminals, and utilizing diversion programs.[4]

Some changes result from the normal processes associated with passage of time and tides of political fortune. Other changes follow shifts in population and in patterns of crime. Thus, some of the flux that court communities exhibit falls under the control of no one in the criminal court community. Conscious decisions made by important decision makers outside the community can also, however, affect profoundly the work of criminal courts. Nowhere is this influence more evident than in the alternatives to incarceration made available. The capacity of the local jail and the state prison system effectively limits the number of people who can be incarcerated and the length of time they serve. Excess capacity allows for harsher sentences. When such institutions fill up, sooner or later the courts must adjust their going rates to reflect the reality that they have no room to house newly sentenced defendants without releasing others. The policies of law enforcement agencies on allocating investigative resources and the criteria used to arrest and charge defendants are another significant source of externally generated changes. The court community cannot ordinarily halt such changes. It must accept and adjust to them.

Other changes can be traced to a community member's conscious decision. Prosecutors in particular may undertake changes, and for various reasons. Some reflect obligations to implement campaign promises. Others are meant to respond to problems that arise in administering the office. The departure of several experienced assistants may force reassignment of remaining veteran prosecutors and even reorganization of the office. Or an effort to make the office

---

[4]Herbert Jacob, *The Frustration of Policy: Responses to Crime by American Cities* (Boston: Little, Brown, 1984), Chapters 4 and 6.

more "professional" can produce changes. Such motivations may prompt a decision to switch from horizontal to vertical prosecution, so that the same assistant will handle a case from the time it enters the office to final disposition. Judges and the public defender's office also initiate similar changes for numerous reasons. Judges may require all preliminary hearings to be conducted in the main courthouse to better enable them to prompt lower judges to screen out weak cases.

These individual initiatives display some common characteristics. First, they often can be undertaken without approval by or even advance knowledge of the rest of the community. Second, they force the other members of the community to respond and to adjust. Like it or not, such changes affect everyone. Third, the changes produced by such initiatives and the adjustments that others subsequently make are often inadvertent and unpredicted. Shifting assistant prosecutors previously assigned to one judge's courtroom under a horizontal case-assignment procedure to a vertical scheme, causing them to follow their defendants all over the courthouse, destabilizes the triad of judge, prosecutor, and defense attorney who dispose of cases. In larger communities, it can also reduce familiarity. Centralizing preliminary hearings formerly scattered throughout the county makes it possible for the DA's office to attend them and implement early screening or plea-bargaining policies previously impossible to accomplish. Both changes may not have been undertaken with the intent of producing these effects. Indeed, those who initiated the changes may have been unaware of their full ramifications. Nonetheless, such changes spread ripple effects throughout the court community.

Lesson 4 provides a new perspective to the assessment of reform. It suggests that we need to look beyond efforts explicitly identified as reforms to consider the influence of other changes made for reasons that do not overtly include consideration of changing the way in which criminal courts operate. Any alteration in the method for recruiting key participants, in the resources made available to them, or in the procedures they are required to follow can induce significant unanticipated change.

Lesson 5. Reforms from Within Court Communities Face Significant Obstacles

Efforts by any participant in a court community to bring about significant change face formidable obstacles not unlike those encountered by reforms from above. The resiliency displayed by a court community that thwarts externally imposed reforms also stymies individual participants' ability to induce change. A prosecutor's efforts to change the going rate for some offenses can be countered by cooperation between defense attorneys and judges in working out sentences.[5] Judges' policies designed to speed litigation can flounder on the rocks of resistance put up by prosecutors and defense attorneys.

Incomplete commitment to a policy or failure to understand what successful implementation requires also impedes reform, as we see clearly in the Oakland County prosecutor's plea-bargaining policies. He wanted a "minimalist" guilty-plea system, with few changes in counts. Presumably, it was in his power to move the system unilaterally to a minimalist pattern. Why was Oakland, then, in the "middling" category of guilty-plea systems? One reason was that his office failed to screen cases at arrest as stringently as Kalamazoo, despite its ability to do so. Whereas Kalamazoo eliminated 36 percent of the arrests brought to it, Oakland's figure was just 8 percent. Thus, more of the weak cases and cases carrying charges that could not be sustained came to Oakland's trial court, making it difficult to apply its stringent policies at disposition.

Explicit efforts to reform made from within do not, though, inevitably fail. Although plea bargains in Oakland may not have conformed to the minimalist pattern, defendants nevertheless may have been treated more severely merely by having to undergo the burden of prosecution or by having additional, if somewhat less serious, convictions added to their criminal record.

Reforms from within stand a better chance of success if the major residents in the court community agree that change is needed. Such agreement, however, is not often achieved. Court communities commonly experience bruising battles over policies and practices and must live with their lingering effects. New proposals for change often awaken old rivalries and resentments and provide new opportunities to refight previous battles. Changes supported by one segment of a court community may succeed partially or produce unintended results. Furthermore, their effects may become entangled in the web of other changes occurring constantly in court communities, changes

[5]For an excellent description of just such a sequence of responses, see Thomas W. Church, Jr., "Plea Bargains, Concessions, and the Courts: Analysis of a Quasi-Experiment," 10 *Law and Society Review* (1976), p. 377. For a description of attempts to maintain going rates in the face of changes in sentencing law, see Milton Heumann and Colin Loftin, "Mandatory Sentencing and the Abolition of Plea Bargaining: The Michigan Felony Firearm Statute," 13 *Law and Society Review* (1979), p. 393.

that participants introduce for reasons other than bringing about specific reforms. Finally, some court communities, reflecting the political culture and tradition of the larger community in which they operate, simply are not imbued with the spirit of reform. Nothing in
the recent history or dominant beliefs of political elites of St. Clair
County, for example, inclined them to seek reform.

In evaluating the likely effects of an announced reform by judges,
prosecutors, or public defenders, the same general rules useful for
evaluating reforms from above apply: Be skeptical. Be cautious. The
complex, continuing interactions that form the life of court communities make it difficult to implement planned change fully; not
that change does not come from within — it sometimes does. Change,
however, rarely succeeds in turning out as intended. Kalamazoo's DA
sought on-the-nose pleas and succeeded. Oakland's prosecutor also
wanted to restrict plea bargains. He failed, but may nonetheless have
produced harsher outcomes for defendants, the ultimate goal of his
reforms. Du Page's DA also increased the harshness of sentences,
but encountered strong opposition, which ultimately contributed to
his failure to win re-election.

CONCLUDING THOUGHTS

Proposed reforms of the criminal justice system in the United States
may be meant to address problems for which there is no good solution. Americans will not cease trying to eliminate crime. Also, however, they probably will never succeed in doing so. The discontent,
anxiety, and frustration this failure will generate provides an unend-
ing supply of political opportunities that will be exploited. As long
as society continues to function in an organized and democratic fashion, opportunities to apply the metaphor of courts as communities
to the analysis of reform proposals will be plentiful.

Reform proposals face another difficulty. Often they are designed
to resolve conflicts over underlying values about which there is no
agreement. One such conflict is whether criminals should be punished or rehabilitated. Another deals with whether we want more
equality of outcomes, so that similar defendants charged with the
same crimes get the same punishment, or whether we want local
communities to be better able to control their own affairs. Enhancing the autonomy of criminal court communities favors the value of

community control, but raises major questions about equality. Efforts to impose uniformity not only encounter resistance from court communities, but raise questions about the desirability of imposing standards from the outside against the wishes of the community.

These enduring conflicts guarantee that issues involving performance by criminal courts will remain on the political agenda. Courts embody competing impulses to control simultaneously both crime and the power of government. These impulses directly touch everyone's material and psychological well-being and ensure that courts will always attract attention from both citizens and the mass media. Americans will struggle to understand criminal courts as long as they remain aware of and interested in the conditions of social life. Inevitably, we will draw upon the legal metaphor, the image of Law. Success in knowing what *really* is going on, however, requires an alternative view. In this book we suggest a powerful yet simple alternative metaphor — the court as a community. If it changes readers' way of thinking about criminal courts, it has achieved its principal purpose.

Illustrative Responses to the "Belief in Punishment" and "Due Process" Attitude Scales

Figure A–1 lists the questions used to produce the "belief in punishment" and "regard for due process" scores and shows the answers actually given by a prosecutor and public defender in sharp disagreement.[1] Agreement with the first six questions and disagreement with the last three indicates belief in punishment. The prosecutor chose a response indicating greater belief in punishment on every question. The length of the line between their answers represents the size of the difference in their response. The scale scores, derived from a statistical procedure that summarized responses, were +4.73 for the prosecutor and −6.14 for the public defender.

The responses of another prosecutor–public defender pair with very different attitudes toward due process appear at the bottom of Figure A–1. The public defender achieved the highest possible standardized scale score, +2.92, the prosecutor's score was −2.36.

We can compare the attitudes of the PD and DA offices by presenting the average score of their members for each question. Figure A–2 indicates the answers to the first question for all the prosecutors and public defenders who filled out the attitude questionnaire. Differences within each office were extensive, of course, and using the office average conceals this variation. But the average nonetheless summarizes the central tendency of opinion in each office. Figure A–3 indicates only the office average on each question. Prosecutors as a group, as one would expect, believed in punishment more and due process less than did public defenders.

---

[1] For a complete discussion of how the questionnaire was constructed and the scales derived, see Peter F. Nardulli, Roy B. Flemming, and James Eisenstein, *The Tenor of Justice* (Champaign-Urbana, Ill.: University of Illinois Press, 1987), Appendix 1.

Figure A–1

Response of a Prosecutor and a Public Defender to Questions Used in the Attitude Scales

"Belief in Punishment" Questions	Strongly agree	Agree	Disagree	Strongly disagree
	1 2 3	4 5 6	7 8 9	10 11

1. Criminals should be punished for their crimes in order to require them to repay their debt to society. — P ———————————— D

2. Most of those who advocate rehabilitation of criminals do not attach sufficient weight to the seriousness of the crimes they commit. — P ———————— D

3. The frequent use of probation is wrong because it has the effect of minimizing the gravity of the offense committed. — P ———————— D

4. The failure to punish crime amounts to giving a license to commit it. — P ———————————— D

5. Most people charged with serious crime should be kept in jail until their trial, even if they have strong ties to the community. — P — D

6. Criminals should be punished for their crimes whether or not the punishment benefits the criminals. — P ———— D

7. It is important to sentence each offender on the basis of his individual needs and not on the basis of the crime he has committed. — D ———— P

8. Even with a prior record, most people with strong community ties should not be detained prior to trial. — D ———————————— P

9. Our present treatment of criminals is too harsh. — D – P

Belief in "Due Process"

1. The Supreme Court's decisions in the past twenty years expanding the rights of defendants are basically sound. — D ———————— P

2. It is better to let ten guilty persons go free than to convict one innocent person. — D ———————— P

3. Existing Supreme Court decisions protecting the rights of defendants that jeopardize the safety of the community should be curtailed. — P ———————————— D

P = Prosecutor's response   D = Public Defender's response

Figure A–2

*Distribution of Individual Prosecutors' and Public Defenders'
Responses to the First "Punishment" Item*

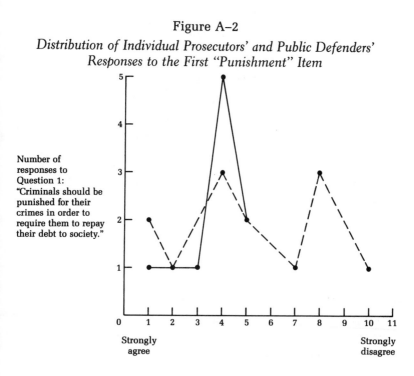

Number of
responses to
Question 1:
"Criminals should be
punished for their
crimes in order to
require them to repay
their debt to society."

———— Prosecutors' responses[a]

— — — Public defenders' responses[b]

[a]Prosecutors' response average 3.78

[b]Public defenders' response average 5.36

Figure A–3

*Average Office Response, for Prosecutors and Public Defenders,
to Questions on "Belief in Punishment" and "Regard
for Due Process" Scales, Erie County*

	Response	1	2	3	4	5	6	7	8	9	10	11
Belief in Punishment												
Question 1					P ——— PD							
Question 2							P — PD					
Question 3					P ————— PD							
Question 4					P — PD							
Question 5								P ——— PD				
Question 6						P ———— PD						
Question 7						PD ———— P						
Question 8						PD ————— P						
Question 9									PD ——— P			
Regard for Due Process												
Question 10					PD — P							
Question 11			PD — P									
Question 12						P ————— PD						

See Figure A-1 for wording of questions.

P = Prosecutor's response   PD = Public Defender's response

Index

311